Dawn Hill was born in Launceston, Tasmania, and spent most of her childhood on King Island in Bass Strait. Although she began training as a nurse, circumstances prevented her finishing the course, and she now describes herself as a writer with an interest in psychic research.

Also by Dawn Hill in Pan Books

REACHING FOR THE OTHER SIDE
LIFTING THE VEIL

EDGE of REALITY

Dawn Hill

Pan Books Sydney and London

For June, my mother
and Darryl, my son . . .
just because I love them

First published 1987 by Pan Books (Australia) Pty Limited
63-71 Balfour Street, Chippendale, Sydney

Reprinted 1987, 1988, 1989
9 8 7 6 5 4

Hill, Dawn, 1946-
Edge of reality.

ISBN 0 330 27096 6.

1. Psychical research. 2. Spiritualism. I. Title.
133.8

Printed and bound in Australia by
The Book Printer, Victoria

Contents

Introduction 7

1 The Quest for Truth 21
2 Development Groups 45
3 Cleansing the Aura 60
4 Psychic Self-Defence 73
5 The Inner Sanctuary 85
6 Relaxation 96
7 The Aura 109
8 Colour and Spiritual Growth 127
9 Trance Mediumship: Communication with Spirits 138
10 Countering Psychic Attack 151
11 Spirituality or Religion? 165
12 Personal Growth 179
13 Dangerous Pastimes 193
14 Creating your own Reality, with your Mind 217
15 Suicide, Accidental Death and the 'Lost Soul' Syndrome 237
16 Witchcraft and Satanism 265
17 New Age Children 273
18 A Message 293

Introduction

I have always to be aware at the outset that I am writing for a range of individuals whose levels of experience and understanding vary. Some of my readers will be people who have years of experience, whilst others are only just beginning to explore their own spiritual potential. Some will have read my first book and will therefore be familiar with my terms of reference, others will not. If I commence at the level of those who already understand a great deal, the beginners will be discouraged and feel out of their depth. If I work on the assumption that my readers know nothing, I will have little to say that will be of value to the more advanced souls. This introductory chapter is my way of resolving the dilemma and placing all my readers on an equal footing. For the more advanced, it will be revision but, although it contains information that you may already know, I ask that you read it anyway. For the less experienced, this chapter should define the basic framework of understanding upon which the later chapters will build.

Whenever I commence work with a new group of people (and I must assume that I am doing so here, even though I am well aware that some of my readers will be old friends), I begin by explaining that, although I have been called a teacher, it isn't really my role to teach you anything. My function is rather to remind you of things that you once knew but may have forgotten: this information may then act as a catalyst to activate the release and unfoldment of the spiritual awareness that lies within each one of us. The answers to every question you are ever likely to ask are already contained within your own mind, which could for the purpose of simplicity be described as a 'cosmic computer'. All you need to learn is how to operate the computer so that it will release into your conscious awareness the information that you seek.

It is important for you to bear in mind that no person currently living on Earth can rightfully claim to be an authority on matters of the spirit; those who know all there is to know are found on levels much higher than ours. I do not claim to know all the answers or to be an ultimate authority; I am simply a person like yourself who has learned to understand something about the nature of the infinite reality that surrounds and interpenetrates the corner of existence that we know as the physical universe. Just as I have been assisted by spirits of higher advancement in my search for knowledge, I seek to share what I have learned with others who seek the same understanding.

I ask that you do not accept anything that I or anyone else may say, purely on face value. Use your discrimination as you read this book and test for truth at every step. If you find something between these pages that seems wrong to you or is difficult for you to accept, put it aside and pass on. Don't throw it away completely. You may find at a later time and with the benefit of hindsight that it is not as outlandish as it first seemed. Perhaps you may never accept it. Either way, try not to accept or reject anything without first testing.

I have occasionally encountered people who have insisted upon setting me on a pedestal and expecting me to be some kind of cross between the Archangel Gabriel, the Madonna and the Blue Fairy, in spite of my vehement pleas to be accepted as the person I am, rather than as something that I cannot be. If I am placed on a pedestal, being human, I will inevitably wobble and fall, at which point the person who set me up in that ridiculous position in the first place will promptly accuse me of fraud. People who place unreasonable expectations on me are bound to be disappointed: I am not superhuman, nor am I obliged to live up to someone else's image of me.

Following on the publication of *Reaching for the Other Side* (Pan Books, 1982), I received quite a few letters from people who expected me to perform miracles for them. For instance, a man who had suffered a permanent affliction as a result of an accident with his hotted-up motor vehicle literally demanded that I repair his injury so that he could get back on the road. Apart from the fact that his injury was clearly the karmic result of his style of driving and that the rest of the population was no doubt infinitely safer whilst ever he was kept off the roads, there were several very good reasons why his demands could not be satisfied. When he finally realised that his badgering tactics were not going to get him anywhere he promptly accused me of being a fake.

That kind of situation is unpleasant for all concerned and to prevent any similar future occurrences, I would point out that my purpose and the purpose of the spirit beings who work with me is to help others explore their own potential. The demonstrations of spiritual healing related in my first book were given by the guides to show what can be done by anyone with an understanding of natural energy and an ability to work with it. These abilities are latent in all of us and the purpose of the spirit teachers is to help us learn to use them. So long as there is someone else prepared to do it for us each time we ask, we will never learn.

On the subject of my first book: I have often been irritated when reading a book, to find the author constantly referring me back to a previous publication, particularly when I am told that the information I need in order to understand the book I am currently reading is contained in the earlier edition. In this book, wherever information contained in *Reaching for the Other Side* is needed, I have included the information itself, worded differently perhaps, but still essentially the same. However, since this book *is* the second in a series, some references to the first book are unavoidable (as in the preceding two paragraphs, for instance) and therefore I make no apology for including such references where they are necessary.

Spiritual truth is universal: it is not limited to any man-made philosophy and, in spite of what certain people may believe, it is not necessary to conform to any particular religious doctrine in order to gain access to the Divine. You have your own channels of spiritual communication and they will function all the more clearly if you do not have a succession of middlemen insisting that you need them to intercede on your behalf. By the same token, I do not advocate the rejection of religion out of hand, for to do so would be to discard a wealth of accumulated wisdom and inspiration. To reject all religion is as unbalanced as being a fanatical follower of one specific ideology. In either case, a large chunk of truth is being ignored. It would be much wiser to make an objective study of comparative religion: that is, to study a number of religious philosophies and seek for the elements within each one that are in harmony with the others, the points on which they all agree. When you find those elements you can be reasonably confident that you are looking at a core of truth.

I have a very dear friend, a lady of my mother's generation, who is a happy Roman Catholic. She enjoys her religion and gets a great deal of fulfilment from it. The fact that she is also a talented medium doesn't cause her any conflict at all; in fact, she finds that each aspect of her spiritual nature tends to enhance her appreciation of the other. She is involved with the 'Charismatic Renewal' movement, which is the Roman Catholic religion's version of born-again Christianity and, a number of years ago, I had a conversation with her which could be of interest here. At the time, in addition to her regular church services and prayer meetings she was also participating in a spiritual development group comprised mostly of sincere Christians who believed that if psychic abilities could be used in the service of darkness, they could equally well be used in the service of the Lord of Light. It was in the course of attending the psychic development meetings that she discovered her talent for trance mediumship and the group received the benefit of the spiritual wisdom and guidance offered by her guide, a female entity I will call Astara.

'You know, life can be quite amusing sometimes,' remarked my friend with a definite twinkle in her eyes. 'I go to the psychic development group, I am entranced and Astara takes over. When I wake up, people say "Isn't that wonderful? The guide has brought us teachings of spiritual wisdom." Then I go to my prayer meetings and I am overcome by the Holy Spirit and spiritual messages come out of my mouth. When I come back to normal, everyone is saying how wonderful it is that the Holy

Spirit has spoken through me. Now, if I were to tell some of the people in the congregation that I was actually in trance and that it was a spirit guide who spoke, they'd accuse me of witchcraft and throw me out on my ear. Funny... it feels to me as though I'm doing exactly the same thing in both cases!'

According to this friend of mine, it is not the priesthood who reject the psychic aspect of her spiritual endeavours. For the most part, she tells me, the priests are quite understanding and willing to accept the spiritual value of her gifts, however they may be manifested. In general the opposition comes from the less enlightened, prejudiced minds within the congregation. I won't deny that there are some prejudiced minds within the clergy, just as there are some opportunistic souls who have jumped onto the Evangelistic bandwagon in order to make a fast buck. There is good and bad in every field of human endeavour but it is important that in the quest for spiritual truth, you keep an open mind. Be prepared to listen to what other people have to say, don't reject anything without giving it a hearing, otherwise you could be guilty of the same kind of prejudice that you find abhorrent in others.

When it comes to finding a path to spiritual truth, the onus is on you; no-one else can take that responsibility for you. Be discriminating: don't accept everything you are told without testing but don't reject anything without giving it an objective hearing.

Every human being has a full range of psychic abilities which can be developed. There is no such thing as a human being who is not psychic, but just people who do not recognise their psychic faculties for what they are.

It might surprise you to know how many spiritually aware and sensitive people consider themselves to be about as psychic as an old boot. Spiritual awareness is extremely subtle and unless we learn to attune our minds to that more refined level of vibration, we can fail to recognise inner perceptions. For instance, how many times have you started thinking about someone you haven't seen for quite some time and haven't thought about for months, only to have that very person contact you within about 24 hours? What do you call that... coincidence? What is it that puts a mother on the alert when her child is exposed to danger, even though the child may be out of her range of vision? How many times have you listened to a person speaking and known beyond a shadow of doubt that the speaker is lying, even though there is not a single hint of dishonesty in his words or his expression? These and many other related incidents are things most people accept without really thinking about them. They're a normal part of life, everybody has experienced them, it isn't 'psychic', it's just natural. True, they *are* just natural: that's the whole point... it is *natural* for people to be psychic.

Psychic development is a process of tuning in to yourself, the person within. You have an infinite range of gifts and abilities that a book such as this can only begin to explore, and then only lightly. You have many layers of consciousness beyond the physically conscious mind and within those infinite depths of consciousness you have the knowledge of All that Is. If you were to become consciously aware at this level of all the things that are taking place within all of your other levels of existence all at once, you would probably go quite insane within a matter of moments. Your waking consciousness is simply not ready to absorb such a massive amount of input all at the same time.

Consciousness grows like a flower; it has to unfold gradually, in its own time and in the right season. For the sake of your physical survival, your conscious mind has to be focussed clearly within the physical. If it were not, you could walk in front of a train and never know what hit you. There has to be a protective mechanism within the structure of your consciousness that keeps your attention focussed where it is needed and, indeed, there is such a mechanism. We call it the Ego. The Ego is programmed for physical survival and when it feels threatened, it has the power to shut out the other levels of consciousness so that all of your energies are focussed into the physical. If you happen to be in danger of walking under a train, the Ego can be an extremely fortuitous asset. It makes an excellent servant: unfortunately it also makes a very bad master.

When the Ego is permitted to dominate the personality to such an extent that the conscious mind is capable of focussing on nothing but the physical world, the spirit is hobbled, unable to fulfil its purpose. Over centuries and centuries of conditioning, the human race has been conditioned to Ego-domination, to such an extent that a large proportion of human beings have forgotten who they really are, where they come from and why they are here. They have lost touch with themselves and as a consequence, they are wandering around in the darkness of spiritual ignorance, quite lost.

By resuming contact with our own inner divinity or spirituality, we can start remembering and releasing the true awareness that comes from spiritual vision, which helps us to see the purpose of our lives more clearly and to understand how our destiny may be fulfilled. We rediscover a sensation of completeness that we lost so long ago, we cannot even remember having had it, until it returns. It is the quest for this feeling of completeness or 'at-one-ment' that draws many people to seek within the spiritual for their fulfilment. Some people seek it in places where it cannot be found, in relationships with other people or in the accumulation of material fortune or power, but as long as they seek it outside themselves they will not find their treasure, for it comes from within.

There are any number of practical exercises that can help you to expand your consciousness but before commencing on any such course, there are universal laws that need to be understood. One of these is Karma.

We will be discussing the principle of Karma in some detail as we progress throughout this book; an understanding of karmic law is vital for your own well-being, therefore it deserves your attention. For the present it is only necessary to understand that Karma is a law of cause and effect that permeates every level of existence. Basically it means that any energies you give out must inevitably be returned to you. This applies not only to your actions but to the energies you emit in the form of thoughts and emotions as well.

The simplest way to explain the principles of vibration and thought energy is to do some quick revision on High School Physics. All matter consists of energy and all forms of energy are in constant motion, or vibration. Every form of energy has its own intrinsic rate or pattern of vibration and each pattern is as individual and unique as a fingerprint: there are no two energies that are exactly the same in every detail, although there are many qualities common to groups of energies which vibrate on a similar wavelength.

The wavelength of a particle of energy can change if its state of being is altered. For example, think of a particle of energy with which we are all acquainted, a molecule of water, H_2O. Water is a substance that is familiar to all of us, yet it has several different states of being in common with other forms of physical matter. These states are: solid, liquid or gas. In its solid form, water is rigid and its particles of energy vibrate slowly by comparison with the vibrations of water molecules in the liquid state. In the gaseous state, as steam, the molecules vibrate so quickly that they are no longer held tightly together but break free of each other and move through the atmosphere. The only essential difference between those three states of matter (apart from the obvious physical differences) is *the rate at which the energy particles vibrate.*

Thought is also a form of energy, although its wavelength is currently beyond the range of measurement of the machines created by our scientific technology. Like physical matter, thought has a number of different wavelengths: some are slow and comparatively rigid, others are faster and more flexible. The power of thought has yet to be fully recognised by the human race in general but any student of psychic energy must be aware that thought is capable of producing tangibly physical results. If, for instance, you were to continually focus your most powerfully negative thoughts onto another person, you could cause them an injury. By the same token, you can focus your positive thoughts to help others, as in spiritual healing for instance. The immense well of infinite human thought potential is only now beginning to be explored. Humanity as a whole has a long way to go before all this potential can be fully realised but even now, merely by scratching the surface, human beings are making achievements that would have seemed incredible a generation or two ago.

Communication with 'Higher Spiritual Intelligences' over the past few decades has indicated clearly that there are many highly evolved beings on levels beyond our own, who are keenly interested in our evolution and willing to guide and assist those of us who will accept their help. Contact with such beings is established through channels of psychic communication available to any human being who cares to make use of them but it is vital to be aware that not all the spirit beings who exist on levels beyond our own have our best welfare at heart. There are spirits who exist at very low levels of evolvement, whose characters and motives are primitive, aggressive, opportunistic and parasitical. It is worth bearing in mind that, whilst such low-level entities are primitive in terms of spiritual development, they are not necessarily stupid: most of them are skilled in the art of deception and, given an opportunity, can be extremely destructive. Psychic communication with high-level entities can be achieved safely if the questor is prepared to spend the necessary time and effort in raising his own level of vibrations to a point at which contact is possible. This may take time to achieve but it is the only safe course to take.

In the words of my spirit teacher, David: 'I cannot come to you. You must first come to me.' In essence, this means that if I am functioning at a low level of spiritual vibration, direct communication between David and me is not possible and, if I open my channels of communication at a lower level, a lower level being will make contact with me. That makes sense to me. To look at it from another point of view, if you want to contact me, you wouldn't begin your search in South America, would you? To find me, you must look for me where I live, in Australia. By the same line of reasoning, if you want to make contact with a highly advanced and trustworthy spirit teacher, you must seek for such an entity *on the level at which such beings exist.*

To use a different analogy, we could liken a spirit teacher to a radio station that is broadcasting on a particular wavelength. To receive that broadcast, you must tune your radio set to the required frequency. The spiritual development techniques given in this book are designed to help you focus your channels of communication in a way that will connect you with the higher levels of guidance and not with the levels at which there are influences that would do you harm. There is, however, one 'wild card' in the deck... YOU.

I can share my knowledge with you and I can offer advice based on my own experience but I have no control over the way in which you choose to apply that knowledge. For instance, I have said that it is possible to physically harm another person by focussing negative thought energy onto that person. I have also made it clear that whatever energies you send out will inevitably be returned to you by courtesy of karmic law. If any of my readers should choose to take the option of causing harm to someone and suffer severe karmic consequences as a result, please don't blame me... I warned you! I cannot stress this point strongly enough; anyone who chooses to use psychic energy in order to do harm or to gain some kind of unfair advantage over others will inevitably be hurt and the only person who can possibly be to blame is that person himself (or herself). Psychic energy is quite safe in the hands of those who use it with care and forethought but those who use it irresponsibly are asking to be hurt.

'You reap what you sow' is not an idle saying; it is an immutable cosmic principle. The spiritual law pertaining to free will is intrinsically linked with the law of Karma. If you deprive another of his free will, you are automatically and simultaneously throwing your own free will away. It is said that in order to confine another person in a ditch, you must be down in the ditch yourself. If you wish to reach the levels of spiritual existence occupied by the Spirits of Light, you need to be following the pathway of Light. The Spirits of Light, whether they be gliding around in some celestial sphere or physically incarnated right here in the material world, *never* knowingly impose on the free will of others. If what you are seeking is physical power and advantage, the pathway of Light will not lead you to it, for it leads into the spiritual, not the profane.

It matters not a scrap to which religion you belong, how much money you have in the bank or what colour skin you happen to be wearing this time around. What matters is the person living on the *inside*. The Spirits of Light are characterised by certain qualities; for instance, they are always motivated by a desire to help others. If they have money, they will use it to help the destitute. If they have a talent in music or art, they will use their creativity to inspire and uplift others. If they are psychically gifted, they will channel their gifts into helpful occupations such as healing or teaching.

We all have something to give and there is no gift that is of less value than any other. Remember the parable of the widow's mite? The two meagre coins she gave as an offering to her God were less than paltry beside the handful of gold thrown in with a flourish by the self-important rich man who strutted where he could be seen easily, making sure everyone could witness his pious generosity to the Lord. The widow quietly prayed, apologising to God because she was able to give so little. Yet, says the parable, in the eyes of God, her gift was by far the greater. The rich man had given but a fraction of his great wealth, and that only for show. The widow had given all she had, for love.

There are so many people who have written to me saying: 'I'd like to be able to do something to help make this world a better place for others, but I have so little to give.' That is the wrong way to look at things. It would be much more correct to say that these people have not yet begun to realise just how much they *do* have to offer. It doesn't matter whether you do something good out in the open where everyone can see you or quietly in your own corner when nobody else is around. What matters is not how much you give but how happy it makes you to give it. If you cannot give with love and joy, it is better not to give at all because a gift that is begrudged is a gift of bitterness.

I write because I enjoy it, not because I think 'I must' or 'I should'. I do it because it's fun, I enjoy talking to people and I enjoy writing. When I was in my early teens I had about eight penfriends, from a number of different races, living in different parts of the world. There was a girl in England, a boy in Singapore, an African princeling, two girls in different parts of India and two other girls living in Germany who wrote to me jointly as a part of their studies in the English language. Now, I write books and my readers write back to me. It's like writing to penfriends but on a much wider scale.

When I wrote my first book, it was based on my personal experiences. As a direct result of having written that book, my field of experience has been considerably widened because I now have information given to me by literally thousands of other people, which is much more data for my personal 'computer'. This sets up a cycle of positive energy in which, by doing what I can to help others expand their field of conscious awareness, I am helped in return to expand mine.

Life, for me, is a little bit like a living storybook and every story in it carries a lesson... and a gift. David has told me many times that the reward for education is further education. If you comprehend the law of Karma, that has to make sense. I learn from life and I learn from everyone who learns from me. It's known as a positive cycle and from where I am sitting, it feels good! The love and light that my readers keep pouring back to me has me on a permanent high. Who needs money?

If you set up cycles of positive energy in your life, Life itself will bring to you the things that you need. Ask and it shall be given to you; seek and you will find... heard those words before? The trouble with spiritual axioms is that they have a tendency to become so familiar that we never think about what they mean.

Thinking is what spiritual development is all about. Spiritual awareness comes through using your mind and through cultivating inner vision, the ability to look *into* things, not just *at* them.

Think about these words, written by Marcus Aurelius Antoninus in the 1st century A.D.: 'The universe is transformation; our life is what our thoughts make it.' Today, around nineteen centuries later, our quantum physicists are saying that 'Consciousness has an essential role to play in the creation of physical reality.' Personally, I think Marcus Aurelius' way of explaining it was easier to understand. I would put it even more simply: With your thoughts, you create your own reality.

In the theme from *Time*, Lawrence Olivier says 'If you want to change your world, my friends, you must change the way you think.' Listen to the words in songs like John Lennon's *Imagine* and *Mind Games*. What are all these people trying to tell us? They are saying that we can create a better world for ourselves and those whom we love, just by thinking about it. The Catch-22 is that in order to achieve it, you must figure out a way to do it without causing harm to another living thing or overruling anyone's free will. In short, you cannot impose your idea of a perfect reality onto someone who prefers another. Sensitivity and balance are the keys. Sensitivity without balance can become a multitude of phobias. Balance without sensitivity would only be cold logic.

There's much more to the spiritual way of life than just being psychic. There are psychics and there are psychics! There are some misguided psychics who use the energies at their disposal selfishly, bringing harm to others. I would not call them spiritual in nature. There are people who seem to believe that being psychic (in the popularly accepted sense of the word) automatically bestows infinite wisdom. There are people who use their energies wisely and there are people who do not. That is true in every stratum of life; the area of psychic activity is no different.

You can't have spiritual development without having a love affair with life. Spirituality pervades every level of our lives; we can find it right here in the physical if we care to look with our minds and not just our eyes. Psychic abilities and senses come into operation quite naturally when spiritual awareness begins to unfold and, when it happens this way, the conscious entity is sufficiently developed to take control of them without fuss. Forcing the development of your psychic abilities before you are spiritually and psychologically capable of handling them is courting disaster. When I speak of spirituality, I am not talking of religion; I am talking of the existence that we all share as spirits at a level beyond the confines of the physical. I call this the spiritual sphere; other people have different names for it. Whatever name you care to call it, I am speaking of developing the immense well of potential that lies within your own thoughts.

With great power comes great responsibility. The nuclear escalation in this world is a classic example of what can happen to great power in the hands of those too spiritually immature to handle it responsibly. You have a great deal of power within your own mind and, if you use it to destroy, it will destroy you. Right from the outset, the advice is: if you don't feel prepared to handle the responsibility, don't play with the energy.

CHAPTER ONE

The Quest for Truth

'Life is what happens to you
while you're busy making other plans.'

John Lennon *Beautiful Boy*

One Sunday when I was about twelve years old, I came home from a church service and informed my mother that I had no intention of attending church any longer.

'It's all lip service,' I grumbled. 'They don't really know any answers.'

'Oh, and I suppose you do?' There was more than a hint of irony in Mum's voice. I shook my head.

'Not yet, but I'm going to find them.'

'I see,' parried my mother. 'And how will you recognise the answers when you do find them?'

'I'll know because I'll *feel* it,' I answered, pressing one hand to my solar plexus. 'In here!'

Had I been a little older and more experienced, I would have known better than to accuse the church of not knowing any answers at all because that statement isn't really true. I would now be more inclined to say that the church was not giving me the answers I needed at the time, which is not quite the same thing. Still, even though at twelve I lacked the ability to express my feelings clearly, I knew I had to find something that would give meaning and purpose to my life and that I would never feel at peace within myself until I succeeded.

Children are very aware and perceptive little creatures; their view of life is often far more clear and realistic than the perspective of adulthood. By the time we become adults, our heads have usually been jammed so full of conflict and contradiction that it is easy for us to forget what the real questions are, as far as life is concerned. As for trying to find consistent answers, many people give it up as a hopeless cause. At the age of twelve, I had been attending High School for the better part of a year and I had been told in Science classes that the universe was created by some kind of cosmic explosion, human beings had evolved from apes and the whole business of living was an almost random process of evolution. This seemingly heretical revelation caused me some considerable degree of concern because it was in direct conflict with the story of Creation taught to me in Sunday School.

I had been raised to believe that my elders always knew best and I found this problem so perplexing that I decided to ask our parish minister for an explanation. I can't recall what he said in answer because it simply didn't make sense to me; it sounded more like an evasion than a reply. I found myself confronted with a seemingly hopeless dilemma which made my life confusing and meaningless. It occurred to me then that if science and religion could not agree with each other it was quite possible that neither side knew the whole truth.

In the years that followed, I became quite accustomed to being told to get my head out of the clouds, come down to Earth and start living in the world of reality. 'It isn't normal or healthy for you to be so immersed in your impossible dream,' I was told. 'The answers you are trying to find have eluded the world's wisest men for centuries: what makes you think that you will have any more success at finding them? Wake up to yourself. Get married, have babies; forget all this nonsense!'

If everyone around you keeps insisting that your view of life is abnormal for long enough you can reach a point at which you begin to believe them and, by the time I reached the age of eighteen, I had begun to accept the possibility that there was something wrong with my way of thinking. I tried to conform, to be like other people and to see life as they saw it but there always seemed to be something missing. What was the purpose of marrying, giving birth to children and struggling to acquire all the physical trappings of security when we all know perfectly well that eventually we will pass out of this world without ever learning to understand why we came here in the first place? There had to be something more and whatever it was, I needed to find it.

When I began to experience vivid premonitions of disaster at the age of eighteen I did not immediately recognise them as the key to the answers for which I had been searching for so long. Although I had never actively rejected the possible existence of the supernatural, I had never considered that it might have anything to do with me personally. As far as I knew, psychics were people who possessed some kind of mysterious abilities which gave them access to realms of existence that were closed to ordinary people like me and, in any case, the whole area of supernatural activity was highly suspect, if not actually sinister. Consequently my reaction to the advent of psychic activity in my life was a mixture of shock, fear and anger. I didn't know how to cope with it; I resented the ill fortune that had brought it upon me and wanted nothing more than to find a way of shutting it out so that I could at least try to live a normal life. As if I didn't already have enough problems!

Looking back, I now realise that I have always been psychic but in earlier years it had manifested in minor, subtle incidents, such as reaching for the telephone an instant before it started to ring or knowing who was at the door before I opened it. Like most other people, I had always ascribed these incidents either to coincidence or to some form of educated guesswork. Once I came to terms with it, however, I began to realise that the strange events which had begun occurring in my life proved that my earlier feelings had been correct and there was more to life than I had been led to believe. This renewed my determination to find the answers and also expanded my field of exploration.

I have often been accused of being a hopelessly idealistic dreamer, out of touch with reality and living in a world of fantasy but I have learned to understand that reality is a matter of personal perception. There are people who operate on the principle that reality consists only of that which can be perceived through the five physical senses. If that were true, it would confront us with some interesting questions: for instance, if you blow a silent dog whistle and your dog responds although he was not in a position from which you were visible to him, to what is he responding? Stuart Holroyd writes that 'To say

"Reality must consist of such-and-such because I've never experienced it any other way" is not only unphilosophical but fundamentally unintelligent, the cry not of the truth-seeker but of the man who seeks the fixation of belief.' (*Briefing for the Landing on Planet Earth*).

Not so very long ago in terms of human history, a man named Louis Pasteur died heartbroken and defeated, ostracised both by society and by the members of his own profession for making the preposterous claim that disease could be caused through the invasion of the body by living creatures too small to be seen with normal human vision. His critics, no doubt, were all people who would accept only what their physical senses told them.

Although the atmosphere today is much more liberal than it used to be, any mention of a personal involvement with the supernatural can still raise more than a few eyebrows. Some people dismiss the whole subject as too wildly fantastic to be possible, others regard it as the work of the devil. Nevertheless an increasing number of people are encountering so-called supernatural phenomena on a regular and frequent basis. When you find yourself actually *living* with the paranormal, you either come to terms with the situation or seriously consider booking yourself into the nearest psychiatric institution.

I don't think I'm any loopier than other normal human beings and, from my point of view, there are many things about life in this world that are much crazier than talking to spooks. The nuclear arms race is one example of human lunacy. Allowing people to starve to death on one side of the globe while millions of tonnes of surplus food are dumped to rot in other countries is another. I do not consider myself to be crazy and, having lived with the reality of supernatural phenomena for more than two decades, I have managed to come to terms with it. The letters I receive from readers have added the reassuring knowledge that, in my acceptance of the spiritual, I am far from being alone. Among the people who have made themselves known to me there are a variety of cultures, religions, philosophies and professions but remarkably few barriers. The search for truth has a way of transcending such man-made obstacles.

The spirit teacher David has explained to me that

human beings are basically in search of the answers to three questions:

'Where do I come from?'
'Why am I here?'
'Where am I going?'

Psychic perception, coupled with spiritual awareness, can provide us with keys that help us to find the answers to those questions, but it would be a mistake to regard psychic phenomena as being answers in themselves.

The fact, for example, that an ordinary housewife can be in telepathic communication with beings from other dimensions of existence is relatively unimportant, in fact it is not even unusual. There are heaps of people who can do the same thing; they do it all the time. It has been happening for literally thousands of years... so what? For me, the important issue is not that we can hear voices from other planes of existence; the real importance lies in what those voices are trying to tell us. It is for this reason that I am making no attempt to convince anyone of the reality of psychic phenomena. If you are prepared to accept the truth of it you will and if not, no words from me will sway your opinion. In this sense, it might be said that I am preaching to the converted but my function is simply to observe and report truthfully what I see. Perhaps my truth is yours also, perhaps not... All I ask is that you read what I have to say with an open mind and think about it from an objective point of view.

There are people who say that I have been especially lucky to have a husband, Roland, who, as a trance medium, makes it possible for me to have direct verbal communication with a spirit teacher advanced enough to take his place among those whom some know as 'The Shining Ones'. I certainly won't deny my good fortune but I am concerned about the number of people who appear to believe that direct contact with these higher intelligences is only ever made available to a special few. Nothing could be further from the truth.

So many people believe it is impossible for ordinary people to communicate with the Higher Ones simply because they have been *taught* to think that way and by believing that it is impossible, they make it impossible for themselves. In the beginning this was true of me also; that is why David had to communicate with me through a trance medium. Through Roland, it was made possible for David to teach me how to get my channels of communication open and functioning clearly so that I could converse directly with David through 'telepathy'. This is the way in which spiritual communication *naturally* occurs and everyone has the ability to do it.

I don't have any special gifts or abilities that are lacking in anyone else: if I did, it would be pointless for me to write books in an effort to tell others how to use abilities they don't have, wouldn't it? There is nothing I can do that cannot be done equally well or better by someone else. It isn't difficult to make contact with higher spiritual intelligences once you know how to approach the project. You don't need half a dozen university degrees, nor do you need to be particularly psychic in the accepted sense of the word. All you really need is some motivation and commitment, along with a willingness to perservere. Nothing worthwhile ever comes without a certain amount of effort. Spiritual illumination cannot be bestowed upon you by a tap on the head from a fairy with a magic wand. If you truly wish to gain enlightenment, you will have the motivation to persevere until you reach that goal. If not, you will not bother to make the effort.

In itself, developing your psychic abilities will not automatically bring spiritual illumination to you. Illumination is one of those lovely big words that people often use when they want to sound impressive but, unfortunately, many of those people never get around to looking up the true meaning of the word. People will tell you that to be illuminated means to be knowledgeable and wise. It is true that a genuinely illuminated person will display knowledge and wisdom but the word itself means something else. To illuminate means to light up: spiritual illumination is a lighting up from within, an irradiation with spiritual Light.

A great deal has been said and written about spiritual Light but many people still are unaware that the reference to it is literal, that the Light really exists. I didn't fully realise this until a few years ago but once I saw the truth of it, I wondered how on Earth I had managed to avoid seeing it for so long. It is one of those truths that is so simple and obvious that people continually fail to notice it.

The discovery of the reality brought me to a level of awareness far beyond the merely psychic and in the process of making that transition I became aware that our conception of ourselves as being alone and powerless in the world is a complete misrepresentation. Spiritually speaking, you and I have muscles we haven't even thought about using yet. The ways in which you can use the spiritual Light in order to develop those 'muscles' is a subject we will be exploring in detail further on.

Mankind in general is only now growing accustomed to the awareness that we are not alone in the universe; even today, there are still quite a few obstinate souls who cling to the belief that the entire universe was created solely for the benefit of we humans on Planet Earth. It takes a flexible mind to live with the awareness that we are not alone in our own tiny corner of the universe but are surrounded by uncountable hosts of intelligent beings who share our space at different levels of existence. For some inscrutable reason we are all encouraged to believe that it is impossible for ordinary human beings to communicate with our unseen companions, even though there are innumerable incidents recorded throughout history in which precisely that form of communication has occurred over and over again. This and other forms of parapsychological phenomena have been researched, witnessed, observed, tested and documented by impeccably erudite and educated personages, such as doctors, scientists and clerics, for centuries. Wouldn't you agree that it's about time we all stopped marvelling at the phenomenon itself and started paying attention to what it *means*?

Those of us who are prepared to listen to the spiritual message are told to use our own spiritual abilities in order to improve the quality of life for all who live in this world. Let's face it, when we look at what human 'civilisation' has done to this world so far, it could *do* with some improvement, couldn't it? We also have to realise that we are not the only intelligent life-forms in this world and that there are many other races of beings living here with us who are being affected by our collective selfishness and destructive activities. The fact that we can't see these other life-forms until we learn how to look properly is no excuse for ignoring their right to share this planet with us without suffering pain and hardship at our hands.

Whether it is seen as a blessing or a curse, I have been granted the ability to see life not only through my eyes but with my mind as well. There isn't anything unusual in that; any human being has the same ability. Whether or not you choose to *use* that ability is for you to decide. There are people who shrink away from this kind of vision, fearing it and calling it names like 'The Evil Eye'. Sometimes I can't help wondering if the attitude of those people is not prompted, at least in part, by a fear of what that kind of vision might reveal about themselves.

Some people do not look beyond the superficial manifestation of psychic phenomena. They cannot understand why I am not interested in telling fortunes at the drop of a hat or why Roland refuses to capitalise on his talent for trance mediumship by putting on public performances, so that anyone who desires to do so can carry on a conversation with the dear departed. We do not do these things for a number of reasons, the main one being that it is not where our interests lie. Besides, David has made it quite clear that if we wanted to play 'psychic parlour games' we would have to count him out.

If a person writes to me and says 'I want you to use your powers to heal my chronic acne in time for my sister's wedding next week', I probably won't have time to answer the letter. If I did answer it, I would tell the person how to make adjustments to his diet, lifestyle and attitudes in order to heal his own acne. In short, I am not here to do for other people what they are perfectly capable of doing for themselves and neither is Roland. We are simply here to share the things we have been taught to do and understand with those who are interested in making the effort to learn.

I have been taught to understand that we are not really physical in nature, that the greater part of our being is non-physical or spiritual. This is by no means a new revelation; it is a fact that has been recognised and accepted by countless people ever since the dawn of time as we know it. Even a person who has difficulty accepting the reality of the spirit is able to understand that, in addition to having physical bodies, we are also creatures of emotion, intellect and feeling, all of which are non-physical aspects of our nature. You can't catch an emotion and put it in a bottle. You have a physical body but there is also a person living within that outer shell.

The ancient Greeks had a word for this inner person; they called it the Psyche, the word meaning both spirit and mind, or either. Today there are people who will argue that the mind and the spirit are separate parts of our nature; there are even some who insist that the spirit does not exist. I'm not even going to start debating such a pointless argument: I know perfectly well that there is a person living inside my body... what the detractors have inside their bodies is anyone's guess. When I use the word Psyche, please understand that I am speaking not of a thing but of a person, the person who lives inside you. This is the *real* you, the immortal being.

Most major religions tell us that a part of us survives death, that in some form or another there is an afterlife. Once it was easy for people to say that the existence of an afterlife could not be proven, since 'Nobody who has died ever comes back to tell us about it'. Since the beginning of this century, however, that argument has become progressively less credible. There are psychics claiming to be in contact with spirits from beyond the veil of death, highly respected universities and scientific institutions studying the occurrence of paranormal phenomena and, just recently, the revelations of a growing number of people who have been resuscitated after a period of clinical death. The latter have told of observing the scene from a position above their own bodies and have correctly related the actions and conversations which took place around the body whilst the personality was considered to be dead and incapable of any form of awareness.

These people have further gone on to state that whilst out of the body they experienced travelling down a long tunnel towards a light, within which they could sense a presence that they seemed to recognise as a divinity. They have also related meeting and conversing with deceased loved ones, who usually told them that they must return to the body because it was not yet their time to leave this world. If there were only one or two recorded cases of this phenomenon there would, perhaps, be reason for scepticism. In fact, there have been hundreds of cases reported and researched by qualified medical personnel, involving people from many different cultures and philosophies all over the world. When only one or two people tell you that the sky is falling, you can shrug about it, but when hundreds more start saying the same thing, it would be wise to glance upwards, just to be on the safe side.

For anyone who is interested in learning more about the 'near-death' experience, I would suggest as reading material *Life after Life* by Dr. Raymond Moody, *Life at Death* by Kenneth Ring, Ph.D. and any of the excellent books by Dr. Elisabeth Kubler-Ross.

If we accept that events of an apparently paranormal nature can happen unexpectedly in the lives of other ordinary human beings, it would be reasonably logical to assume that such things can also happen to us. Even so, accepting this idea in an abstract way is not quite the same as experiencing the living reality, face to face. No matter how well prepared you may think you are at an intellectual level, the reality can take quite a bit of getting used to.

According to David, spiritual awakening with the attendant paranormal experiences is a normal and inevitable stage in the evolution of a human soul. In other words, if you haven't experienced it yet, you will! It is happening to thousands of perfectly sane and normal people in this country alone but, as yet, only a comparative few have been willing to speak openly about their experiences, for fear of being rejected or misunderstood. Many such people who have written to me have also confided that I am the first person to whom they have told their story because among all their friends and family members, there is not one person who would understand. I find that extremely sad.

Because people are naturally reluctant to speak openly

in the face of prejudice, it fosters the illusion that psychic activity at the 'normal' human level is a rare occurrence. This can lead to a number of problems for the person who is experiencing a spiritual awakening, not the least of which is a deep sense of loneliness and alienation. This major barrier can be overcome when you accept that it is natural for human beings to be psychically aware and active. Once you have made that mental adjustment, you can set about learning how to function normally at the psychic level.

Physical perception is limited by the boundaries of the five physical senses but, even so, it is a scientifically established fact that other forms of life exist beyond the range of our physical senses and that these unseen life-forms can have powerful effects on us. You cannot see a virus with the naked eye but if it should attack your life system you will certainly feel its effect. There is no way you would deny the existence of the virus; you can *feel* that it is real. We also know that there are light frequencies that exist beyond our range of vision and that other creatures can see within those ranges of frequency. A bumble-bee, for instance, sees everything in the ultra-violet range. Friends of mine who were given a bee's-eye view of life through the medium of television have informed me that it is quite a mind-blowing vision.

Compared with that of animals, our sense of smell is minimal and many animals are capable of hearing sounds inaudible to us. Because we can see evidence of the existence of those scientifically proven but humanly imperceptible energies around us all the time, we accept them without thinking very much about it. If you have only recently started to encounter paranormal phenomena on a personal basis, you might be interested to know that there will come a time when you will also accept this as matter-of-fact. It can be a bit mind-boggling at first but you do get used to it.

Although there is a growing acceptance of the paranormal, there is still a fairly widespread belief that there is something sinister about the 'occult' and those who meddle with it. You may complacently accept that idea for as long as you are not personally exposed to events of a supernatural nature, but once you do start experiencing them, what then? Must you try living with the idea that you have unwittingly allowed yourself to become an instrument of Satan? Ludicrous as it may seem, this is precisely what many psychic sensitives are expected to believe about themselves and, as one who has had to run that particular gauntlet more times than I care to remember, I can state quite emphatically that it's about as much help as a can of petrol in a bushfire. What a person really needs in this situation is understanding, support and good old-fashioned common sense.

The prospect of coming to terms with a totally new existence, in which everything you have previously thought to be impossible becomes an everyday reality, is daunting enough without having it further complicated by superstition, prejudice and old wives' tales. Psychic ability is not an abnormality; it is simply an extended range of *normal* human ability which can be cultivated by anyone. Psychics are conscious of a range of sense impressions not usually noticed by other people but they are not equipped with extra sense mechanisms; they simply use their standard equipment more efficiently.

In 1973, Brendan O'Regan of the Design Science Institute, Washington D.C. wrote 'Presumably, we in the West believe our senses only as their impressions are verified by the machines we create'. Think about that.

One of my favourite singers is Ivan Rebroff, a giant of a man, whose magnificent voice spans a range somewhere in the vicinity of four and a half octaves, from a bass that could rumble the floorboards to a clear soprano. The average range for the human voice is around two octaves. Now should we classify Mr. Rebroff as some kind of sideshow freak or, simply, allow ourselves to enjoy his artistry with music? It's interesting to note, by the way, that when speaking of his vocal range, Ivan Rebroff has been known to point out that he is equipped with exactly the same number of vocal chords as any other human being, the only difference being that he *uses* more of his. We can apply the same line of reasoning to the way in which psychics use their sensory faculties.

There is some basis for believing that our forebears were unable to see the range of colours that we see today. An ancient Greek writer referred, for instance, to the 'tricoloured rainbow', implying that he saw only three colours where we recognise seven. If this is the case, it is obvious that the range of normal human vision has done some expanding over the centuries. Quite possibly, any ancient Greek who attempted to convince his contemporaries that the rainbow contained seven colours may have been regarded as being a little strange.

If you are only capable of seeing three colours, then three colours are all your world will contain. That does not, however, give you any basis for assuming that if thousands of other people are seeing seven colours, there is something wrong with their eyes. John Denver sings a song called *Boy from the Country* which tells the story of a boy who is rejected and regarded as insane because he calls the Earth his mother, calls the forest his brother and tries to tell people that the animals can speak. 'Who knows?' says the song. 'Perhaps they do. How do you know they don't, just because they've never spoken to you?' I can relate to that kind of logic with no trouble at all!

There are many things in this world that can be classified as evil and, to my way of thinking, the father of all evil is ignorance. Ignorant people fear what they do not understand; because they fear it, they are hostile towards it and from that hostility comes hatred and harm. It really isn't long since hapless psychics were tortured and burned at the stake and, even today, there are quite a few people whose attitudes are still rooted in the Dark Ages. Prejudice and superstition can be hard to take when they are aimed at you but there are times when they can be quite amusing. When my first book was released there was a certain amount of publicity in newspapers, magazines, radio and television. Naturally enough, this was noticed by the neighbours in the Sydney suburb where I lived at the time and, whilst most of them didn't bother to read the book, their reactions to the publicity were quite an education.

Children on their way home from school used to entertain me regularly with robust renditions of the theme from the television series *The Addams Family* as they passed my house and I became quite accustomed to receiving suspicious glances from their older counterparts. A woman who lived several doors away gave vent to her opinions by abusing my son every time he passed her house and loudly hissing 'Witch!' whenever she passed me in the street, in a tone which clearly implied that people like me had no right to exist in a world that has invented penicillin.

There would have been no point whatsoever in making an effort to explain to this woman that, for a start, she was quite obviously making the common error of confusing witches with satanists. It would have been equally futile to try pointing out to her that, if I had been what she clearly believed me to be, her actions would have placed her in imminent peril of being turned into a toad. From her attitude, it was clear that any placatory attempt on my part would only have been rejected with vehement hostility, so I decided to deal with the situation by the simple expedient of ignoring it. Then my cat had kittens.

Now I know that, as a spiritually oriented person, I should hold myself above the temptation to turn the tables on someone who is doing her best to make life unpleasant for me and mine but, when I looked at Mother Cat's new family and saw one little fellow who was coal-black all over, my wicked sense of humour took control. The other kittens all found homes elsewhere but I kept the little black fellow, named him Merlin and went to great lengths to encourage him to be my inseparable companion. He got the message. As he grew, he obliged by following me everywhere like a little four-footed shadow. When he wasn't trotting around behind me, he could usually be seen reclining elegantly on our front steps, surveying the passing parade through a pair of infathomable green eyes.

On the occasions when I happened to be in our front yard as my hostile neighbour passed by, I would drape the cat across one shoulder, caress his ebony fur and croon 'There, Merlin,' in a voice dripping honey, both of us watching intently as she passed, head down and scurrying as fast as her feet would carry her. From that time on, she seemed to lose all interest in making open expressions of hostility, apparently preferring to pretend that I no longer existed. Okay, so maybe I *shouldn't* have done it... but it was fun!

Most of the time, we are forced to accept that some of the people in this world will view us with jaundiced eyes and that it is fruitless for us to make any attempt to alter their opinions. All we can do is smile through gritted teeth, mentally recite a few God-bless-you's and hope that the time when everyone will understand is not too far away. At the same time, we do not have to allow other people's opinions of us to affect the way we see ourselves or the way we express ourselves as individuals. My grandfather, who was to me everything the best grandfathers are supposed to be, had a fund of natural wisdom and one of his favourite sayings was a quotation from Tennyson:

> 'This above all, to thine own self be true. It follows... that thou canst not then be false to any man.'

In times when my self-confidence has been close to faltering under a barrage of criticism, those words have frequently been one of my greatest sources of comfort and reassurance.

Being true to yourself isn't always easy, especially when everyone around you is pressuring you to ignore the truth that you feel within yourself and to accept what they want you to believe. It's even harder when you know those people genuinely love you and sincerely believe that they know what is right for you. Being true to yourself also means being honest about your inner motives and that can be the greatest challenge of all. Nevertheless, if you do not wish to spend the rest of your life floundering in a morass of conflict and confusion, true to yourself is precisely what you need to be. It is not a crime to deceive yourself but, when you start working with psychic energy, self-deception can create situations that are likely to have a number of painful results for you. If you are not already aware of the reasons for this, they will become obvious as you read further into this book.

When people begin to be aware of the immense potential which exists within themselves, it is common to feel a tremendous thirst for knowledge, an impatience to know it all NOW. It is at this point that the psychic channels often seem to dry up and it is not unusual for long months to pass without any notable experiences at all. This happens quite frequently just after the commencement of regular meditation, leading many people into the mistaken assumption that their meditation periods are worse than useless. Many of the people who write to me have mentioned this effect and asked me if I could explain why it happens. It happened to me too and at the time I found it most perplexing, but the explanation is quite simple. The very fact that you start consciously working to develop your spiritual faculties is an indication that the spontaneous psychic occurrences have achieved their purpose.

By actively focussing your mind on developing your abilities, you effectively 'change channels' and proceed to work at a level upon which you will learn to exercise more conscious control. As you progress, you develop the facility of using your psychic channels at will and because you are directly controlling your energies, their function is likely to be somewhat altered. Your abilities do not disappear, they simply undergo a change of direction.

There is another factor to be considered at this point: when you begin to consciously direct your psychic energies you take on an increased responsibility. This is where you need to give serious thought to the principle known as the Law of Karma. This is a law of cause and effect, without which it would not be possible to maintain the balance of the universe. Karma will ensure that whatever energies you project onto others will be returned to you in kind... and magnified. Anyone who starts indiscriminately flinging psychic energy around before gaining a reasonable understanding of how it works is like a toddler who has been given a loaded machine gun to play with: in situations like this, people get hurt.

If I appear to be placing a heavy emphasis on the ethics of psychic activity, it is not without good reason. I have been an unwilling witness to the foolhardiness of a number of people who threw caution to the winds in their eagerness to get themselves involved in all the excitment of playing with psychic energy, heedless of the warnings given by others more experienced than themselves. Without exception, those over-enthusiastic souls inevitably brought harm, not only to themselves, but to other people as well. I would prefer to err on the side of caution than to risk under-emphasizing the very real need for a sense of responsibility, self-control and consideration for others.

The higher spiritual beings who assist in your development are aware that misplaced enthusiasm can lead an eager student into jeopardy, which is why the brakes are so often applied in the early stages of our conscious development while we go about the task of gaining the necessary patience and self-discipline. There are ways of circumventing these restrictions if a person is determined to do so but, since it is not in anyone's best interests to take that course of action, I do not feel inclined to explain how it can be done. It is wise to remember always that *there are no safe shortcuts in psychic development.*

Psychic energy need not be harmful if you handle it with care and wisdom and these virtues can be acquired if you are prepared to put a reasonable amount of effort into the project. In itself, psychic energy is neither good nor evil; it is purely energy and it is neutral until you channel it. To illustrate this principle, we could compare psychic energy with a laser beam. A laser beam is simply a highly potent ray of light and it can be beneficial or harmful, depending on how the user directs it. Put laser technology into the hands of healers and they will find ways of using it to improve the quality of life. Give the same technology to the military and you have a death ray.

A laser beam cannot be held responsible for what its user chooses to do with it and it would be ridiculous to say that, just because it can be used for a harmful purpose, it should never be used at all. It would be equally preposterous to say that because it can be used to cause harm, the laser beam itself is evil. Good and evil are qualities which arise in the minds and hearts of human beings, not in the energies that are available for their use. It is true that psychic energy can be used as an 'instrument of the devil' but it is also true that it can be used with even greater effectiveness on the side of the angels.

If a person's motives are self-seeking, he will use his

abilities in selfish ways and almost certainly cause a great deal of harm in the process: this is commonly known as Black Magic. On the other hand, you can seek to enhance your understanding of life and its purpose on a scale far beyond the limitations of physical experience and to use your knowledge in ways that are beneficial for all concerned. In either case, your actions towards others will be returned to you in kind. Since very few people really want to cause themselves unnecessary suffering, it seems to me that the most sensible course of action is to opt for the unselfish approach. It may be more difficult in the initial stages but the long-term benefits are infinitely more desirable than the fate which awaits those who follow the alternative pathway.

It has been said many times that the magic of today is the science of tomorrow and the more I learn to understand about the principles of psychic energy, the more I comprehend the profound truth in that statement. It is possible to understand the workings of psychic energy in terms that any average junior High School Science student could easily understand. If you want to develop your psychic abilities and explore the worlds of spiritual existence in safety, the sensible way to go about it is to take a scientific approach: learn to understand the principles by which the energy is governed so that when you set anything into motion, you can be reasonably sure that you know what results to expect.

Many of the psychic development groups in operation during recent years have tended to function on the principle that, if everybody sits around and does their best to open their channels of psychic awareness, something interesting is bound to happen sooner or later. This course of action is roughly equivalent to thrusting your bare hand into a hole in the ground in order to find out whether it is inhabited by a rabbit or a snake. It is not a method I can recommend.

In this book, I shall endeavour to provide an explanation of psychic energy principles that is comprehensive without being complicated, and to set out a program for psychic and spiritual development that is simple to follow, effective and safe. From the outset, it is necessary to bear in mind that it is impossible for anyone to set an arbitrary division between what is and is not psychic. Many of the commonplace incidents that we accept as being physical in nature are actually psychic and although most of us have been taught to believe in a clearcut division between the world of physical existence and the world of spirit, no such division actually exists. In reality, the physical is a *part* of the spiritual and the only barriers between the two are those which exist in our own minds.

While I'm exploding popular myths, I may as well disillusion anyone who believes that spiritual awareness is some kind of panacea that will miraculously remove all the problems, tribulations and hassles of life in the physical realm. Sorry to disappoint you, folks, but it doesn't work that way! The spiritual world is not a haven somewhere over the rainbow to which you can retreat when you want to get away from this world and all of its problems, although I will agree that it would be very nice for all of us if it were. If you learn how to look properly, you will be able to see the spiritual right here in the world around you but, in order to see it, you must be willing to look life squarely in the face.

Many of the people who try to ignore the physical side of life and devote their attention solely to the spiritual are, in fact, seeking an avenue of escape from their personal problems. Trying to run away from your troubles only makes them worse. Spiritual awareness can increase your problem-solving ability by giving you an expanded perspective on life and helping you to harness your energies more effectively, but trying to escape is a self-defeating exercise. It is by facing problems and learning from them that we grow in spiritual strength and stature. One of the greatest challenges in life is to take an apparently negative situation and turn it into something positive: that is how the *real* magic happens!

What do everyday, down-to earth physical problems have to do with spiritual development? The answer is simple: everything. People in quest of spiritual understanding sometimes tend to turn their backs on the physical as though it were unconnected with spiritual matters and, when they do so, they miss the whole point of the exercise. The world of spirit is not hidden behind some intangible barrier that can only be crossed at death or through the use of unusual psychic abilities; it is all around and within you. We are spiritual beings and the world we inhabit is a part of the spiritual world. As David has often said, if you cannot come to terms with life on the level at which you are now living, how can you possibly hope to understand it at a higher level? When you can see the spiritual *within* the physical, you are on the way to achieving your true potential.

Sometimes people expect spiritual assistance to come in the form of some extraordinary psychic intervention and, because of this, they tend to overlook the opportunities that reach them through seemingly ordinary and mundane channels. Not long ago, I heard a clergyman illustrate this theme with a tale about a man who sincerely believed that, if ever he desperately needed help, God would come to his aid. According to the story, the man was fishing from some rocks when an enormous wave came along and swept him into the water, where a powerful current swiftly washed him out to sea. Struggling for his life, the man frantically called for help.

'Lord, save me!'

It wasn't long before a fishing boat came along but when the crew attempted to rescue the drowning man, he waved them away.

'I don't need your help,' he told them. 'The Lord will save me.'

So the fishing boat sailed away and the man went on calling to the Lord for his salvation. Meanwhile, some people who saw the man swept off the rocks had contacted the Air-Sea Rescue Service and, no sooner had the fishing boat disappeared from view, when a fully equipped rescue helicopter appeared on the scene. Again, the man sent his would-be rescuers away, saying the Lord would save him. The helicopter flew away and the man went on struggling in the water and calling on the Lord for help until finally he drowned. When he arrived at the Pearly Gates, he stomped up to confront the Lord in a state of high indignation.

'I trusted You and You deserted me!' he declared in irate tones. 'I always believed that if I ever really needed help, You would come to my aid but, in my time of greatest need, You ignored my cries for help and let me drown. Why?'

Sadly shaking his head, the Lord replied. 'Have you any idea how much planning and co-ordination it required for me to get the fishing boat and the helicopter to you? Twice I reached out to help you and twice you refused to accept the assistance that was offered to you. Instead, you let yourself drown. Why?'

As spiritual entities, we come into this world in order to grow and to learn; the means by which this process is made possible are already provided in the very structure of our environment. Our purpose is to look at life, see it as it really is, face the challenges that confront us and learn how to overcome them. The only way to achieve this successfully is to get in and start *doing* it. If you can see your problems as blessings that are given to help you grow and achieve your potential, rather than curses sent to bedevil you and weigh you down, you have the means to turn your negatives into positives. Feeling miserable and sorry for yourself doesn't help, it only makes things worse. By taking a negative attitude, you will only increase the amount of negativity that surrounds you. Besides, why should you feel miserable about having an opportunity to overcome a challenge?

There is no point in looking outside of yourself for spiritual truth. You will find it only by learning to clear away the accumulated flotsam of unbalanced human conditioning and to look within yourself. See yourself as you really are in all your spiritual brilliance and start bringing that inner essence through into your physical life. When you are living in accord with the laws of the Creator, which are simply the laws of Nature, then you will find life working with you. If things are going against you all the time, it is usually an indication that you are working in opposition to the natural order and not perceiving your own purpose clearly. This is probably the result of the faulty human conditioning to which you have been subjected.

The human race seems to have a tendency to get itself into difficulties and then look for some miraculous intervention to get itself out of the mess. I don't know how many times I have heard people say 'If there really is a God, if He really is omnipotent and if He really does love us, why does He allow war, violence, corruption and cruelty to continue? Why doesn't He just step in and put a stop to it?'. This would seem to imply that the Creator is obliged to fulfil the role of some kind of cosmic cleaning lady, whilst we have the right to make as much mess as we feel inclined to make. Would that really be in our best interests? Would it help us to achieve maturity? I think not.

At the time of writing, my son Darryl is eighteen years old. Throughout his childhood, he was a typically messy little boy, whose bedroom habitually resembled the aftermath of a cyclone. I don't know how many times I waded in and cleaned up the mess for him, only to see his nice tidy room reduced to a shambles again within a matter of hours. When Darryl reached an age at which Roland and I felt that he should be capable of shouldering some responsibilities of his own, he was told that I would not be held responsible for the state of his room any more. If he wanted to live in a room that looked like a garbage dump, he could do so. I simply affixed a notice to the wall outside his bedroom which read 'The Management is not responsible for the state of this room'.

It took time and there were many occasions on which I had to restrain myself from attacking the room with pails of disinfectant but we left it as it was and Darryl had to live in it. When his friends came to call, they would simply be told 'He's in his room', and if Darryl felt embarrassed when they saw the mess, that was his problem. When he complained about having no clean clothes to wear, I pointed out that I would wash any clothes that were placed in the laundry basket but I had no intention of searching through his room to find them.

Gradually, the message penetrated. Darryl's clothes started appearing in the laundry basket and his room began to take on a tidier appearance. It still gets a bit cluttered at times but it is no longer a health hazard and we don't have to shudder every time we walk past his door. If I had continued to clean up after him, it would still be as it was before we dumped the responsibility onto his shoulders.

The Creator has given us a beautiful world in which

to live. There is no cathedral more magnificent than the star-studded sky at night and no painting that can surpass the glories of nature. Planet Earth is capable of providing food in abundance for all her children and, if we really wanted to do so, we could be living in a garden of paradise, in peace and plenty. We should not have to work ourselves into the ground in order to scrape together a few crusts of bread to keep ourselves from starvation. It isn't the Creator who messed it all up and made things so difficult: that responsibility must be collectively shared by every member of the human race.

If we, as a race, wish to live in a world of beauty, in peace and abundance, we have everything we need to create such an environment. As for the mess that currently blights this world and makes life a trial and a torment for so many human beings, why should we expect the Creator to clean it up? The human race made the mess and it is the human race's responsibility to clean it up. If God were to step in and do it for us, we would probably only set about getting it into another mess, just like little children who mess up their rooms after Mother has done all the tidying. The only way to teach little children not to keep making messes is by leaving them to live in the conditions they have created for themselves.

If we were all living in accordance with natural law, we would not have war, famine, pollution, ecological disaster and ugly grey piles of concrete cluttering up the landscape. If we tended the Earth, instead of raping it, there would be an abundant variety of food for all and our world would be a garden of happiness, not a place of heartbreak and horror. We would not be sitting around in idleness, by any means; there would be enough work to keep us from becoming bored but even that would be a pleasure instead of a burden.

Perhaps it may seem to some people that such a world exists only as a Utopian fantasy, but it does not appear that way to me. I am far from being the only person who carries this vision and it is certainly not an idealistic daydream. Every day there are more and more people working to bring this vision into reality, right here and now. Certainly we have obstacles to overcome, chiefly in the form of opposition from people who do not share the vision and cannot comprehend what we are working to achieve. They fear a loss of security and do not yet understand that they stand to benefit much more from our combined efforts than would ever be possible if the current trends were to continue.

It is time for our world to be transformed into the place of abundant beauty that it is meant to be and nothing on this Earth, no matter how fearsome, will prevent that transformation from happening. Unrealistic? Idealistic? Not at all. If you will open your mind as well as your eyes, you can see the transformation taking place. Not only that, but you also have a great deal to contribute in helping to make it all happen. Perhaps it isn't easy at the start and maybe it will require some effort and commitment but, when you consider the alternatives, have you anything better to do with your energy?

By now it should be apparent that when I speak about spiritual development I am not referring to telling fortunes or bending teaspoons. Those things are certainly possible but when their benefits are weighed against the advantages of putting your considerable spiritual energies to work for the improvement of life in this world for all who live in it, there is no comparison.

When you understand the truth about who you really are and what you are capable of achieving through your inner potential, you will not need me to tell you why it would be tragic if you were to allow it all to be wasted. We are capable of achieving wonders that most of us haven't even begun to imagine yet and it all starts with you. The answers to all the questions you have ever asked or are ever likely to ask are there inside you. All you need to do is learn how to look inwards and see the truth. When you have done that, the whole universe will be open to you, just as it is open to those of your fellow human beings who have already begun. It's time to come out of your shell and find out where you really belong!

CHAPTER TWO

Development Groups

People who set out in search of spiritual enlightenment tend to have a number of things in common. Chiefly, they are sensitive: this quality of sensitivity endows them with an awareness that there is more to life than they have been taught to believe. They may not be sure exactly what awaits them beyond the boundaries of physical life but they know there is *something* and, whatever it is, it holds a fascination that draws them into a quest for understanding.

Contrary to uninformed opinion, the majority of these people do not think of themselves as being particularly psychic in the commonly accepted sense of the word. If they are truly seeking for spiritual enlightenment, they are usually not interested in becoming involved with the more sensational aspects of psychic activity. Although such things might generate a passing curiosity, these people are generally in search of something deeper, something that will satisfy their hunger for understanding and give their lives a heightened sense of purpose. Spiritually oriented people usually prefer to avoid referring to themselves as psychics, largely because of the connotations placed on the term by society. If we must have labels at all, the term that creates the least discomfort is 'sensitive' which is, on the whole, much more appropriate.

Although it is in their nature to be deeply spiritual, sensitives tend to be disenchanted with orthodox religion, primarily because it has failed to answer their deeper needs or to give them the kind of guidance they seek. Often too, they have felt rejected by the more conventional philosophies because they are representative of something unknown and, therefore, suspect in the eyes of the followers of orthodoxy.

The sensitives who have come to me for assistance are

usually looking for a way to find contact with higher forms of spiritual intelligence who can provide them with guidance to help lift themselves onto a higher level of awareness and understanding. It is this urge that frequently leads spiritually sensitive people to consult mediums and clairvoyants, a course of action which does not always produce the most desirable or satisfactory results. Such communications can be inspiring, especially when the medium is highly spiritual in motive, but it is an unfortunate fact that many professional clairvoyants are not on a very high level of advancement and the messages they transmit are at best trivial and at worst misleading.

Everyone has, within themselves, the potential to achieve communication with higher spiritual intelligences and it is far better to work at developing those inner channels than to rely on information transmitted through another person, no matter how sincere or well advanced that person may be. Spiritual development, as its name implies, is a process of getting in touch with your own spiritual abilities and raising them to a level of function at which it is possible to draw guidance and information through a direct channel, usually with the assistance of a spiritual guide or guardian. In the information that follows, I have structured guidelines in accordance with the needs expressed by those people who have come to me for advice. I have also paid particular attention to the need for safety, simplicity and the kind of flexibility that will make the program equally effective whether it is carried out by one person alone or by a group.

Some of the principles given here may already be known to you, but I should stress that my object is not to invent anything new and revolutionary. I consider it wiser to use techniques and principles that have been tested successfully by as many people as possible and can therefore be considered both safe and reliable. Whilst I am aware that the explanatory material covers territory that will already be familiar to some of my readers, it is necessary for me to bear in mind that others will only recently have begun their quest for understanding and, for them, it is all new ground. From my experience in working with groups of people, I have found it most effective to begin on the assumption that everyone is a beginner. Those who have already acquired a certain amount of experience usually don't mind revising the basics, whilst those who are only just starting out are not left feeling out of their depth.

A high level of psychic ability or expertise does not automatically imply a high level of spiritual awareness or wisdom. There are people who are versed in the use of psychic energy, Satanists for example, who are brilliantly psychic but I doubt that many of us would regard their motives as being particularly spiritual.

It is worth remembering that to see is not always to understand. I could sit in the cockpit of a jumbo jet forever, just staring at the control panel but that wouldn't teach me how to fly the aircraft. I have never seen any evidence to indicate that it is particularly safe, or even worthwhile, to concentrate on the development of psychic abilities without giving at least an equal amount of attention to the spiritual energy principles involved. Therefore, whilst you will certainly find psychic development techniques given throughout this book, you will already have noticed a great amount of attention given to the relevant principles. To ignore those principles and concentrate only on psychic development is definitely not the wisest course of action for anyone to follow: this is something I have learned both from observation and experience.

As your spiritual awareness unfolds, the psychic senses will automatically come into function, naturally and in harmony with the order of things. This principle does not function in reverse: forcing the development of the psychic faculties is unlikely to lead into spiritual wisdom. Playing with forces you do not fully understand and therefore cannot control is an invitation to disaster: psychic energy is not a toy.

Roland and I once visited a psychic development class in which a group of people were hoping to learn how to become trance mediums. The person conducting the class had begun trancing only eighteen months previously and had been running the class for twelve months which signifies that, after just six months of trancing, that person considered herself qualified to teach others.

I know that in some philosophies, trance mediums are regarded as the elite and to be a trance medium is considered an indication of superior spiritual knowledge, but that can be a very dangerous misconception. Roland is a brilliant trance medium and in trance he has been the vehicle for communication with some extremely high levels of spiritual existence but when he first began trancing, he didn't even *believe* in psychic phenomena, much less understand it. Over the past ten years, Roland has made significant progress in terms of acceptance and understanding but even now, if you ask him to explain his function as a trance medium, he will reply with a shrug.

'What's to explain? I sit in a chair and go to sleep.'

In the aforementioned trance class, it was clearly demonstrated to me that the 'teacher' knew little or nothing about the basic safety precautions for trance mediumship. When Roland showed signs of entering a trance state she leapt from her chair, grabbed him by the shoulders and started shaking him roughly. At first I was too stunned to move and it is fortunate that Roland was only in the first superficial stages of trance because if he had been in full trance, the shock of her actions could have killed him. This sort of behaviour is what I call 'The Wild Card in the Deck' — unpredictable human nature, otherwise known as the Absurdity Factor!

This woman tried to justify her actions by informing me that, since *her* guide hadn't warned her in advance that Roland would trance, it was obvious that the spirit involved had been a low-level entity, probably malicious. In fact, the spirit concerned was David, who had intended to offer the class some helpful advice.

The actions taken by the woman told me a number of things about her, the first being that she was completely oblivious to the danger of even touching an entranced medium unexpectedly, let alone handling him as violently as she had done. Secondly, her remarks about low level entities indicated that she had made no attempt to protect the trance room against invasion which indicates either that she did not know how to do so or that she had failed to realise that it was necessary. Finally, even if Roland had been in the process of being taken over by a low-level entity, grabbing him and shaking him would *not* have been the way to deal with the situation. The only conclusion possible for me to draw in this case was that the woman was not only spiritually incompetent but also a danger to her students.

These days it is quite fashionable to be psychic and anyone can set themselves up as a guru. Unfortunately, there are too many self-styled teachers who are sadly under-qualified and whose motives owe more to a desire for ego gratification and/or financial gain than to genuine spiritual understanding. There are some genuinely gifted and sincerely spiritual teachers around, I've met quite a few of them, but it isn't easy to distinguish one from the other if you are just starting out. This can lead to a Catch-22 situation: how are you to learn if you cannot find a teacher and, if you do find one, how do you know the person is reliable unless you already have a reasonable amount of knowledge?

Relax! The situation is not as hopeless as it may at first appear. Provided that you understand the basic principles and necessary safety precautions, you can be your own best teacher. You can also get together with a small group of like-minded friends and form an effective development group of your own. This is probably the best way to proceed because, in a group, you can pool your energies, share knowledge and experiences and also give each other some much-appreciated understanding and support. You don't need a large number of people; three or four can be enough. Any more than six can become cumbersome and difficult to co-ordinate.

If you are working with a group, there are one or two pitfalls that should be avoided right from the start and the biggest bogey amongst them is egotism. There is no room for egotism in spiritual development and any competitive elements within a group should be thoroughly discouraged. The moment you have one person taking a dominant role and dictating to the other group members, you may as well disband the group. Admittedly, you need a certain amount of organisation and there has to be someone to direct the order of proceedings during your meetings but it needn't be the same person every time. In fact, it is best to take turns so that everyone has an equal chance to experience all of the functions and responsibilities within the group as a whole.

There are some basic procedures that should always be included in your activities, such as the cleansing and protective procedures which guard against negative interference. These techniques are explained in the following chapter. There is also a certain necessity for the kind of repetition that reinforces understanding and promotes spiritual growth. In this respect, the development of spiritual abilities can be compared with athletic training, where the working muscles need to repeat specific sets of exercises. Within that framework, however, there is still plenty of room for variation and there is a wide range of meditation techniques and exercises that can be used with excellent results.

Nothing could be more boring and disheartening than an endless repetition of the same old routine, which can happen if you have the same person leading your group activities at every meeting. In addition, it is counter-productive to place the onus of leadership on one person. If each member is aware that they will be taking the chair in turn, it is an incentive for them to engage in private study and research so that they will be able to bring greater insight and fresh ideas into each group meeting.

While you are working to develop what is commonly known as your sixth sense, there are two other senses that should also be exercised: common sense and your sense of humour. Just because your motive is spiritual it doesn't mean that you must act as though you're attending a funeral. The hallmark of a really good group is the ability of its members to relax and enjoy themselves. Laughter raises the level of spiritual vibrations and lightens the atmosphere, thereby encouraging healthy spiritual growth. It is possible to be serious in your endeavours and light of heart at the same time and, if you are not enjoying your spiritual growth, you aren't doing it right. Remember that the angels rejoice to hear your laughter!

It is not advisable to let yourself be too carried away with the psychic aspect of your endeavours; whilst psychic activity is a natural facet of spiritual growth, it is a means to an end, not and end in itself. I have known development groups in which there is a chorus of Oohs and Ahs whenever a candle happens to splutter and the most trivial incidents are regarded as omens of the greatest import. Candles do splutter and it is most unwise to exaggerate small incidents in a way that is totally out of proportion to their significance. If you permit this to happen, you can find yourself running off at a tangent away from the spiritual objective. Take note of these things certainly, but do not let them become the prime focus of your attention.

While your mind is alert to the possibility of psychic communication, try to remember that the physical world itself is a manifestation of the spiritual. It is often through events of an everyday nature that the spiritual will seek to reach you. By accepting only the unusual or waiting for a sign from the heavens, it is likely that you will overlook the clear and explicit messages that flow towards you in the natural order of things.

For example, let's take an ordinary housewife, doing her weekly shopping at the supermarket. Nothing could be more commonplace and the supermarket is probably the very last place in which you would expect anyone to receive a psychic 'message'. Don't close your mind to the possibility; it *can* happen. For instance, our housewife may find her attention caught by a display of disposable blade razors, so strongly that she has an urge to pick up a packet and drop them into her trolley. It so happens that her husband has used an electric razor for as long as she has known him, so she dismisses the impulse as a momentary aberration and passes on, leaving the disposable razors on the shelf.

Next morning, her husband emerges from the bathroom half-shaven, holding a very dead electric razor in his hand and muttering a string of imprecations. He is now forced to grump off to work without shaving and she is probably going to do some extra running around to arrange for his razor to be repaired or replaced. 'Funny!' she thinks to herself. 'I almost bought some disposable razors yesterday. They'd have been very useful right now.'

Some time ago, Roland and I were planning a journey

to Melbourne during which we had arranged to spend a few days with a friend. As it sometimes happens, we had to alter some of our plans at the last moment and there wasn't time for us to advise our friend by mail and get the necessary reply before we were due to leave so I decided to contact him by telephone.

It was a Sunday morning and since our friend Marc shares a house with four other people, it was reasonable to assume that there would be someone on hand to answer the call but the telephone rang and rang interminably with no response. After trying fruitlessly for some time I began to wonder if there might be a faulty connection and decided to call in some help from 'Upstairs'.

'C'mon fellas!' I implored heavenwards. 'You know how important it is for me to get through, how about some assistance?'

I dialled the number again and this time I heard the click of a connection, followed by what was obviously the tail end of one of Telecom's recorded messages. '... please check the number in your telephone book and dial again,' it instructed me, with irritating smugness. I was beginning to feel more than a little annoyed! I had written the telephone number into my address book several weeks previously and knew that I had been dialling correctly.

'Damn it, that's all I need!' I grouched. 'Why on Earth do I keep getting faulty connections?'

For the next half-hour or so I kept trying the number, to no avail. Finally I slammed the receiver down in fierce exasperation. 'This is *impossible*!' I fumed. 'There are five people in that house; why doesn't someone answer the wretched telephone?'

I stomped away from the telephone desk and flopped down onto my bed. As I did so, something fluttered to the floor. It was Marc's most recent letter, with his telephone number written in bold capitals at the head of the page. I picked it up and stared at it in astonishment. I don't know how it happened but I had somehow managed to copy the number into my book with the last two digits transposed.

I called again and this time the telephone was answered on the third ring by a pleasant-voiced young woman.

'I'm sorry, Marc isn't here just now,' she told me. 'He went out half an hour ago.'

Half an hour earlier I had been *told* to check the number in my book and because it had sounded like just another Telecom message and I was so sure that I had written the number down correctly, I had ignored it. Trust me to forget that our friends Upstairs will often use facilities that are already available. I don't know how much clever manipulation had been required on their part to make the message play as it had but I do know they were not impressed with my lack of perception. They had responded to my plea for help promptly enough, but I had been too dense to recognise the message.

Being as human as anyone else, I can occasionally forget that the world is my schoolroom and every experience in life carries a message or a lesson to be learned but, whenever I forget, I can usually be confident that life will manage to rap me across the knuckles before I stray too far from the path. I have learned to understand that to disregard the mundane and spend all my time searching for the extraordinary would be to throw away countless opportunities for learning. Spiritual vision is not so much a matter of what you see as how you look. By looking beyond the surface, we can see how all life in its infinite variety fits together as part of an overall pattern.

If you are working with a group, don't fill all of the time with meditation exercises and organised activities. Take the time to discuss what you are doing. If you have just completed a meditation exercise, follow it with a discussion. How did the group members react to the exercise? Did they receive any impressions during the procedure? If so, what form did the impressions take: mental images, physical sensations, emotions, thoughts or a combination of things? Did they enjoy it? Do they feel that they gained something from it? Would they like to do it again in future? Listen to what the others have to say. You can learn as much from the comments made by your companions as from books and psychic impressions, sometimes even more.

When I was running development classes in Sydney, I found that I learned a great deal by listening to my students instead of just talking at them. By their reactions, I could tell which exercises were the most productive. By taking note of the questions they asked, I could tell whether or not I had explained a particular principle clearly enough. Often the students would make remarks that provided me with an added insight into a subject that I had thought I already understood. As I taught them, my students taught me in return, even though they were usually unaware that they were doing so.

Be selective and practise discrimination by all means: you must, if you are not to become bogged down under a pile of conflicting ideas but, at the same time, try to be open-minded. Be prepared to listen to others and, when differences of opinion arise, search for common ground and find areas in which your ideas agree, rather than arguing over who is wrong. The idea is to learn from each other and in this way you will come closer to an understanding of universal truth. Isn't that what you are seeking?

Many people are inclined to be hesitant when it comes to relating their inner impressions in a group situation, for fear of sounding ridiculous. Often they are uncertain as to whether an impression is valid or merely the result of an overactive imagination. This is a natural reaction when we consider that most of us are conditioned to ignore our inner impressions and to dismiss them as fantasy. Sensitives frequently have difficulty in deciding whether an inner impression comes from a reliable source or is merely a product of wishful thinking. I wouldn't mind having a dollar for every time I've heard someone say 'I don't know whether this is for real or whether I'm only kidding myself.'

I can sympathise with people who find themselves in that predicament; I've felt that way myself and there are still occasions when I can feel uncertain. It would be less difficult if I could always see spiritual visions emblazoned in the sky in three-dimensional colour or if I could hear spirit voices in the same way as I hear human speech but, in practice, such things rarely happen, to me at least. More commonly, a vision will form inside my head, as though it is projected onto a screen behind my eyelids. Clairaudient or 'verbal' communication will occur as words in my mind, as though I'm having a mental conversation with myself. Some impressions can be even more nebulous, such as an emotional mood or a funny sort of roller-coaster feeling in the solar plexus.

We can't be one hundred per cent sure of ourselves all the time. There are bound to be some occasions when things are misinterpreted but, if you try to censor your impressions, you will only succeed in stifling them and that won't help your development at all. This is one of the areas where the support and understanding of other group members is invaluable. We all feel uncertain at times and we can all blunder but, if we can have confidence that we aren't expected to be superhuman, we can at least relax, be ourselves and learn to go with the flow.

Another question which bothers a number of people concerns the nature of reality. How can we know for sure what is real and what is unreal? Everything is real at some level of existence and more often than not, it is our physical senses that deceive us, not our subjective impressions. Things in the physical world are never quite what they appear to be on the surface and our inner impressions are usually closer to the truth. How often have you ignored a gut feeling in favour of logic, only to discover that your inner feelings were correct? Instead of asking 'Is it real?', it would be better to ask 'Is it relevant?'. Even then it is possible that, although an impression may seem irrelevant to you, it could have significance for one of your companions, so don't hold back... communicate.

Whilst meditating with a group of friends not long ago, I had a strong physical sensation as though someone unseen were placing a ring on the middle finger of my left hand. At the same time, I had a mental picture of a gold ring set with a ruby which had been cut into the shape of a rose. The impression meant nothing to me but I shared it with my companions anyway. A young woman in our group, who had been widowed some eighteen months previously, spoke up almost immediately.

'I think that might be for me,' she told us, a little shyly.

Before leaving home that evening, the young widow

had felt strongly impelled to place her husband's wedding ring on her own hand, something she had never done since his death. The ring was too large to fit on any but the middle finger on her left hand, so that is where she wore it although I hadn't noticed it when she arrived. The ring was a plain gold band so I was a little puzzled about why I had seen it with a ruby rose until she explained further. On the birth of each of their sons, her husband had presented her with a bouquet of roses.

'I've been hoping that one day he might find some way of getting through to me, just to let me know he's alright,' she confided. 'Because he died in an accident, I was concerned in case he might have become earthbound. I'm glad he passed on his message through someone else because I mightn't have dared to believe it, had he contacted me direct.'

Seeing her eyes light up with a quiet glow and imagining how much that message must have meant to her, I felt a warm surge of pleasure and a sense of privilege. How sad it would have been for the young husband who had reached out to reassure the wife he loved if I had dismissed the contact as a trick of the mind or if I had lacked the confidence to share it with the group.

It isn't always a good idea to try analysing or interpreting the impressions you receive, particularly in the early stages of your development. Better simply to describe them and let the course of events show how and where they apply. In this way you are more likely to develop an intuitive understanding of their meaning. It is also a mistake to try to interpret another person's impressions for them, chiefly because an image that has a particular meaning for you may mean something subtly different to another person. For instance, a vision of a sword might give you an impression of a guardian or a defender whereas someone else may interpret it as a warning of danger.

I have found it easier to share impressions if they are prefaced with a remark like 'I'm seeing an image of . . .' or 'There are words going through my head . . .'. It then becomes a simple matter of describing your impression as it occurs. Don't neglect to describe any accompanying feelings as well, even when they seem inappropriate. As an example, if you are mentally seeing a young girl dancing in a field of daisies under a glorious summer sky but have a feeling of heaviness and foreboding, it may indicate a situation which appears good on the surface but conceals a serious problem.

If you are working alone rather than with a group, it is a good idea to write down your impressions in a notebook. This way you can keep a record of your progress. People are often surprised when they read back over their notes and realise how much headway they have made when they may have been feeling that they were not making very good progress at all.

In group situations, two or more people will often share an impression. In a group that I used to attend, this happened regularly. On one occasion, four of the five members shared an impression of looking down from a height over a sweeping expanse of lush countryside. Superficial details varied: I had an impression of drifting on a cloud while someone else saw the scene as though from the ramparts of a castle but the basic elements were too much alike to have been coincidental.

You may find that as one person makes a statement, another will say 'You've taken the words out of my mouth! I was just thinking exactly the same thing'. It is very gratifying when such things happen but it can sometimes lead to a babble of discussion which loses direction. To deal with such situations, Roland and I devised a game called Psychic Snap, a variation on the children's card game. It works quite simply: when you hear someone else putting your thoughts into words, you just say 'Snap!' or snap your fingers. Everyone in the group will then be aware that a connection has been made and the person who is speaking can continue without interruption. Afterwards, you will be given the chance to explain how your thoughts or impressions have tallied.

It isn't unusual for two or three group members to call a Snap at the same time and, when Snaps happen, they provide excellent feedback for the group as a whole. If someone else receives an impression similar to yours it can reinforce your confidence in the validity of your perceptions. When two people repeatedly put each other's thoughts into words, it is possible that they share a telepathic link, which could provide an opportunity for some worthwhile experiments. In any case, Psychic Snap is fun and can add to the enjoyment shared by the group.

Ideally, there should be a sense of unity and kinship so that the group takes on an identity of its own, becoming a cohesive unit rather than a collection of assorted personalities. A group that can successfully establish such a rapport has many advantages in terms of strength and progress. With everyone pulling together as a unit it is possible to make much better progress than could be achieved in a group where the members are intent on doing their own thing. Any group will function most effectively when the energies within it are balanced and in harmony. In addition, a well-balanced group has a much better chance of attracting the close assistance of highly advanced spirit teachers.

A successful group will develop a character that is a composite of the personalities of its members, yet has a unique quality of its own. The group personality can develop to such an extent that it becomes a living essence which can be tangibly felt. I was present at one group in which the group personality had become so complete that it actually *spoke* to the members through a trance medium. That may sound far-fetched if you know nothing about the creation of thought-forms, but I was there and I can assure you that it did happen! When a group can achieve such a blending of energies that it develops a unified personality, we refer to it as the Group Entity.

The first goal of a development group should be the formation of the group entity. This will set into motion a cycle of energy that is beneficial not only for the group as a whole but for each individual member as well. The group entity represents a whole that is greater than the sum of its parts. The energies generated within it are available to all of its members. To be present at a meeting of such a group is a fortifying and uplifting experience which is exactly as it should be.

Relaxing together, sharing insights and experiences and providing each other with loving acceptance and support goes a long way towards the development of a cohesive group entity. Additionally, there are a number of conscious exercises that can be employed with the specific intention of bonding your energies together in ways that stimulate the formation and growth of the group entity. Some examples of these exercises will be given in a later chapter. Of course it is not for me to say that you *must* proceed in this way but I have noticed that the groups who are successful in forming a group entity also seem to have the greatest success in terms of growth and productivity.

On a wider scale, the successful construction of a group entity helps members to gain an appreciation and an affinity for the greater spiritual unity which is the hallmark of all advanced souls. There is no loss of individuality, yet each soul gives its best and purest energies for the highest good of all. In return, the combined energies of all flow back to the individual, bringing strength, inspiration, upliftment and unconditional love.

For any sensitive, there is always a need to have the feeling of belonging and the fulfilment of a higher purpose. Although, in the beginning, we may not be able to define precisely what we need, we know there is something and usually we cannot be content until we have found it. A lady who paid me a visit some time ago expressed it in this way: 'I have a wonderful husband, two lovable kids, a nice home and plenty of material security. I should be on top of the world... and I am happy, but I'm not *satisfied.* I feel a bit guilty at times because there are so many people worse off than me and I really have no right to feel discontented but I can't help it. There has to be something more. I don't know what it is but I won't really feel satisfied until I find it.'

The contentment we crave is a feeling that comes from unity of spirit. Physical consciousness is only a fragment of our overall essence, or the Higher Self, as it is usually called. Our drive to find that indefinable 'something more' is the expression of a desire for wholeness, a need to feel complete. When we achieve a tangible form of unity with a group of kindred spirits by forming a group entity, we bring ourselves one step closer to union with our Higher Self, which is the true aim in spiritual development.

CHAPTER THREE

Cleansing the Aura

Whether you are working alone or with a development group, your most important priority should be the protection of your personal energy field, otherwise known as the aura. If you neglect this area of basic and essential importance, you are literally asking for trouble. The danger of possession or, more correctly, auric invasion should never be under-estimated. In the course of my work I have been required to deal with a number of these cases and the effects are never pleasant to behold.

Auric invasion occurs when an alien energy form, such as an earthbound spirit or a malicious entity, penetrates the aura. The effects can range from physical illness and psychological disturbances to the classic 'possession' syndrome which can cause insanity, violence and even death. The technique of psychic rescue, used to remove an invading entity from the aura, can be both arduous and dangerous for everyone involved and, in the majority of cases, it would not have been necessary if the people concerned had known and practised the necessary protective techniques.

Prevention is always better than cure and the basic technique of auric protection is so simple that it could easily be taught to a child. To understand how and why it works, we need to know something about the function of the aura itself. We will be exploring that subject in some depth as we progress through this book but, as with anything else, we must commence with the basics.

We are spiritual beings and, as such, our personal energy fields extend well beyond the material form that constitutes the physical body. That part of our life energy pattern which extends beyond the physical is known as the aura and it has a number of functions that are vital to the maintenance of our health and well-being. It is not usually visible to human eyesight (unless you happen to be clairvoyant) for the simple reason that it is composed of a substance much finer than physical matter.

The presence of the human aura, although known to mystics and occultists for centuries and even graphically represented in the works of early artists as the 'halo' surrounding the head and sometimes the entire body of saints and other spiritually advanced beings, is only beginning to be recognised by scientists and members of the medical fraternity. Dr. Walter Kilner, a physician and surgeon involved in the investigation of electrotherapy at London's St. Thomas' Hospital (where London's first X-ray department was established in 1897) believed in the presence of the aura. He discovered that, if a human figure was viewed through a glass screen coated with dicyanin dye (a derivative of coal tar), a whitish luminescence could plainly be seen following the outline and contours of the body.

The Kilner Screen, as it has come to be known, made the aura visible to all. The British Medical Journal in its January 6, 1912 issue, however, said 'Dr. Kilner has failed to convince us that his aura is more real than Macbeth's visionary dagger'. Dr. Kilner's book, *The Human Atmosphere*, was not well received by either the medical or scientific fraternities.

Scientists in the U.S.S.R. have been investigating the field of psychic phenomena for a number of years and, although a cloak of secrecy has been thrown around their investigations in recent times, a number of their findings are quite well known. One of the earlier experiments conducted by Soviet scientists revolved around a young woman named Ninel Kulagina, who demonstrated some rather remarkable telekinetic abilities, causing lights to turn on and off, crockery to fall from shelves, doors to open and close, all without apparent human intervention. During the course of these experiments, Dr. Gernady Sergeyev measured the electrostatic field surrounding Ninel's body and found that, during moments of intense concentration and stress, the energy in this electrostatic field, or aura, pulsed at four cycles per second.

Despite science and medicine's seemingly dogmatic stance against the presence of the aura, Semyon Davidovitch Kirlian and his wife Valentina, again from the

U.S.S.R., experimented with and perfected a technique for capturing the aura, with its startlingly vibrant colours, on film. This technique, like the Kilner Screen, bears the name of its discoverers and is known as Kirlian photography.

So much then for the presence of the aura and the proof of its existence through the work of a few dedicated and far-seeing individuals, when the weight of contemporary thought in scientific and medical circles has been that no such thing exists. Given that the human aura does exist, the next most obvious questions are: Why? What are its properties? What does it do? What is its purpose for existence? These are questions that cannot be completely answered with words alone. To fully comprehend the nature and functions of the aura, you must attune your consciousness to it and feel it for yourself but, nonetheless, there is a great deal of information available.

At this stage, the most important thing to understand about the aura is that it literally *breathes*, drawing in essential life energies from the atmosphere around itself. The fuel which powers your physical organism is absorbed by the body in the form of food, air and water but the life essence that supports the framework of your total energy pattern is absorbed directly from the atmosphere, through the aura.

Within the aura there are a number of levels, or layers, which become progressively finer as they move away from the physical. The closer to the physical, the more dense is the energy. The first few layers of your aura extend outwards from your body to a distance usually between one and two metres. Think about this for a moment; imagine that you are walking down a crowded city street or travelling on a train packed with commuters. Your aura's first few layers extend, shall we say, to a distance of two metres from your body surface... and so do the auras of everyone else around you. This means that if anyone passes within a radius of four metres or so from your body, the energies in your auras will mingle. Your aura will pick up some of the energies of the people with whom you come into proximity.

Now, how do you know that the man quietly reading

his newspaper in the seat beside you hasn't just murdered his grandmother? Take a look at the people you pass in the street; how can you possibly know where their auras have been and what sort of energies they are carrying?

Thought is a form of psychic energy; so is emotion. Believe it or not, it is the combined effect of our thoughts and emotions which creates the world in which we live, both individually and collectively, as a race. Take time to absorb and understand this statement: *the physical world is a product of the spiritual.* It is not the other way around. Whatever you create within your mind will eventually percolate its way through into physical reality in some form or another. In other words, what you think... IS.

Take a good look at the world in which you are living. What sort of world is it? At present the world of mankind is full of violence, insecurity, suffering, starvation and bloodshed. What does this tell you about the nature of the thoughts and emotions being broadcast by the human race as a whole? It doesn't take the mind of a genius to figure out what kind of energies are floating around in the nearest levels of the psychic atmosphere, does it?

If the air that you breathe is polluted, you know that your body is certain to suffer damaging effects, just as it will suffer from the effects of tainted water or contaminated food. The same principle operates on the levels of psychic existence. If the psychic atmosphere is polluted, that contamination will be drawn into your aura. Once there, it will generate energy imbalances or conditions of dis-ease. These unhealthy conditions, should they be permitted to remain, will inevitably be passed on through the mind and emotions and into the physical body itself as the energies drawn through the aura are circulated throughout your life system.

Just as you cannot have clear vision through a window that is clouded with dust and grease, you cannot operate efficiently or effectively at the psychic level if your aura is saturated with negative energies. Additionally, while those energies are allowed to remain within your aura, you will find yourself crippled with negative thoughts, turbulent emotions and debilitating physical ailments.

To make matters worse, your aura's defences against negative external energies will be virtually non-existent.

It is pointless, even dangerous, to make any attempt at contacting higher intelligences whilst your aura is filled with negative energies. At psychic levels, there is an energy principle stating that like attracts like. The energy vibrations within your aura will attract other life forms which vibrate on similar frequencies. If your aura has been contaminated by negative and destructive energies in the atmosphere, those energies will attract other energy forms of like nature. Negative energies must be removed from your aura before you dare to open channels of access between yourself and the psychic spheres.

If this basic precaution is not taken, the chances are high that you will attract life forms which are likely to prey on you and will ultimately do you harm. That is a complication you definitely do not need! Before you even think about attempting to proceed any further, it is in your own best interest to become familiar with the technique of cleansing your aura and sealing it against unwanted and disruptive energies.

The cleansing and sealing of your aura is a routine that should be practised on a daily basis, like taking a shower. In fact, you can regard it as an extension of your normal hygiene procedures.

Some people are often strongly tempted to skip the boring basics and get into the interesting stuff but, when it comes to psychic energy, this course of action is about as sensible as crossing a six-lane highway at peak hour with your head stuck in a bucket! Anyone who can't be bothered with the basic essentials of safety would be well advised not to tamper with psychic energy.

The method for cleansing and sealing the aura is quite simple and once you have become familiar with the process, it doesn't require much time. In the beginning stages, while you are acquainting yourself with the technique, it is best to allow a period of five or ten minutes. Ideally, the exercise should be performed a minimum of twice a day but, if your daily schedule is really hectic, once will suffice.

Remember, at the psychic level upon which the aura functions, what you think *is*. Thought is the only reality, therefore when you work on the energies within the aura, you will work with the power of directed thought energy. This concept may seem a little difficult to grasp at first but the only way in which you can make an accurate assessment of the technique's effectiveness is to do it and judge by the results.

The effect of the cleansing exercise is both cumulative and progressive. You will notice the effects after a time but don't expect overnight miracles; they do happen but not all that often. It took a long time for those energies to build up in your aura and, over the years, some of them will have become quite deep-rooted. It may take a little while to get rid of the accumulation but, once that is done, the daily routine is enough to keep your aura clear, sparkling and resistant to invasion.

Apart from cleansing and sealing the aura, the cleansing technique has a number of functions, which include clarifying and strengthening your psychic channels, raising your level of vibrations and helping you to attune yourself to the level of spiritual existence at which the higher guides function. The more practice you give to the exercise, the more noticeable these effects will become. You will probably also notice an improvement in your general state of health and a heightened ability to cope with situations of stress. Another advantage of the technique is that it helps you to master the first stages of mind control, which is essential if you hope to make significant progress spiritually. By mind control, I am, of course, referring to your own mind and to self-control. It is never wise to try controlling the minds of other people; it can be done but the repercussions for the person who does it are likely to be most unpleasant!

The time of day at which you perform the exercise is not important; any time you can find a few minutes to sit or lie quietly and uninterrupted will do. Most people find that the few minutes just after waking in the morning and the time in bed at night just before going to sleep are the most practical. Shift workers can adjust the times to fit their lifestyles. It is not necessary to adopt a rigid schedule of doing the exercise at precisely the same time each day and, in practice, human conditions often render such a course impossible. An overall pattern of regularity is important for the sake of self-discipline and optimum effectiveness but the pattern can be adapted to suit your needs.

Remember these two basic principles:

1. Like energies attract.
2. What you think . . . IS

You are going to draw on a universal or cosmic energy stream and pass it through your aura, where it will commence cleansing and revitalising your personal energy pattern, right through to the very centre of your being. To achieve this, you use the law of attraction. Like attracts like: if you wish to attract a particular energy into your aura, you must generate a corresponding energy within the aura to act as a kind of magnet. How do you generate the energy within the aura? Simple . . . you THINK it there. You are operating on the plane where thought energy is the reality, remember.

To focus your thoughts in order to generate the effect you wish to achieve, you will use imagination, which is creative thought energy. Although a number of meditation techniques require that you actually visualise the effect you wish to generate, it is not essential in this procedure. If you have difficulty with visualisation, focus instead on the feelings that you wish to produce. It is the focus of thought, not the method you use to focus it, that achieves the desired effect.

White Light Meditation

To begin, sit or lie down and get as comfortable and relaxed as it is possible for you to be without actually dropping off to sleep. Let your breathing become regular and even, the way people breathe when they are sleeping. It is permissible to join your fingers together but your legs and arms should not be crossed. Your spine should be straight but not ramrod stiff.

Close your eyes to shut out external distractions and focus your thoughts inward. To help you attune yourself to the aura, imagine yourself as a large cell, with your body as the nucleus and the aura as the surrounding sphere of protoplasm. Remember that you are the *com-*

plete cell, not just the body in the centre. Take as much time as you need to create the attunement within your mind.

Feel yourself being irradiated with pure White Light that pours down on you from above. Perhaps you may like to imagine that you are beneath a waterfall where, instead of water, Light cascades down over you. Some people like to imagine that they are being surrounded by a cloud of Light. The images you choose are up to you; it is only important that you draw the White Light to yourself.

Let the Light flow over you and through you, penetrating every level of your being. As this Light penetrates every particle of your life energy it cleanses, uplifts, energises and purifies your energy pattern, raising your vibrations and bringing you closer to the source of life that is your Creator.

Feel a warm, lifting, tingling sensation as the Light effervesces through all of your energy streams. Let it flow into your mind; imagine that inside your head is a dusty old attic and someone has just flung all the windows open to the Light, letting in a heavenly breeze that blows all the dust away. Feel your mind becoming crystal clear, calm and full of Light.

Now follow the energy as it moves downwards from the top of your head to the soles of your feet, cleansing everywhere as it flows. Follow it every inch of the way as it dissolves away every shadow of darkness from within your aura until your energy field is clear, shining and crystal pure.

Feel the Light build and grow, welling up inside you until it permeates every level of your being, through the body and out through the aura until you feel transformed into a being of pure Light, radiating white brilliance far out into the universe.

Still maintaining the flow of White Light, now imagine that your aura has been enclosed in a sphere of one-way glass. From the inside you can see out quite clearly but on the outside the sphere is a mirror that reflects away from you any energies that should not be allowed to penetrate your aura. The positive energies that you want to attract will penetrate easily because you draw them to yourself in the stream of White Light but the combined effect of your reflective mirror and the powerful stream of Light energy that radiates out from you will repel negativity. Your aura is now sealed.

Be aware in your mind that the Light flowing through you is the living energy from your Creator, the Giver of Life and remember that where all is light, darkness cannot enter. Bask in the Light for a while and enjoy the feelings that it brings to you.

Now... *hold the awareness in your mind* and bring these sensations back with you as you gradually allow the focus of your consciousness to return to your physical reality. Take a deep breath, open your eyes and relax for a few moments before going about your business.

The White Light technique is based on the principle of Spiritual Light, which is at least as old as Creation, if not older. From the moment when you first begin to perform this exercise, you will be setting an energy cycle into motion within your aura. The more of the revitalising energy you draw into the aura, the more you will attract. As the energy builds, you will notice that a lot of interesting changes for the better start happening in your life. Apart from personally experiencing the uplifting effects of this meditation for myself, I have also seen its effects in other people. The amount of spiritual progress achieved by these people in a comparatively small period of time has often been quite remarkable.

How many times and in how many spiritual philosophies can you find the basic teaching: 'Look for the Light. Follow it and it will lead you home.'? It is so familiar that most people take it for granted, regarding it only as a metaphor, an allegorical turn of phrase used to represent that which cannot be described in words. That is a pity because, in fact, it is a living reality, not merely a symbolic description. By failing to recognise the *truth* of the Light, people deprive themselves tragically.

As spiritual beings, we draw our life force from a Supreme Being, the Creator. At our present stage of development, it is little short of impossible to imagine the totality of this Ultimate Being. It is easier for us to understand the reality in a symbolic way, provided we don't forget that behind the symbol there is a living reality. So it is with the Spiritual Light.

To teach this principle to their students, the ancient masters used the sun to symbolise the Creator. Everybody knows that without the life-giving white rays of sunlight, no form of life on this planet could continue to survive. The sun is the energy source from which our planet draws its life force. The Creator is the ultimate source, whose energies sustain the whole of Creation. These energies stream out through the living universe, just as the rays of the sun pour through our atmosphere. To attune yourself to this universal stream of living energy, all you need to do is think of your aura as being filled with White Light. Simple, isn't it?

The basic White Light meditation exercise will form the foundation for several of the development exercises that are to follow, so I do advise that you take the time to become proficient with it. Even if you choose not to progress any further with the development exercises, this one simple cleansing routine can be of benefit to you in a number of ways and it is worth your while to practise it regularly. An aura that is clear, bright and radiant with White Light energy has a naturally high resistance to invasion and, for this reason alone, it is in your own best interests to take a few minutes each day to perform this simple routine.

There is only one way to find out for yourself just how effective the White Light meditation can be and that is to test it. As the technique has been devised to be used on a daily basis and to accumulate its effects over a period of time, that is how it should be tested. Doing it once or twice and then giving up or doing it haphazardly every now and then is unlikely to give you any idea of its efficacy. A few people may find the idea of discipline irksome and I really can't criticise because I also have to school myself to maintain any kind of a routine; however once it is established and you feel the benefits, you'll probably find that your daily period of cleansing becomes a pleasure and you won't need to discipline yourself to carry it out.

I would suggest that you perform the exercise regularly for at least a month before you try to assess the results.

It is quite likely that you will be feeling some effects long before the month is up but it will take time for the cycle to become established. As I have already mentioned, it took time for your aura to accumulate the pollution it has become accustomed to carrying and it would be unreasonable to expect it all to be removed overnight.

If you find that you are inclined to become a little emotional during the initial stages of cleansing, don't be disconcerted. Some people find themselves becoming quite weepy during this period and unless they are aware that it is a natural part of the cleansing process, it can be rather disturbing, especially if you have formerly prided yourself on being able to hold your emotions under control. In fact, there is a considerable difference between emotions that are under control and emotions which have been suppressed. Emotional tension bottled up inside you is like an abscess that keeps festering, releasing poisons into your energy system. If you fight the urge to cry and hold back your tears, you will not be doing yourself any favours. Instead, understand that with your tears you are releasing inner tensions that you do not need and which have probably been doing you a great deal more harm than you realise.

One of my former students kept her tears locked inside herself for years and her determination not to 'give way to feminine weakness' was so strong that she managed to maintain this state of affairs for several years after commencing her spiritual training, in spite of regularly performing the White Light meditation. Outwardly she was always bright, vivacious and full of fun but there was a brittle quality in her gaiety. Beyond the surface, I could see a great well of tears dammed up behind all that determined cheerfulness. Even when her marriage came to an end, she was able to maintain an attitude of down-to-earth acceptance and there were occasions when I wondered just what it would take to release all the pent-up pain and grief inside her. Knowing something about her life history and having been through similar experiences myself, I knew how it felt and I found it quite remarkable that she was able to hold it back for so long.

I was sympathetic but not surprised when I heard about the car accident in which she had broken her leg and when I was told that in spite of the ministrations of the finest healers and her own youth and general good health, the leg was taking an abnormally long time to heal. Where she had formerly been able to fill her life with projects and activities, she was now forced to sit still and be alone with her thoughts. She resisted for several months, during which time the leg steadfastly refused to heal properly. Finally, in a lengthy late-night telephone call, she told me that she had at last come to the realisation that she *must* let go and cry. At first she felt angry at her own weakness but, as the tears flowed, she came to feel the cleansing, the relief and the lightening of spirit.

That young woman has a great deal of spiritual potential and has proven to be an excellent teacher, whose help and guidance (much to her own surprise) has been instrumental in helping quite a few other people to find their feet on the spiritual pathway. In spite of all her achievements, however, she would not have been able to achieve her full potential if she had continued to refuse to cry. Tears are a natural and necessary part of the cleansing process.

I have been asked by a number of parents to suggest a way in which they can protect their children against harmful psychic energies. Under normal circumstances, children have a natural form of protection but in the face of the concentrated negativity and savagery to which they can be subjected in the current atmosphere, this is often not enough and it is a good idea for parents to do whatever is in their power to increase the level of psychic shielding around their children. For this purpose, a variation on the basic White Light method is eminently suitable.

With a very small child you can adapt the technique as follows: first irradiate your own aura by following the basic routine and then mentally project a stream of pure Light into the child's aura. It is best that you imagine the Light pouring down on the child directly from the Creator rather than channelling it through your own aura. In this way, you will ensure that the Light reaches the child in its purest possible form. There is no need for you to give the Light instructions as to what you wish it to do for the child; the Light has been around for quite a long time and it knows its job better than we do. All you need to do is direct it, for the highest good of all concerned.

Incidentally, the projection technique is equally successful whether it is directed to a child, to another adult, to an animal or even to a place. I know of quite a few people who 'White Light' their cars or the cars of their loved ones whenever they are about to go out on the road. It doesn't matter how much White Light you pour over a person, it will never do anyone the slightest harm.

When a child is old enough to hold a conversation, you can begin teaching him to perform the White Light exercise. Naturally it is not a good idea to be too technical or detailed in your explanations and in any case, detailed explanations are usually unnecessary. All you need to do is explain to the child that there is a part of every person that most people cannot see and that it gets dirty, just as our bodies do, so it needs to be cleaned. It might help if you were to draw a simple diagram, showing a human figure encapsulated in an egg-shaped 'cocoon' to illustrate the aura in a way the child can easily understand.

Children being the open-minded and responsive little characters that they are, you will probably find that your child will develop a mastery of the technique with almost insulting ease. It is also likely that the child will actually start seeing auras without even trying. The earlier you begin teaching your child the basic elements of protection, the better. These days, children learn cynicism at a very early age and the older they are, the more difficult it becomes to teach them anything.

Happy White-Lighting!

CHAPTER FOUR

Psychic Self-Defence

The White Light meditation will give you effective day-to-day protection against free-floating psychic pollution and it almost goes without saying that it should always be used just prior to the practice of any psychic development exercise and/or attempts at making contact with higher levels of spiritual intelligence. When you are actively practising spiritual development techniques, there is another factor that needs to be considered which is the possibility of *deliberate* interference by negative entities.

Low-level spirit beings are crafty little devils, many of them are skilled in the art of imposture and capable of giving an impressive imitation of a spirit guide. I have seen entities manifesting through trance mediums and copying David's mannerisms, right down to the distinctive pulsation in the medium's right arm and David's most subtle nuances of speech. Had it not been for the fact that David had instructed me always to check for certain private 'call-signs' known only to him and me, it would have probably been possible for me to have been deceived.

I have no doubt just succeeded in giving anyone who has yet to establish a direct link with their true guide an attack of the screaming jitters! An obvious question now comes to mind: if you are not in direct communication with your spiritual guidance and therefore do not have the advantage of pre-arranged passwords, how can you protect yourself against outright deception? That, my friends, is what I am about to explain. Ever heard the saying that prevention is better than cure?

The first and most important principle to bear in mind is that it is never safe to assume that you have automatic protection. Far too many people operate under the assumption that if their motives are sincere, full protection is guaranteed. I even saw this perilous misconception published in a popular psychic advice column in a weekly magazine some time ago. Someone had written to enquire whether ouija boards are really as dangerous as they are reputed to be. The answer given by the supposed 'expert' was that they are perfectly safe, provided the user's motives are pure.

That piece of advice was wrong. Ouija boards are NOT perfectly safe, under any circumstances. I realise that some people have used them without coming to harm; I even experimented briefly myself, before I learned enough to know better. No doubt I caused my celestial guardians a few headaches in the process and I was swiftly guided into safer channels of exploration and warned to avoid the use of ouija boards. In the course of my work since then, I have been required to deal with numerous cases of possession and, in at least 50% of these cases, there had been some association with ouija boards just prior to the onset of the problem. The fact that some people have used these deadly little toys without undue harm is no indication of safety. There are also people who have played Russian roulette without blowing their brains out, but I wouldn't recommend that you take a chance on your luck!

As for the idea that innocence is a protection against evil, we all know that doesn't hold true in the physical world so why should we assume that it is true at the psychic level? I have dealt with cases of possession in which very young and innocent children have fallen victim to viciously destructive psychic infestation, for no other reason than that they were vulnerable. They had usually suffered some illness which left their auras weak, thereby lowering their resistance to attack. If an innocent child can become a victim, what basis is there for assuming that adults who deliberately open themselves to attack will be safe? To make a ouija board work, energy must be drawn from the lowest level of psychic existence and, if you open a doorway into that sphere, you open yourself to the influence of the beings who dwell at that level, none of whom are likely to have your best interests at heart!

Having said all that, I must now emphasise that there

is no reason why psychic activity should be dangerous or frightening, provided that you *use your common sense*. Learn to understand how the energies operate and take advantage of the channels of protection that are available to you.

As a spiritual being you have the right of free will, to choose your own spiritual pathway and to follow it without interference. You also have access to guardian spirits who will defend your right to proceed without molestation, but it is your responsibility to call them into action on your behalf. Unless you do so, they are not permitted to interfere, for to do that would be to overrule your right of free will; this is something they will not and must not do. Unless you specifically ask for protection, they are bound to assume that you do not wish to have it. They may do their best to find a way to warn you about the dangers to which you are exposing yourself but, if you do not heed the warnings, there is nothing more they can do. To interfere, even in your best interests, would be a transgression against the cosmic law. If you want their protection you have only to ask for it; the response will be instantaneous but you must remember to ASK!

The spirits of darkness are no respecters of rights, divine or otherwise. If you are careless enough to leave yourself open to invasion, they don't require an invitation to take advantage of the chance. Once they gain a foothold, they can be very destructive and difficult to dislodge so use your brains; don't leave yourself open to attack.

Your guardian spirits may sometimes respond to a request for protection in a way that is quite unexpected, which can be rather baffling if you are unable to grasp the reasoning behind the action. I had a letter some time ago from a young lady of seventeen years who had been telling fortunes for money ever since she left school. She had a natural talent and the readings that she gave were apparently quite startling in their accuracy but she had no idea as to how it worked. All she knew was that when she wanted it to happen, it did. In fact she knew nothing about the spiritual spheres at all and until she happened to read *Reaching for the Other Side* she had been quite unaware that there were such things as spirit guides.

After reading the book, she decided that it made sense to call on her guides for protection at the commencement of each fortune-telling session. Her letter to me was prompted by the fact that, every time she asked for protection, she found herself unable to do her readings. Her mind would simply go blank and she could get no psychic impressions at all. This was not good for business so she wrote to ask me for an explanation.

To me, the answer was glaringly obvious! In all innocence, the young lady was exposing herself to more danger than she realised and her guides were simply doing what she had asked them to do. I have several friends who have given professional readings at some time or another and they all agree that the greatest danger they face comes from the clients. As one of my friends puts it: 'The clients usually know nothing about psychic hygiene or protection and, until they walk through the door, you don't know what kind of people they are or what influences they carry in their auras.'

These friends of mine are not only talented and spiritually aware, they are also well-educated in psychic techniques and very well protected. Before and after each reading they perform thorough cleansing procedures and, when they do a reading, they aim not so much to tell the future as to give an insight into spiritual principles that can help their clients take a positive approach to life. Their readings could more readily be described as psychic counselling than fortune-telling and, in fact, they are primarily aiming to provide spiritual guidance. Even so, they often find their work quite exhausting and they would be the first to warn others not to attempt this kind of occupation without thorough training and preparations.

In the case of our teenage seeress, training and preparation were precisely what she lacked. By opening her sensitivities indiscriminately, she made herself an open target for negative influences. The fact that her clairvoyance failed her every time she asked for protection was a clear indication that her guides were warning her to stop. I wrote and explained this to her, suggesting that she concentrate on gaining a spiritual education before she attempted any further psychic exploits. I have never received a reply from the young lady so it is impossible for me to say whether or not she followed my advice. It may be that the quest for a higher and fuller understanding of herself has not yet begun within this girl.

It is not my place or purpose to tell other people how their lives should be run but I would be failing my responsibility if I did not point out that when you seek an active involvement with the spiritual, some important choices must be made. I would suggest that you consider your decisions with care because the course of your life from this point forward will be decided by the choices that you make now.

If you were to ask, most people would say that they wish to follow the pathway of Love, Light and Truth but many of them are not prepared to make the kind of commitment this pathway requires. Life is a bit like a bank account; if you want to get anything out of it you must start by putting something in. The type of currency that you deposit will be the currency in which you are paid. To put it another way, if you plant thistles, you can hardly expect to reap corn. When it comes to psychic protection, don't expect the angels to shield you from harm if you feel justified in causing harm to others. To walk the pathway of Light... and to have its protection... you must recognise the sacredness of all life. You cannot do that and be prepared to inflict harm on another living being.

If you choose the pathway of Light, there are commitments involved and it isn't sufficient to make those commitments verbally. You must also be prepared to do your utmost to live up to them. Nobody expects you to be perfect from Day One and it is understood that any one of us can make a mistake. Honest mistakes are understandable; deliberate acts of injury are not. This principle applies to the thoughts that you project onto others, as well as the actions you take. Think about that! It may be easy to see why I have said that a disciplined mind is a necessity if true progress is to be made.

Actions speak louder than words and, as the Bible says, a tree must be judged by its fruits. If you follow the pathway of Light, it will be evident in your attitude towards others. You don't have to wear fancy robes or perform elaborate ceremonies to prove that you are truly spiritual, it's what is in your heart that really counts.

I've known people who could bowl you over with the pious nobility of their words and many even believe that what they are saying is the truth, yet I have seen in their actions towards others that the words are less substantial than air. I have heard people vow to me that they are deeply committed to the Light, yet in almost the same breath they have declared their readiness to attack anyone who stands between them and the fulfilment of some object they desire. I have had experiences of my own, with some 'devoted friend' openly declaring the purity of their regard for me, whilst in the process of stabbing me in the back... or trying to. The most heartbreaking tragedy in all of this is that the people concerned had actually convinced themselves that they were speaking the truth.

There is no line of division between the physical and the spiritual. Your actions towards others in this world are a precise indication of your level of spiritual maturity. If any person is not prepared to accept the obligations associated with spirituality, entry to the spheres of Light is barred, by their own hand.

A deliberate act of harm can never be justified under principles of Love and Light. A conscious and deliberate harm is an act of darkness that could never have been generated by love. There are two distinct and opposing pathways in spiritual life and, as a member of the human race, you are rapidly approaching a point at which it will no longer be possible for you to sit on the fence. I am aware that the majority of my readers will have made their decisions already but, for those who have not, it is time to start thinking.

Once your psychic channels have begun to operate at the conscious level, it is time for you to make a commitment. If you choose not to do so, you become what is known as an open channel. This means that your psychic doorways may be opened by any influence that cares to enter. You could be lucky, it might be an angel; on the other hand it is just as likely to be a demon... you have opened yourself to either. As an open channel you are at the mercy of the tide and you will simply drift with whatever current happens to prevail. Maybe I'm the over-cautious type but I prefer to take the slightly harder route in safety than to risk being washed up on the rocks.

Invocation to the Spirits of Light

You have the right to choose which influences are to be permitted within your personal energy field. To exercise that right, you call on the services of a spiritual doorkeeper and this can be done quite simply, in the form of a prayer or invocation. You may put the request in your own words if you like but, if you prefer to follow a prepared format, you are welcome to share the form of invocation that I use:

> 'In the name of Christ, I call on the spirits of Light to stand guard at the doorway of my soul. Protect me from the forces of darkness and deception and guide me on the pathway of Love, Light and Truth. I commit myself to the Light.'

You will note that I have used the name of Christ but this is not meant to imply that it is mandatory. For me it represents the highest and purest power for good that I personally can understand. I have also experienced its protective potency often enough to have absolute confidence in it. If you have been raised within a philosophy other than Christianity, that name will not carry the same potency of meaning for you. In this case, you would use the word which has the corresponding meaning in your philosophy.

I should mention here that my concept of the Christ spirit may not be in accordance with certain orthodox Christian doctrines but then, I have never believed that it is necessary to be a church-going Christian in order to have an affinity with Christ. For me, it is the meaning *in* the name, the spirit behind the word, not the name itself that is of the greatest importance. What is Christ for me might be Krishna or Ahura Mazda for someone else. The most important issue is that the name used should represent the purest spiritual essence that you personally can identify. The name is simply a focus for a particular quality or a living pattern of spiritual energy.

When you focus your mind on the name, you draw the essence of that spirit into your energy field. This is one of the purposes that the Invocation is designed to achieve.

By speaking the name, I identify myself at the spiritual level and I also attract the attention of those spirit beings who recognise the same authority. The Invocation is actually a formula which contains several active elements. Having drawn the attention of this group of spirit beings, I follow with the phrase 'I call on the spirits of Light' which is the spiritual equivalent of saying 'Now that I have your attention, I have something to ask'. This is followed immediately by the request '... stand guard at the doorway of my soul' which clearly states what I am asking of them.

The request is further qualified by adding the details of what you want to be protected against and the request for spiritual guidance. The formula is almost deceptively simple but I am not the only person who can vouch for its effectiveness. There is no need for any spiritual concept to be complicated and, in fact, the simplest procedures are usually also the most effective.

With regular use of White Light meditation, in combination with the Invocation to the Spirits of Light, you are protecting yourself from any influence by negative psychic forces outside yourself. The next logical stage in the spiritual development process is magnifying the potency of your own inner light. Yes, you do have one and so does everybody else! Spiritual philosophy teaches that within each one of us there is a light, a flame or spark of divine essence. It is this part of the Creator within us that is our source of life. The flame burns more brightly in some of us than in others but in all of us it's in there somewhere, even if it sometimes seems to have subsided to a feeble glimmer. The more robust and healthy our inner flame becomes, the further we can advance in terms of inner strength and certainty, love and happiness.

Feeding the Flame

Obviously, since the flame exists at the spiritual level, you will need to feed it with spiritual energy and, as always, the energy you will need is focussed thought energy. Again, you will use creative visualisation or imagination in order to achieve the desired results and you should be able to feel the effects of the energy you are generating within yourself. It should feel as though the sun is coming out, inside you.

To carry out this procedure, begin with the White Light meditation and the Invocation. Take a few moments to focus on the sensation of Light radiating through your energy streams, raising them to the clarity of sparkling crystal. Feel it. Next, turn your thoughts within. Focus your mind on a point at the centre of your being. It is within the still centre that you will find the flame. Tune in to the flame, Feel it, feed it with your thought.

Be aware within your mind that the flame is the living presence of the Creator, the God within. It is the core of your very existence, your inner self. Concentrate on this presence, feed it with your thoughts and feel it begin to pulse and grow. As you do this, there is a mantra taught to me by David, to recite over in your mind:

> 'God is within All that Is,
> God is within me,
> God within, grow strong.'

Words that are merely recited parrot-fashion are meaningless. *It is the thought behind the words that gives them potency and meaning.* So don't just say the words: *think* about what they mean. By repeating the words, you are giving conscious direction to your focussed thought energy. Hold the flame in your mind and as you form the words, feel it respond, pulse outwards and well up through every level of your being. Give yourself over to it, let it overwhelm you. Feel yourself becoming a radiant being of pure Light, at one with your Creator.

Take a few minutes to bask in the Light and to enjoy the sensation to the full before you return your consciousness to the everyday reality. Hold the awareness of the Light and the feeling it gives to you. Keep it in the forefront of your consciousness as your mind gradually returns to a focus in the physical here and now. As you come back, feel the light radiating out through your body and into the atmosphere around you. If you can't reach a natural 'high' on that feeling, you aren't trying!

Once you have your consciousness relocated in the physical, take a deep breath, open your eyes, wriggle your toes, have a stretch, then relax.

You will have noticed that our emphasis so far has been on the purification and enhancement of the spiritual energy streams within and around your aura, rather than on the development of your psychic abilities as such. It's called groundwork. I know there are other systems of development in which this basic procedure is either skimped or ignored, whilst the main emphasis is placed on psychic ability but, from what I have seen, these systems have little to recommend them. Your safety and well-being should be at least as important to those who lead you as it is to you. In my observations, I have found that in a system where the need for spiritual groundwork is ignored, the casualty rate is alarmingly high.

The idea that spiritual enlightenment will follow as a matter of course once the psychic faculties are developed seems to me a classic example of putting the cart before the horse. It works the other way around. To be psychic does not automatically endow anyone with spiritual awareness or wisdom. I know of more than a few psychics who demonstrate as much understanding of spiritual principles as a bricklayer's labourer might understand about classical architecture. When a person concentrates on *spiritual* development however, the psychic faculties develop naturally, as a matter of course.

As I have mentioned previously, the White Light techniques are not an invention of my own. People were using these principles centuries before Dawn Hill ever arrived on the scene! After *Reaching for the Other Side* was published, I came into contact with literally thousands of people who share an affinity for the spiritual. A large number of them have expressed their awareness of the need for a step-by-step training program that is safe, effective, simple to perform and easy to understand. The need was evident to me also, in the letters and requests I have received from other people.

In the course of my research, I have talked with as many people as possible, visited a number of groups and read I-forget-how-many letters. Invariably, I have found that the highest quality of safety and spiritual advancement has been found among those groups and individuals who apply the principles of White Light energy. If I am to judge the tree by its fruits, I would have to say that the White Light methods produce the best results.

I am keenly aware that many of the peple who read this book will be carrying out the development methods I am recommending, therefore I am conscious of a hefty onus of responsibility. Could you imagine what the karmic results would be for me if I caused several thousand people to follow a direction that led them into harm? *I* can!

This second book, promised years ago when I wrote the first, has taken form over a number of years. It has taken until now for me to do the necessary research and observation. If I would not be prepared to take a certain course of action myself, I will not recommend that anyone else can safely do it. The techniques and exercises that I recommend are those that I have tested and which I personally use. If you prefer not to use them, that's your prerogative. Many things are only a matter of choice; I'm sure there are many people who do not share my taste in perfume but it doesn't stop me from enjoying the fragrance I've chosen to wear. If you find that other techniques work better for you, use them.

I have done my best to make the development program given here as safe and as sure as it can possibly be. There is only one 'wild card' in the pack and that is you. David told me a number of years ago that humans have one major characteristic: unpredictability. 'We may have worked out everything around them in perfect detail and absolutely faultless, then they will do something totally unexpected and throw the whole thing into confusion!' he remarked.

To put it another way, I can write down the recipe for you, but you're the one baking the cake. If a person chooses to start experimenting with the recipe, I cannot be held responsible for the results. There is a saying that the most safely constructed motor vehicle is only as good as the nut behind the wheel. The same yardstick can be applied to the use of psychic formulae: the most brilliantly effective technique is only as good as the person who performs it. As your Junior Science teacher must have told you at least once, handle the elements carefully. If you make a mistake with your mixtures, it could all go bang in your face, with very painful and probably long-time consequences for you. Psychic energy is potent stuff and if you play with it carelessly, you are liable to be hurt.

I strongly suggest that you take the time to be sure that you are thoroughly familiar with one step in the program before you move on to the next. Don't try to force the pace; that could easily cause you to lose your balance. Competition is both unnecessary and dangerous. It really doesn't matter who reaches the finish line first. Why not slow down, be more careful and enjoy the journey? Patience is not an easy lesson to learn but it is an excellent virtue! Take your time, pay attention to detail and observe all safety precautions to the letter, for your own sake.

CHAPTER FIVE

The Inner Sanctuary

When you are working to stimulate the energies within your aura, it is only logical to assume that your efforts will produce certain results. We would expect, for instance, that your personal energies would increase in power and potency, causing you to have an increased amount of impact on those who come into your sphere of influence. This is an area in which we need to be painstaking in the effort to ensure that the effect of our energies upon others is always beneficial. Power can have an intoxicating effect on the personality and power without responsibility can be a source of corruption. Be warned: in any of this work, make sure of your intentions as the law of Karma is swift and just against the careless or unwary.

I believe that any reasonably intelligent human being who truly understands the law of Karma would prefer to take meticulous care with their attitudes rather than to risk the consequences of harmful acts. If people were to understand what they are doing *to themselves* when they project negative energies onto others, they would practise a great deal more caution than most people seem to be practising on this poor mistreated planet of ours right now.

Your thoughts create your own reality. *Think* about that. Look at your reality; is it exactly the way you would like it to be? If there are areas with which you feel uncomfortable, you can change them by making some alterations to the energies that you radiate out from yourself.

Does that sound complicated? It needn't be. The process can be as easy and as simple as you make it. All you need to do is think about how energy works. All forms of natural energy are governed by cosmic law and they will function in accordance with that law. One basic law is that energy moves in a cycle which will ultimately return it to its point of origin. In the process of traversing the cycle, the energy also picks up speed and velocity so, by the time it returns to its source, the impact has been magnified.

This is all good news if the energies you beam out are full of love, light and laughter. On the other hand, what about the gripes, the snarls, the flashes of temper and the cutting words? What about the malevolent thoughts projected onto others in moments of mental darkness? What effects do these energies have on the world around you? It would probably horrify quite a few people to know just how potent and far-reaching those effects can be. People seem to think of thoughts and emotions as something like insubstantial wisps of cosmic smoke, but nothing could be further from the truth.

The physical plane is a product of energies which have their origins on the planes of thought. This whole world is a *product* of thought energy. All energy forms are in constant motion: even in a rock that appears stationary to human vision there are countless atoms, all in constant motion, each one buzzing around in its own characteristic orbital pattern. Between these atoms there is a matrix of energy and their movements set up chain reactions, like ripples spreading outwards in a pool.

Think of yourself as an atom, buzzing around in the ether with billions of other little atoms zinging happily around you, each in its own perfect state of balance. Now if one of those little atoms should decide to get obstreperous and start pushing and shoving, it's going to disrupt all the atoms in the immediate vicinity. They will lose their balance and disrupt others and before too long we have a situation of chaos, all because one little atom decided to get stroppy and throw everyone else off balance. Eventually this disruptive energy will reach the outer limits of its cycle and turn around for the homeward run. By the time all that strife and chaos returns to the rambunctious little atom who started it off, it's going to be packing a considerable wallop!

From basic High School Science you will understand that all life consists of energy and that every tiny, minute speck of energy has its own particular imprint or pattern of vibrations. Think of all the specks of energy that comprise your physical form, then think of yourself as another speck of energy in a greater reality. It shouldn't be difficult to imagine the immense scope of this pattern of cosmic energy, in which you are a vital component. Every action you take, every thought you think and every emotion you feel will have an effect on the other life forms around you. This can be a blessing or a curse, it's up to you.

A person whose nature is predominantly aggressive will find an aggressive outlet for whatever energies may be at his disposal, psychic or otherwise. We have already looked at one example of this in the uses of laser technology. Energy is only energy until you give it purpose and direction. How you choose to channel it and for what purpose is a decision only you can make. In making such choices, I would strongly suggest that you consider the effect you will have on those around you, for these effects will return to you in kind and multiplied.

We are not the only life-forms in the universe and every form of life is equally precious to the One who created it. We do not have the right to cause disruption and suffering for other living beings: those who do will be repaid in kind. This is a cosmic law that has been known and taught for centuries. Our problem at the moment is that people haven't been choosing to listen. It would be wonderful if people learned to understand what a beautiful world they could create for themselves, just by learning how to direct their thought energies in ways that are creative instead of destructive. If people would only change the way they think, they could change the world into a garden of wonder, just by joining their minds together for the highest good of all. It isn't just a fairy-tale... it CAN be done, and we can do it! This is working in harmony with cosmic law when we do it, cosmic law works with us.

I'm sure that almost everybody would love to see our world transformed overnight but, in order to change the world we live in, we need to change the way we think and, for most of us, that takes a little time. Even so, it isn't impossible to achieve and it doesn't have to be difficult if we just keep taking one step at a time. A certain amount of knowledge can be relayed to you in words but although you may agree with everything those words are saying, they will not give you wisdom. Only by putting the knowledge into practice and experiencing the results for yourself can you build up your store of personal understanding, which leads to wisdom. This program of development is designed around exercises that can enable you to *feel* the changes taking place within you as your energy patterns are altered. Realise that all these changes aren't happening by magic. It isn't the formula that makes things happen, it's you. It is your own thought energy that is being focussed, is it not?

True spiritual guidance arises from within and it comes through your own mind, whether you consciously realise this or not. In order to hear the voice of guidance clearly, it is necessary that your own thoughts should be peaceful and still. Spiritual guidance, by its very nature, comes from the realms where thought is the only reality, therefore the logical place to start seeking it is within your own thought patterns. In order to do this, you need to tune out all the voices you don't want to hear. That makes sense, doesn't it? You are continually being bombarded with thoughts and emotions from the atmosphere around you and, if your head is full of static and interference, how can you isolate one voice from the multitude?

You need to have a place inside yourself where all is still and the hubbub has been silenced. Those of you who have commenced the procedures outlined in the foregoing chapters will already be clearing this space for themselves. Next comes the use of creative visualisation to produce within yourself a special sanctuary, in which you may commune both safely and clearly with your spiritual guidance.

Remember that spiritual communication is subtle; it operates beneath the surface and comes to you chiefly in the form of feelings, mental impressions, pictures in your mind, even in emotional spaces. Most times it doesn't feel as though it's coming from elsewhere at all; it's more like a mood or a state of mind that arises within you. That is the natural order of things.

Learning to distinguish the true guidance from false impressions is partly a matter of attitude and partly a matter of experience. Once you have learned to recognise The Voice, you will notice that it has a unique pattern of resonance, a quality of *rightness* that strikes a chord of truth inside you. The more you practise tuning in to this guidance, the more readily you will be able to recognise it. If you practise enough, you will eventually be able to hear it speaking in your mind, even in the midst of a crowd of spectators at a football match. The key that unlocks this awareness is inside yourself: the door opens from your side and no-one else can open it for you.

The quiet space within can be brought into being, nurtured and strengthened through the use of creative thought energy, which forms the basis of all the exercises given so far. The first steps consist of clearing away external interference and focussing into the spiritual, to generate the kind of energies that we seek to draw unto ourselves. The exercises given in the preceding chapters are designed to set this process into motion. The next step is to create a peaceful space within your mind. This will be your inner sanctuary, to which you can come anytime you feel a need to do so. Whatever you create within your mind is *real,* even though it may not be physically visible to those around you.

Before you commence this stage in your journey it would be wise to spend some time in preparation with the cleansing procedures. You do not want to be taking negative energies into your personal sanctuary. When you feel ready to start shaping your inner space, perform each step in the following order.

Commence with a thorough White Light cleansing, the Invocation and the Feeding of the Flame. Any conscious psychic exercise should *always* be preceded by those exercises, to provide the maximum protection, guidance and assistance. When you feel sufficiently prepared, imagine within your mind a special place that gives you a feeling of peace and spiritual upliftment. It could be a deserted beach, the top of a mountain, a grassy bank beside a stream or a point somewhere out in space, drifting among the stars. The place should be one that feels right for you. Take your time and let it grow naturally in your mind.

Mentally place yourself within the scene. Make yourself a part of it and help it to grow as vivid and alive in your mind as it can possibly be. Sit yourself down, rest your hands on the ground and feel the texture of the earth. Feel the flow of the air currents around you. Breathe them in, savour the freshness and fragrance of the air. Look around and take in the details of the scenery, right down to tiny little wildflowers peeking above the grass or little crabs crawling over rocks. You can even have pixies sitting under toadstools if you want them! Use your imagination.

This is your personal place of sanctuary, the place where you come to feel at peace and attunement with the spirit of life itself. Take the time to make this space inside yourself as beautiful and as real as you can possibly make it. Don't try to hurry things, savour every tiny little detail. You are building a spiritual sanctuary, so give it your best.

Once this space inside you has been created, it is there whenever you need to enter it. By focussing your thoughts into this space, you can draw yourself into it at any time. You carry it with you wherever you go. It is not only a focus for spiritual meditation, it can also be a haven that you step into when you are feeling pressured, when you need space to think or simply when you feel like dreaming.

After a time you will begin to notice a living presence in your sanctuary, a loving, spiritual presence that greets you whenever you enter. You may 'see' the presence as a human figure or you may simply feel it as an invisible personality. Don't make the mistake of trying to create this presence if it doesn't seem to be there in the beginning. It will come of its own accord when the place has been made ready for it.

You will probably find that the process of creating your inner sanctuary is a whole lot easier than you expected and you may even wonder whether it's all *too* easy. Don't dismiss it as a product of your own wishful fantasy. It is characteristic of sensitives to doubt their inner impressions, especially when things seem to be happening easily. We have been conditioned to believe that spiritual advancement should be a difficult process and that if it happens easily, it must be false. On the contrary: if you are following instructions correctly it should not be difficult. Challenging at times, perhaps, but if you are having an inordinate amount of trouble, there might be a problem somewhere. When things are happening as they should, your inner impressions will flow naturally and with ease.

Learning to trust your inner perceptions is a process that can take a while and the older you are, the more obstructions you may need to remove. In this society, we are conditioned to disregard inner feelings and impressions on the basis that they are purely subjective and, therefore, neither valid nor realistic. Have you ever seen one of those cartoons depicting a character torn between the voice of his conscience and the voice of human nature, represented respectively as a little angelic version of himself on one shoulder and a little devil on the other? Whimsical, perhaps, but still a good illustration of the conflict that we all experience at times between the voices of our inner selves and the voices of conditioning.

Among the letters that have struck the deepest chords in me, there was one from a young lady who told me that in early childhood she had been in regular communication with an inner voice. When she felt troubled, the voice gave her comfort and reassurance. When she had problems, the voice gave her advice which never failed to provide the most beneficial solutions. As far as the child was concerned, she was talking to God. She accepted this quite happily as the natural way of things until she reached the age of nine, when a paralysing thought occurred to her: 'What if I'm only talking to myself?'

From the moment self-doubt entered the girl's mind, she lost the ability to communicate with her inner voice. She simply stopped hearing it and, from that time forward, she lived with a continual sense of aching loneliness. All the colour and joy faded from her life, replaced by an all-pervading sadness and a sense of bitter loss. She told me that when she first started reading my book, she thought she was reading fantasy because the things that I described could not happen in the world that she knew. Then she thought: 'Wait a minute... those things mightn't happen in the world as I know it but they can in the world *as it really is.*' With that realisation, she thought again of the voice that had spoken to her in childhood and realised that she had been wrong to doubt herself. The voice WAS real! All those years of loneliness need never have been, but for the voice of doubt and its murmured words of poison in her mind.

When I read that young lady's story, deep personal memories were aroused in me of a time far back in my childhood when I had my own wonderful friend who spoke to me silently inside my heart. I could see him in my mind, tall and beautiful, with a radiant smile, eyes that beamed with love and a tender lilt in the voice that spoke only to me. It never occurred to me to wonder if he had a name. He was just... there. For me, there had never been a time when he had not existed and I accepted his presence as naturally as I accepted the flowers and the breeze.

At night when my body was sleeping, his hand would take mine and we would walk together in a place of indescribable beauty and fascination, where I felt utterly happy and at peace. We'd talk and he would teach me things but mostly I just adored being in his company. When morning came in the physical world and I had to return to my body, I would cry.

'I don't want to go back there, it's dark and it hurts. I don't want to go!'

At those times, his countenance would grow sad and I knew that my distress was his also, for he had to send me back.

'I know it hurts and it seems like an awfully long time while you're there, but when you're here with me, you can see that it really isn't very long at all, can't you?'

'But it FEELS long!'

'I know, but you understand that there are things you must do before you can come home to stay and once you're home, it will hardly seem as though you've been away at all. And I am with you. I'll always be with you, even when you forget.'

'I WON'T forget!' I vowed. He only smiled.

One day, I was told that I was old enough to go to Sunday School. I was dressed up in my best clothes, a threepence was tied into the corner of my handkerchief for the collection plate and off I toddled in the care of an older cousin, to the local church. There I listened in wide-eyed rapture to the stories of Jesus, who came down to Earth to lead us all into Heaven, who healed the sick, comforted the lonely and had a very special kind of love for little children. There was no doubt in my mind as to whom they were describing.

'They know you, too!' I whispered in delight and, in my mind, I saw him smile.

Inevitably, of course, I told the Sunday School teacher about my special friend. I was stunned when she reacted with horrified disapproval.

'I hope you don't think you've been talking to *Jesus*!' she exclaimed. 'Jesus is the Son of God and we are only sinners. Sinners can't talk to Jesus and, if he were to speak to anyone in this world, it would not be you. That person you're talking about is just someone you've made up. He isn't really there.'

With those words, the light was taken out of my life. I saw him a few times more but, each time, he seemed more hazy and indistinct.

'You aren't really there,' I lamented miserably and inside me, something withered and went dark. From that time onward I learned to live with hopelessness, despair and rejection. I felt myself defiled, stained with sin and unworthy to be loved by my Creator. I must have been all of five years old at the time and suddenly my life became something fearful. I was nothing but a wretched, worthless sinner, doomed to Hell.

It was to be almost three decades before I rediscovered my wonderful friend and realised that I had not imagined him, that it was the people who denied his existence who had been wrong. He *was* there all the time... even when I did forget. These days, whenever someone accuses me of being out of touch with reality, my answer is a simple question: 'Whose reality, yours or mine?'

It seems to me that human conditioning is designed to turn us away from the truth and freedom of spiritual awareness and to lead us into a form of imprisonment in the physical world. It makes us forget who we really are and where we come from: it turns us into lost souls, at the mercy of unscrupulous exploiters. The sheer effort of surviving in this world is enough to keep most people's minds so occupied that they lose all awareness of anything but the physical. Spirituality is sneered at, sensitivities are trampled. Dare to be different and you invite persecution.

When the human race as a whole is living in a state of peace and plenty, working in harmony with nature and demonstrating that it understands the laws of creation, then the voice of human conditioning will have some worthwhile things to say. Until then, it isn't worth the bother of listening. As long as human society allows itself to be ruled by aggression, greed, hypocrisy and violence, it has no right to set itself up as an arbiter of truth or sanity.

Spiritual development is a voyage of self-discovery. To find the truth, it is necessary to peel away the layers of ignorance, self-doubt and illusion that have been woven around you by the voices of conditioning and to go back to the open-minded simplicity and instinctive wisdom of childhood. Place your trust in the spirit that moves within you and not in the world of mankind.

I don't care how many fancy robes a man might wear, how many letters he has after his name or how many years it took him to learn how to put his collar on backwards; that man is still a human being with two eyes, two ears and one brain, just like us. His concept of reality is no more valid than yours or mine. Whatever the concept of God may mean to you personally, most of us acknowledge the existence of a divine presence that is the ultimate in terms of spiritual existence. According to the greatest spiritual teachers who have ever walked this earth, the way to reach that essence is to look within. We are specifically told that we will not find it by looking elsewhere. According to the teachings of Christ (Luke 17:21) the kingdom of God is *within* you. It follows that so long as you seek outside yourself, you will be unable to find your God.

Take the time to tune into yourself and explore your own divinity. Enter your inner sanctuary as often as you wish. Listen for the inner voice and you will hear it. Dismiss the voices of doubt and discover your own truth. So, maybe you will make a few mistakes along the way;

so what? Mistakes are only lessons in disguise and besides, you're likely to make worse mistakes if you *don't* listen to your own voice of truth.

It may seem at first as though you are only carrying on a mental conversation with yourself; that is why we often tend to dismiss the inner voice as a quirk of the mind. If you really listen, you will realise that whenever this particular voice speaks in your mind, its words are always correct, even when you might prefer it to be otherwise. The advice it gives to you may not always be the easiest to follow but it always brings the most worthwhile results. The more you listen, the more clearly you will be able to hear . . . and to understand.

If you have gone to the necessary effort to cleanse your energy streams, protect yourself against deception and attune yourself to the highest level of spiritual purity that you can imagine, you have cleared the way for spiritual communication. From here it is a good idea to spend some time just letting that sense of attunement grow inside you. It doesn't matter if you aren't progressing in impressive leaps and bounds; it matters that the spiritual bridge you are building is steady and strong.

For a time you might enjoy simply getting into that spiritual space and soaking up the atmosphere, for no reason other than the fact that it feels good. If that is what you feel like doing, do it! You are not wasting any time, believe me. As you raise the levels of spiritual radiance and contentment inside yourself, so you also give that radiance out to others. Just by *feeling* good inside, you can make those around you feel good too.

The hallmark of your spiritual guidance is that it will always tell you the literal truth. There are no half-truths or veiled hints, only truth. If it were any other way, how could you trust the voice to guide you truly? Your awareness will grow quite naturally as your levels of spiritual attunement are deepened. The spiritual experience should be a joyful one, so let yourself enjoy it. It's your world, after all!

CHAPTER SIX

Relaxation

If you have been experiencing some trouble with the exercises given so far, the most likely possible cause is that you are not sufficiently relaxed when you commence. The ability to construct a mental bridge between your physical consciousness and the Cosmic Mind depends to a large extent on your ability to relax. This means relaxing not only physically but within your mind and emotions as well. Where there is tension, spiritual balance is upset and your energy currents cannot flow as they should. This will have an adverse effect on your ability to make contact with the levels of spirituality that you seek.

You cannot focus into the spiritual with clarity and strength if your muscles are stiff with tension, your emotions are taut and your mind is preoccupied with nagging worries. By the time we reach adulthood, many of us have become so enmeshed in the fight for survival that we forget how to be really relaxed. Tension and stress have become so much a part of our lives that we hardly notice them any more. Even when we think we're relaxing, the chances are high that the residual level of tension is much greater than we suspect, particularly for those of us who must live and work in big cities.

To make progress in the development of your spiritual awareness, you need to achieve inner stillness and for that, you must be relaxed. Tension and stress have the effect of locking your consciousness into the physical sphere to such an extent that the more subtle vibrations coming from the spiritual spheres cannot reach the surface of your mind.

If we want spiritual experiences to take place, we will not achieve that goal by trying to force them to happen. It is more effective and considerably less strenuous to relax, sit back and *allow* things to happen naturally.

It may well be possible to cause events to occur through a single-minded effort of the will but it's an awful strain on your energies, especially when it is possible to achieve results by much simpler and far less stressful methods.

The energy that powers the Universe is available for your use but, in order to make use of it, you must be in attunement with it. For instance, if you want to generate an energy that can soothe and heal, you must be attuned to the appropriate wavelength. There's not much point in trying to do it when your vibrations are set on a frequency that is noisy and disruptive. That would be the psychic equivalent of applying rock and roll music to cure a migraine!

In the process of attunement, it is essential to shut out any extraneous influences and enter a space that is clear and still. The channels that bring spiritual energies into your sphere of influence flow *through* you. You will find them when you look within, not when your attention is focussed on the influences that come from outside yourself. This is why the most effective systems of mystical training are those which teach the value of inner attunement and tranquillity.

Even if you consider yourself to be a fairly relaxed sort of person, a course of relaxation exercises may surprise you. More than likely, you will discover that you were nowhere near as relaxed as it is possible for you to be. Some people carry more tension than others but people who are sensitive tend to be particularly vulnerable. Anyone who feels drawn to pursue a course of esoteric study and research is bound to be sensitive.

You should be able to make some time available each day in which you can just let go and relax, let your body go limp and your mind empty itself of care so that you can rest and have your energies recharged. Sleep is not an answer in itself. There are quite a few people who do not relax properly even when they are asleep. Ten minutes of total relaxation will produce more benefit than any amount of trouble-tossed sleep. It will also heighten your receptivity to the spiritual influences you are seeking to cultivate.

It may take some time, in the initial stages, for you to program yourself to relax properly but until you master it, don't expect any startling results with your development exercises. To achieve the most effective results, your relaxation program should not stop with the physical body. You must also include the aura. The exercises suggested here have been widely used for a number of years and have proven effective provided, of course, that you are prepared to persevere.

The degree of commitment you are willing to make will determine the effectiveness of the program for you. Naturally enough, a person who is not prepared to exercise a reasonable amount of self-discipline cannot expect to achieve the best results. If at first you don't succeed, persevere.

Allow yourself between fifteen and thirty minutes each day, to be set aside as your relaxation period. Use a quiet room in which you will not be disturbed and lie down comfortably, on your back with your arms lying alongside the body. Give yourself a few minutes to get comfortable, close your eyes and let your breathing become regular and even, as you do in meditation.

The first stage is the relaxation of the physical body, from the tips of your toes to the top of your head. Begin with the toes: wriggle them around, stretch the feet then allow the muscles to relax. Now imagine a warm, soothing current of energy flowing right through your toes, melting every hint of tension out of the flesh and even making your joints feel loose and relaxed. Everywhere this relaxing energy touches, tension disappears and a feeling of comfortable warmth fills all the spaces.

Allow this relaxing energy to keep flowing and feel it rise up through your lower legs, relaxing the ankles, the calves, even the shins. Keep the energy flowing... follow it with your mind as it moves through the body. Up through the knees to the upper legs, thighs and buttocks, then feel it flowing into your arms through the tips of your fingers. Feel it flow upwards through the arms, into the shoulders.

Now focus on your lower torso and feel the flow of relaxation moving up your spine, soothing in every place it touches. Through the neck, up over the scalp and down the face. Feel the expression leaving your face as the facial muscles go limp. Focus your attention onto the throat.

Swallow, then let the throat muscles relax. Feel your tongue resting lightly on the floor of your mouth and let your jaw relax. Feel your body totally relaxed, comfortable and at ease.

Don't be in too much of a hurry to rush into the next stage of your activities; take the time to tune into the delicious sensation of being completely relaxed. Enjoy the feeling.

When you feel ready for the next stage, you can focus on clearing emotional tension away from your aura. Although there are some similarities between this procedure and the regular aura-cleansing routine, there are some subtle differences. Having dealt with the negativity that arises from outside you, we are now working to clear away the tensions that you have generated inside yourself. I call this technique the 'Magic Hands' meditation, for reasons which will shortly become obvious.

To begin: 'White Light' yourself and invoke your protection. Now, with your eyes closed, imagine that you can see your body surrounded by the aura. While the aura is usually seen as a field of shifting, luminous colours, for the purpose of this exercise it should be visualised as being suffused with a light grey mist, through which the colours appear clouded. The grey mist represents all of the tensions which have been generating negative energies within your auric field.

Focus your attention on your feet and imagine them being gently stroked by a pair of soothing hands. As the hands sweep through your aura, they gather up the grey mist from around your feet and form it into a ball. The hands continue until they have gathered all of the mist from around your feet, then they deposit the ball of mist in the air, about half a metre above your head where they leave it hovering, like a small cloud. I'll come back to the cloud later but for now, leave it floating there.

Send the hands to stroke away the mist from around your lower legs. As before, have the hands gather up every scrap of grey mist from around the lower part of your legs and when it has all been gathered, add it to the cloud above your head. Now move on to the upper legs, thighs and buttocks, gathering up all the grey mist and adding it to the cloud above your head. Continue in this way moving up through the lower arms and up to the shoulders then from the lower spine up the torso, neck and head.

Take your time with this exercise, there is absolutely no need to rush. Focus on the soothing, calmative energy softly radiating from the magic hands as they sweep all the tiredness and tension out of your aura. As the hands move along through your energy field, feel a mild and blissful wave of serenity permeating your mind.

When all the mist has been removed, turn your attention to the grey cloud, bobbing around just above your head. This cloud now contains all the negativity that has been cluttering up your aura. Examine the cloud and you will see that it is rather like a little package, held together by a number of darker grey threads. Each thread represents a negative emotion which has been holding negative psychic energies inside your aura.

Emotions are the carrier waves over which psychic information is modulated. Negative emotions which are permitted to remain within your aura will continue to attract negative psychic energies to themselves and hold them. All of those negative emotions are the dark threads in your cloud of oppression. When those threads are taken away, the cloud of negative energy will be dispersed like a puff of smoke in the breeze. We are now going to have the magic hands remove each thread from the cloud, one by one. As each thread is removed, we will give it the name of a negative emotion that has been causing affliction. I will suggest names for the first few threads and you can name the rest. Ready?

As the magic hands touch each thread, it slides away easily and as the hands draw it from the cloud and send it drifting away, we give it a name... ANGER.

Now as the next thread is removed, we have another name... GRIEF. Then come more: JEALOUSY, REJECTION and FAILURE. Let them be drawn away and sent off into the beyond. You don't need them, do you?

Continue naming the threads until each one has been removed. Now see the cloud dispersing like drifting smoke on the cosmic winds, which will carry it far away from you. Again, 'White Light' yourself. This time, feel how much stronger and brighter the light is. In your imagination, see how much clearer and more vibrant your aura has become. Enjoy the feeling.

The only negative energies that can now exist within your aura are those you generate within yourself. It is a good idea to perform this clearing exercise on a fairly regular basis, once every few days or once a week perhaps. We have yet to break all the old habits of thinking which have been causing us to feel those negative emotions in the past. I don't know about you, folks, but I can assure you that all my accumulated bad habits could not be broken overnight. We need to keep a watch over our emotions; they make excellent servants but we need to keep them harnessed. When they are allowed to take control, there can be big trouble: emotions have no common sense at all.

This is the point at which we all start paying serious attention to the challenge of cultivating the quality of patience. Until this hurdle is jumped, you will find your patience being tested, probably quite sorely, at almost every turn you take. Each time it happens, you will find yourself confronted with a decision... to give way to negative emotions or to stop and think.

A person who continually gives way to negative feelings sets into motion a cycle of energy that can best be described as a Negative Spiral, although it could be more commonly known as a Vicious Circle. The soul becomes enmeshed in a destructive pattern of thought and behaviour, which will ultimately result in self-destruction unless the pattern can be reversed. A fully mature and competent spiritual being does not give way to negative emotions... ever. I doubt that any one of us was born with the quality of patience but it can be cultivated and in this field of activity it is not only a virtue, it is essential.

When you are at peace within yourself, your world will be at peace with you. With every thought that you think, every emotion you feel, every word that you say and every action you take, you are sending ripples of energy out through the atmosphere around you. Simultaneously you are receiving energy from the atmosphere and in what it brings to you can be found all the qualities you have been projecting. If you do not like some of the energies that life brings to you, it is in your power to change things.

Energy cannot be destroyed, it can only be transmuted; that is why it is so pointless to try bottling up your negative emotions. They won't go away, they will only fester inside you and continue releasing destructive energies into your aura, long after you have forgotten about having imprisoned them deep inside yourself. The most effective way to neutralise negative energy is to turn it into something positive. Think of yourself as an energy transformer, receiving energy from the atmosphere around you, processing it through your own patterns of energy and then radiating it outwards.

If you can grasp the concept of the karmic cycle you will understand why this world's greatest spiritual teachers have always advised us to harm no living thing and to return good for evil. The less negativity you radiate, the less you will receive, which means that your personal energy field will be able to maintain a more even keel. You will be more relaxed and at peace within yourself, the energies that you radiate will be harmonious and constructive and you will have set into motion a cycle of positive energy that will lift you up instead of weighing you down.

Obviously, you can't flop down onto the floor and perform your 'Magic Hands' routine every time life starts rocking your boat so it is helpful to have one or two little emergency measures up your sleeve which will help you to minimise negative reactions to situations of stress. When the boss is making things difficult for you at work, when you are caught in a traffic bottleneck, when a shop assistant is being rude to you or in any situation where you can feel your hackles starting to rise, you can neutralise the negative effect with a simple 'Centering' procedure.

Take a deep breath and hold it for a few moments. While you are holding a breath, mentally say to yourself: 'The negativity I am feeling is not mine. It comes from outside me and I have the power to send it away. As I breathe out, the negativity will be blown away from my aura and I will remain calm,' or words to that effect. Then breathe out quite forcefully, imagining, as you do so, that the cloud of negativity is being blown away from you. Depending on the circumstances, you may need to perform the exercise more than once but don't do it more than two or three times in a row; we don't want you to run the risk of hyperventilation.

In a situation where another person is directing negative energies at you, a slight variation on the method used for sealing the aura can be most effective. Care is needed here to ensure that you do not, even unwittingly, allow yourself to consciously feed negative thoughts or emotions back to the person who is opposing you. This is quite a challenge, especially when you are inclined to think that your opponent deserves a good kick in the pants but, if that is the case, life itself will deliver the kick at the most appropriate time.

It helps if you can understand that a person who gives out excessively negative energies probably doesn't know any better and is probably feeling miserable inside. You know from personal experience that it is not difficult to be nice to people when you are feeling happy and peaceful but if you are feeling depressed the world turns grey, everything is a hassle and other people seem to go out of their way to get on your nerves. A person who gives out negativity is feeling bad inside and the best thing you can do in such situations is to send the person some positive energy. Firstly however, you need to make sure that your own energy field is doubly insulated.

Even while you are outwardly dealing with the situation as it confronts you, inwardly you can be working at the psychic level to counteract the negative energies swirling around you. Focus on the 'glass bubble' within which your energies are contained. Remember that on the outside, this glass has a mirror surface that reflects away from you any energies you do not wish to receive into your aura. Imagine that you can actually see it happening. You may like to see the negative energies as little arrows that hit the auric shield and glance off harmlessly. If you do not allow yourself to react to the situation with corresponding negativity, these harmful energies will not be able to penetrate because there will be nothing in your aura that can attract them.

Having reinforced your auric shield, you can now start

beaming White Light towards the person who is directing the negativity towards you. Anyone who is being unpleasant could benefit from a nice shower of White Light. It will not harm them, it will absorb and transmute negative energies and it might even help to alter their state of mind but, remember, you cannot use it to retaliate. If you visualise the Light heaping punishment onto the other person to 'teach him a lesson' you have immediately altered its character. It will no longer be White Light but something harmful and, since you were its source, you will also be its ultimate destination.

Remember that you are not trying to change the other person, simply to prevent yourself from giving way to the kind of destructive emotional patterns that will throw you off balance and keep you from achieving your personal aims. If you happen to cause your opponent to feel a little better so that he is no longer so inclined to throw negativity around, you will have done him a favour and that's good Karma for you.

Another way of neutralising negative energies is called 'Earthing' and it simply consists of putting your hands onto the ground and imagining the turbulent energies being drained away from you and into the earth, where they will be converted into the kind of energy that helps things to grow. It is quite effective when you have an opportunity to do it but if you work in a high-rise city office, you might be better advised to concentrate on shielding and centering.

If your office happens to have a few pot-plants close by, you may care to follow the example of one of my former students, who worked in an office where the boss was in the habit of taking his frustrations out on his employees. He was having one of his bad days, stomping grumpily around the office and finding fault until his employees' nerves were all stretched to screaming point. When he came bearing down on my student like a battleship in full steam, ready to fire off another tirade of criticism, she raised one hand and asked him to wait a moment then calmly walked to the nearest pot-plant and stuck her finger into the soil.

'Now,' she smiled at her boss. 'What did you want to say?'

Flustered, taken aback and totally forgetting for the moment what he had been intending to say, the boss pointed weakly at the pot-plant.

'What are you doing?' was all he could manage to utter.

'Earthing myself,' she replied blithely. 'I need to drain off the negative energies I've been absorbing all day so that I can cope with whatever it is you want to lecture me about. Now Sir, what did you want?'

'It doesn't matter,' muttered her bewildered employer. He turned and wandered back to his office and she returned to her seat, wearing a huge smile and feeling great.

In addition to the performance of specific relaxation exercises and ridding yourself of emotional tensions, it is also advisable to give some attention to your physical energies. If there are chemical imbalances within your body, every other level in your energy pattern will be thrown out of balance. While we are setting our sights on the development of our spiritual faculties, we need to remember that our bodies also require care, attention and proper maintenance. In our society, there is a tendency to ignore the body until something goes wrong, then we trot off to a doctor, who does whatever he can to correct the problem. We usually give our cars better treatment than our bodies receive!

Cars are expensive pieces of machinery and we know that, unless a car is regularly serviced, it will wear out and break down more quickly than it should, so we take the precaution of having it regularly overhauled. In the process, small faults can be found and corrected before they cause major problems and the machinery runs more efficiently. We could use the same kind of preventive maintenance for our bodies!

I have no wish to denigrate the very real and valuable help provided by the medical profession, but any doctor is at a disadvantage from the outset because he usually only sees you when you are already ill. The time to give your body proper care and attention is *before* things start going wrong. I personally have derived a great deal of benefit from the attentions of my naturopath friends, who have given me excellent care and advice over the past few years. According to these practitioners, even a person on a normal 'healthy' diet can suffer from vitamin and mineral imbalances to some degree and these in turn will generate disorders within the life energy pattern. Optimum results cannot be achieved at the spiritual level if the energies are being drained and thrown out of balance within the body.

People who have a strong focus into the spiritual are sometimes inclined to forget that they have bodies or to dismiss the body as being 'of the physical' and, therefore, little more than an impediment. This can lead to the kind of imbalances that can generate disease. While we exist in this reality, we need our physical vehicles and it is in our own best interests to have them running as smoothly as possible so that physical problems don't get in the way of the things we really want to do. A body that is in poor health, loaded with toxins and pushed beyond its limits cannot make an efficient vehicle, nor can it provide a clear channel for spiritual energies.

When it comes to the need to take proper care of the body, I am speaking not from hearsay but from personal experience. Anyone who knows me personally can tell you that my focus in life is almost exclusively spiritual and that, mentally, I am away with the pixies most of the time. Like many other sensitives, I have often felt uncomfortable in the physical world and have not identified very closely with my body. According to David, my balance of energy is 'ninety-nine per cent spiritual' and this is reflected in my physical expression. Naturopaths are always telling me that my levels of earth energy are low. From a strictly personal point of view, the situation doesn't cause me great concern but I have chosen to perform a specific task during my stay in this world and I would like to fulfil it to the best of my ability.

If I allow my body to become so run-down that it cannot function efficiently, my ability to fulfil my chosen purpose will be affected and that would cause me some considerable bother and frustration. What applies to me in this respect can be equally applicable to anyone. Whether you are a public figure, a mill-worker or a housewife, you express yourself through your body. If you don't look after it, the body will inevitably let you down, no matter how zealously you tend your spiritual energy levels. None of us expect our bodies to last forever but, for as long as we need them, we might as well look after them so that they don't break down on us at inconvenient times.

From a spiritual perspective, your body is a part of your life energy pattern. The physical is a part of the spiritual, remember? Anything that affects the balance of energies within your body will have a corresponding effect on your energies at other levels. For instance, if you have a pounding headache and your stomach is churning, how are your moods affected? Do you feel happy and lighthearted, brimful of energy and raring to go? Can you think quickly and cope with everyday problems efficiently, without falling to pieces? Hardly! More than likely you feel irritable and short-tempered, you want to be left alone to lie down and find an escape from the pain, you feel thoroughly out of sorts and can't even think straight. Your mind and emotions are not physical in nature but they are affected by the condition of your body. So are your psychic energies.

Perhaps you aren't suffering from any noticeable illness but your physical condition can still be running just a little below par. You may not even notice it; you may be so accustomed to this condition that you think of yourself as being quite healthy. One of my naturopath friends tells me that when he asks new patients about their general state of health, the reply is often: 'Oh, apart from the normal headaches and occasional back pains, it's fine.' Headaches and back pain, says my friend, are *not* normal; they are indications that there is something out of balance within the body. We often tend to accept these conditions as being natural and unavoidable phases in life but, in fact, they are neither. Physical imbalances not only impede our physical performance, they also restrict spiritual progress. When the situation can be corrected with proper maintenance and preventive therapy, it seems irrational for it to be allowed to continue.

According to the research I have been able to undertake in this area, naturopathic or wholistic therapy differs from the medical approach in that it aims to treat the whole person, not just the body. The goal in wholistic therapy is to keep the life organism functioning at peak efficiency and to rectify conditions of imbalance before they lead to serious problems, rather than trying to repair the damage after it has occurred. Of the naturopaths I have met, the majority have been spiritually sensitive, with a keen understanding of the relationship between universal energies and the individual. Some are more aware than others and there seems to be a direct correlation between the level of spiritual awareness and the degree of healing ability. If you're looking for a good wholistic healer, you may need to do some shopping around in order to find a practitioner with whom you feel comfortable and confident but it is worth making the effort. The consultant's job will be much easier if you are able to relax and talk as friends.

Feeling comfortable with yourself is really important, especially from the spiritual point of view. In physical society we can be subjected to heavy negative conditioning that makes us see ourselves through jaundiced and critical eyes. Our flaws and imperfections are magnified whilst we are discouraged from feeling pride in our talents or successes. This creates an imbalance and often causes people to view themselves with contempt, if not with outright disgust. This is an unnatural situation that generates inner conflict, causing imbalance, unhappiness and tension. No one is perfect, nor are we expected to be, at least not in this life. If you work at accentuating your positives and eliminating the negatives, you'll reach perfection eventually and you'll also start feeling a whole lot better about yourself right here and now. You are a pure spirit, as good and as beautiful as any other. Start seeing yourself that way!

The aim in spiritual development is to help the pure and beautiful spirit within you to grow and rise to the surface. In this way you will become the glorious butterfly you were meant to be, no longer a sad caterpillar crawling around in the dust. If you want to fly, you must first spread your wings. Don't limit yourself in your thinking: you can achieve anything at all if you will only believe in yourself.

CHAPTER SEVEN

The Aura

Many people have written to ask me questions about the aura, its colours and what they signify. This topic is not easy to cover as an isolated subject because the energies within the aura are inextricably bound up with every other aspect of our being. As we have already discussed, the aura absorbs energies from the atmosphere around it and distributes them throughout the living organism. This process operates through the chakra system; so to understand the functions of the aura, we need to know something about the chakras, how they operate and the purposes they serve.

Colours are produced by light-waves vibrating at specific levels of frequency. The colours in the aura are governed by the types of energy that flow within it, therefore, to understand the colours, we need to understand something about the qualities of energy at the different levels of frequency. There are several distinct levels of energy within the human pattern of existence and each level has its own particular properties and colour frequencies. To start with a basic understanding, let's return to High School Physics and revise some of the fundamentals of energy.

All forms of energy have a distinctive rate and pattern of vibration, which gives the energy particular properties. This applies to the properties of colour, since colour is simply a form of light energy operating within a specific frequency range. This frequency of wavelength can actually be measured in nanometres (a nanometre is a millionth of a millimetre or 10^9 smaller than a metre!). The colour red, for example, operates on a frequency of around 610 nanometres (nM) whilst blue is 430 nM. The wavelength of an energy gives it other characteristics aside from colour and we often assign certain properties to a colour without consciously realising that we are describing something that actually exists. For example, red is frequently associated with passion and when you look a little deeper into the qualities of energy, it won't be difficult to understand why this is so.

Just as a crystal or prism will break down white light into a spectrum or rainbow of colours, the aura absorbs White Light energy and separates it into its various frequencies, which are fed into the life organism through the chakra system. At the same time, the organism (this means you!) is processing those energies, converting them and feeding them back through the aura, which radiates them outwards. The process is two-way, like breathing in and out.

The Sanskrit term 'chakra' translates as 'revolving wheel' and aptly describes the wheel-like vortices of energy located at definite intervals along the spine and within the head. Man is a composite being made up of physical, emotional, mental and spiritual components and the chakras are energy centres that relate to his make-up as a complete being. Man is said to exist upon seven levels or planes of existence. These are the Physical Etheric, Astral, Lower Mental, Higher Mental, Spiritual Causal, Intuitive and Divine or Absolute planes. There also happen to be seven colours in the rainbow and if you think that's a coincidence, you've got some learning to do!

Just as there are seven planes, so man is said to have seven subtle bodies. The seven primary chakras are the energy centres for each of the subtle bodies. It is through the composite aura, which comprises all seven levels, that a person's state of health, spiritual development, educational standard and frame of mind may be read by someone who is psychically sensitive to the aura. To a clairvoyant, the aura appears suffused with colour, the most predominant colour giving a fair indication of the overall characteristics and qualities of the entity concerned.

The colours in the aura come from the energies operating through the chakras. Each is of a specific wavelength or frequency within the spectrum of light peculiar to each chakra. For instance, the colour relative to the Lower Mental plane is yellow. Therefore if there is a predominance of yellow within a person's aura, then this is the main energy being suffused into the system and such a person would be said to be operating upon the Lower Mental plane. Knowing something about the qualities relative to that plane would then give us the ability to deduce certain things about the person concerned.

Understanding the properties of colour energy can also help us to deal with situations that challenge us in physical life. For instance, blue is a soothing, cooling colour which is very useful in the treatment of inflammatory conditions, whilst orange is good for alleviating the constriction of asthma. Green can help us to maintain inner balance and red can boost physical energy. The science of chromotherapy or colour healing was understood by the ancient mystics and has been undergoing a strong revival in recent years. There is really no limit to the ways in which an understanding of colour energy can be usefully employed.

The colours in your aura are not static; they move and change in accordance with your moods, thoughts and activities but there is one basic colour to which the aura will keep returning. This colour gives an indication of your level of development, basic personality, characteristics and state of health. Since the levels of consciousness are in harmony with vibrations of particular colour frequencies it is possible to use colour in meditation as a means of getting in touch with those levels within yourself.

Although each level has its own distinct properties and can be experienced individually, all the levels are interrelated and each can affect the others. Thus an emotional problem will affect your state of health or your imagination will influence your ability to learn. The activity in the chakras, or energy centres, has a direct influence on the nervous system, hormone secretions and the state of the body in general. Imbalance in any of the levels will ultimately lead to a condition of dis-ease in the body.

A person whose chakras are all open and functioning in perfect balance will have all the colours combined in a strong golden-white aura; however, most people only have two or three chakras operating most of the time. With safe and practical techniques, it is possible to stimulate the chakras and control the flow of energies within the aura, thereby generating a healthy balance of energy and promoting spiritual growth.

Having established a basic framework of understanding in respect of the aura, the chakras and the properties of light energy, we can examine each level individually and in detail.

The Base or Root Chakra

So known because of its location at the base of the spine between the coccyx and the gonads, this centre is the home of the 'serpent fire', the Kundalini. Its energy frequency within the light spectrum is in the *red* range at approximately 610 nanometres. This is the energy frequency of the *Physical Etheric* plane, which is the level immediately above the materialised physical world.

Just as we have a physical body, composed of matter which is attuned to the physical range of frequencies, so we also have an etheric counterpart. The Physical Etheric is also known as the Lower Astral and from this level we draw the primal energy that gives life its power and thrust. This is the 'fight or flight' energy of adrenalin in our system that sets our blood racing, gives us courage and boosts our willpower.

Red promotes heat and body temperature, gives us vitality and gets us going. You need a good level of red energy in order to achieve your physical goals successfully. Red level people are good at physical occupations and getting things done. They make excellent sportsmen and athletes. Red is also the colour of the sex drive and it is closely linked to the physical senses, so that red level people tend to seek sensory stimulation and excitement. These people are also inclined to live for the moment and give little thought to the past or future, relying greatly on external stimulation to satisfy their sensory appetites.

Red people are inclined to react without thinking and tend to be aggressive by nature. Given sufficient opportunities to channel their energies positively in work, creative activities, sports and lovemaking, a red level person can be a tower of strength; however if those positive outlets are denied, the energy can easily become brute force, violent and destructive.

In its negative form, red energy gives rise to lust, hatred, rage and intolerance. Because it feeds the ego, the passions and the sex drive, people with an excessive build-up of red energy can be dangerous characters. Here we find the bullies, rapists and violent criminals, for instance. Paradoxically, this energy can also be found surging through the auras of some of the crusading, hellfire and brimstone preachers who continually harangue their congregations on the evils of sensuality and the torments of damnation. In reality, these people are usually terrified of their own powerful carnality and, in the energetic bible-thumping and fervent tirades of condemnation, they are actually finding an outlet for this energy.

At the other end of the scale, people with insufficient levels of red energy are the ones who tend to be always tired, listless, run-down or anaemic. These are the people whose 'get up and go' has got up and gone. Both extremes indicate a lack of control, a personality that is out of balance at the red end of the spectrum. Between these two opposites there is a point of balance, the Middle Way, or Way of Moderation.

If you tend to have an excess of red energy, look for ways to channel it in physical occupations that involve an output of physical energy and leave you with a feeling of satisfaction and accomplishment. Something as simple as working in the garden or giving your home a thorough spring-cleaning can burn up all the excess energy in a positive way, leaving you feeling that you have done something worthwhile rather than letting off steam in a burst of destructive temper.

Meditation on the colour pink can help to tone down excesses of red energy, This principle has been used effectively in the United States with the management of young drug offenders. There is a particularly lethal concoction known as Angel Dust, which stimulates tremendous excesses of red energy and, under the influence of this drug, the users become extremely violent. Their level of physical strength is so intense that it can take several burly policemen just to hold them, even though their bodies may be puny. It was found that when these people were confined in a cell that had been painted pink throughout, they quietened down to such an extent that within about half an hour, some even went to sleep.

The red range of frequency can be said to represent the physical element in man. It is essentially egocentric, vital and active, giving our lives a quality of dynamism.

The Spleen Chakra

This centre operates within the *orange* frequency (580-590 nM) and is centred in the small of the back, to the left-hand side of the spine. It relates to the *Astral* plane, just above the Physical Etheric. Whereas the primitive surge of red energy provides thrust, this frequency adds motive.

Although it is more subtle than its companion red, orange is nonetheless an extremely potent force. It is still quite egocentric, in the sense that orange people seek to be admired by others but, at this level, the desire for gratification is emotional rather than physical.

Orange energy within the system has a wonderful tonic effect on all of the body processes. If you want your family to have good appetites, try decorating your dining room in orange; it stimulates the digestion! It also assists in the distributory and circulatory processes and gives a boost to both the physical vitality and the intellect. If you suffer from shyness, think orange. This is a colour that helps to relieve emotional tension, open the mind and encourage tolerance.

Orange is an expansive and outgoing energy, so people in this category are always seeking social contact and prefer to move with groups. They crave social acceptance and prefer to be one of a crowd rather than to stand apart as an individual. Even when they pursue an occupation that places them 'out front', there is usually a crowd around somewhere. For instance, an orange person may choose to be an actor; they thrive on applause and adulation. This does not, of course, imply that *all* actors and actresses are orange-level personalities, only that entertainment is a field that presents an attraction for people in the orange group. These people also love parties and thoroughly enjoy being social butterflies. Communal living also holds a strong attraction for them.

On the positive side, people in the orange group have strong humanitarian instincts and are more inclined to be concerned with the welfare of the community than with their own sensory gratification. This inclination, combined with their outgoing and gregarious nature, makes them excellent social workers.

In the negative aspect we have the trendies, cult-followers and dedicated devotees of fashion who wouldn't be caught dead wearing last week's hairdo. These people are often social climbers, groupies and camp followers. They simply *have* to be in with the In-crowd, are very concerned with appearances and constantly worrying about everyone else's opinion of them. They are strongly narcissistic and usually emotionally insecure. They can be extremely vain and temperamental and seem to be continually seeking praise and emotional reinforcement.

Where the red level is the level of childhood, in which the personality is busily exploring the body and the world of the senses, orange is the colour of adolescence. Just watch any group of teenagers all dressed in the latest way-out teen uniform, following all the current fads and crazes, constantly seeking the approval and acceptance of their peers. If you could see the auras of these young people, you would find a strong predominance of orange.

A person in whom the orange energy is balanced has a character that is sensitive, generous, mobile and warmly serene. The orange level of energy is said to represent the emotional element in our nature.

The Solar Plexus Chakra

This centre operates within the *yellow* frequency (570 nM) and is located in the middle of the back, over the kidneys. It relates to the *Lower Mental* plane. Here, in the quality and clarity of the yellow in the aura, a person's intellectual make-up is revealed. It is at this level that thought and feeling are joined.

Thoughts, ideas, reason, intellect and knowledge all arise at this level. As the energy transcends the orange

range, it moves towards the gold of wisdom. Emotion is linked to understanding. This is the level at which the personality begins to seek wisdom and purpose through understanding and communication. It is the level of intellect. Whereas red energy provides thrust and orange gives motive, yellow adds conscious direction.

Yellow is exhilarating and sunny, intellectually stimulating. Yellow people are walking computers! They love to analyse, evaluate, categorise, debate and generally have a great time playing around with the process of logic. These people just love to THINK; in fact, they can spend so much time just thinking that they often don't get around to following up any of their brilliant ideas. As soon as they finish exploring all the computations and ramifications of one idea, their minds zoom off in search of something that will present a fresh challenge to their reasoning ability. They like change and new ideas.

The yellow level represents the psychological element in human nature and, with their natural capacity for analysis, these people can make excellent psychologists, provided that they don't get so caught up with their analytical logic that they lose touch with their emotions. One of the negative aspects of the yellow level is that the personality can become blinded by the light of its own power of reasoning. Yellow people can become so involved with pulling life to pieces and figuring out how it works that they don't get around to doing any real living. They can tend to spend so much time analysing their emotions that they don't really *feel* them and this can make them rather superficial. They may sit back and observe to such an extent that they separate themselves from the mainstream of life and they can often be quite maddeningly egotistic.

The shade of yellow that is associated with cowardice is actually a polluted colour, murky and tending towards olive. The clear yellow is bright and inquisitive, always alert for new fields to explore and new problems to solve. In its pure form, yellow is bright and optimistic.

Yellow energy stimulates the nervous system and the digestive processes. It assists the eliminative functions, particularly through the liver and intestines. Yellow is a cleansing colour that purifies the whole system, particularly the skin. Since it stimulates the intellect, the logical mind and reasoning powers, yellow aids self-control through inspiring the higher faculties.

A restricted flow of yellow into the system will indicate itself in a person with bad eating habits, poor digestion and a nervous disposition. Depending upon the degree of restriction, the effects can vary in severity. One person may only feel generally a bit sluggish, and then only temporarily, whilst someone else may permanently be intellectually a bit slow on the uptake. Yet another may display either or both of the above and suffer from skin blemishes too: eruptions, eczema, acne and rashes.

Balance is achieved through clarity. The soul first must learn to know itself, then to develop an awareness of its actions, and then to learn to comprehend the consequences. Whatever thoughts we entertain in the mind are relayed to the emotions, which stimulate a corresponding feeling, which generates action. By controlling our thoughts we can control both ourselves and our effect within the collective environment. When we master this level of awareness, we are well on the way to understanding how, with our thoughts, we create our own reality.

The Heart Chakra

The heart chakra occupies the *green* frequency in the light spectrum at approximately 550 nM and is located between the shoulder-blades, in line with the heart. It relates to the *Higher Mental* plane, the level at which the Higher Mind, or Soul principle, comes into being.

The Emerald Kingdom is an expression of love, abundance and fertility, balanced and in harmony with itself. The primal drive of creative energy gives rise to new growth. Physical drive and emotional sensitivity, balanced with clarity and awareness, are at harmony in the heart.

Green people are sensitive and imaginative. They need to feel completely secure, especially within their emotions. Insecurity can bring out their most negative characteristics, which is how we arrive at such expressions as 'green with envy'. Green people like to store things up, whether in the form of possessions or knowledge. If they are stable and secure they will be naturally generous and willing to share, not only their possessions but also of themselves.

One of my friends is a lovely green person who likes collecting pieces of fabric from the remnant tables in department stores. She has bags upon bags of material squirrelled away, and I'm sure she could sew from now until doomsday without using it all up. On several occasions I have been lovingly presented with beautifully sewn outfits made from some gorgeous pieces of fabrics from Beverly's treasure trove and it gives her no end of delight when she sees how much her gifts of love are appreciated.

A negative, muddy green will produce a personality that is miserly, selfish and acquisitive. Once again, security is the key. Scratch a greedy person and, underneath, you are likely to find someone who is frightened, insecure and badly in need of comfort and reassurance. Greed is only a manifestation of insecurity. People who are afraid to open up and let themselves love are often sensitive green people who have suffered rejection or had their trust abused. Their nature is inherently loving and giving but, because they are so very sensitive, they can be driven to hide away in their shells like little hermit crabs.

Positive green people are among this world's most beautiful inhabitants. They have a strong affinity with nature, love getting their hands into the soil and helping things to grow and have a deep concern for animals, birds and all living creatures. It is no accident that the conservationists and those who fight to protect Earth's wildlife and ecology are known as 'Greenies', nor that the international foundation which fights so hard in defence of nature and the quality of life goes by the name of Greenpeace.

Green is a colour that generates balance and harmony. The home of a green person will usually have a deliciously pleasant, serene and soothing atmosphere and there will probably be indoor plants thriving everywhere. The home may not always be tidy on the surface, in fact, it is quite likely to be overrun with a horde of cheerfully energetic children and an equally exuberant assortment of animals, but there is an underlying sense of order and balance, even in the midst of domestic chaos. It may seem jumbled on the surface but you can bet that your green person will know exactly where to find anything at a moment's notice.

This is the level of the dreamer, the idealist, the artist and the decorator. Green people love to make things beautiful. Green energy gives a quality of empathy and compassion, along with love and generosity of spirit. In its pure form, love is a life-giving force that swells outward to encompass the whole of Creation. It is totally unconditional because it asks nothing more than to be allowed to give of itself. Thus the message of the Creator, exemplified in the positive green personality, becomes not 'Love me or be damned,' but 'Just let me love you'.

Green is the colour of nature itself. When your nerves are frayed and the ratrace is taking its toll on you, the green of trees, grass and plants has a wonderful refreshing effect, instilling a sense of renewal and restoration. Because of its harmonising qualities, green helps to restore balance within the energy pattern, which gives it a quality of healing. A negative, murky or purulent green is associated with imbalance, disease and infection. This colouring indicates that the pure life-force has been contaminated.

In balance, the energy through the heart chakra is one of calmness, serenity and inner strength. Just as the yellow energy of the solar plexus chakra provides conscious direction, so the green energy of the heart chakra provides balance and selflessness. Green energy represents the harmonising element in our life pattern.

The Throat Chakra

This centre operates within the *blue* range of light frequency around 430 nM and is centred at the nape of the neck, near the base of the skull. This is the level of the *Spiritual Causal* plane, the level where spiritual awareness begins to unfold.

All of the levels so far discussed pertain to the individual consciousness but, at this level, the fifth chakra, the individual is linked to the ocean of human consciousness or group mind. The energy from this centre surrounds and interpenetrates all the lower planes of consciousness and draws to itself an awareness of all the sensations, ideas and experiences gathered through the lower levels. In this sense, it acts as a data bank for information. Everything you have seen, felt, learned or experienced throughout your lifetime is stored here; nothing is ever lost.

Because this level is the junction between the physical consciousness and the higher planes, it also acts as a receiving station for information, sensations and influences from the upper levels of spiritual existence. Blue light energy is the colour specifically associated with healing, and it is no coincidence that the colour most frequently chosen for nurses' uniforms is blue. The aura of a dedicated healer is predominantly blue and, if you could see your doctor's aura, you would be able to tell, at a glance whether he entered his profession because of a genuine calling or because it represented a lucrative or socially prominent career opportunity.

Blue level people are deep thinkers with a high level of moral commitment. They like to think things through carefully before taking action and, unlike their counterparts on the preceding levels, they are anything but impulsive. Classically, they are the still waters that run deep and their depths are profound. They are inclined to be conservative and resistant to change. To people who like fast movement, change and rapid progress, blue people can seem to be stuffy stick-in-the-muds.

Blue people are inclined to be pacifists who seek peace at any price, even if that may mean tolerating bullying and oppression from others. They are usually deeply religious and this, in conjunction with their highly moralistic nature, can have its negative side in bigotry and puritanism. Fanatical religious wars and bloody purges such as the Inquisition, in which thousands of 'heretics' were hideously tortured, would seem to be more the type of activities perpetrated by violent red-level personalities than peaceful blues but, in fact, a negative blue can be intolerant to an extreme.

Blue helps ideas to crystallise. It is a cooling, soothing colour that exerts a slowing and steadying influence. It promotes quietness, tranquillity and peace of mind. As the mind clears, it begins to examine the accumulated information drawn from all its conscious levels of experience. This is the point of union with the higher self, the level at which you can consciously influence the pattern of events that will occur in your life. In order to chart your course, the higher self draws on the information stored in your data banks. What lessons remain to be learned? Are there any tasks left uncompleted?

Here the soul is beginning to experience the first clear rays of spiritual awareness. They occur in the mind as fleeting images at first, flashes of higher awareness that become more numerous and frequent as the understanding progresses. A clairvoyant can see this effect within the aura in the form of dancing blue sparks of light. The turbulence of the lower levels is being transmuted; there is growing peace.

As you move closer to the stream of universal consciousness, the membrane that surrounds you becomes thinner and more translucent, allowing more light to penetrate the capsule of your conscious awareness, but *you* must dissolve the last of the membrane. Blue level people need to beware of the tendency to become stuck in a mental rut, allowing their thought patterns to freeze into icy rigidity, taking a narrow-minded approach and refusing to accept change or progress. Nothing in life remains stationary: everything is transient, moving, changing and constantly evolving. If you can go with the flow, keep your mind open to new discoveries and changing concepts, then you can transcend the lower levels, pass through the membrane and enter the world of higher spiritual awareness.

In balance, the blue level has movement, flexibility and wit. The personality is alive and vital, but tranquil also. There is warmth and an outflowing of positive emanations; a comfortable warmth laced with cooling breezes, not an all-consuming body heat. It is subtle and delicate but penetrating. It bathes the sensitivities and puts the mind at rest.

Blue energy provides spiritual direction and gives the life energy pattern the specific healing element.

This is the traditional 'Third Eye' centre, in the middle of the forehead between the eyebrows. It draws energy from the *indigo* level (400 nM) and relates to the *Intuitive* plane, the origin of all the psychic faculties such as clairvoyance, clairaudience, telepathy, prescience and, of course, intuition.

The indigo light gives clear perception but, until the lessons of the preceding levels have been thoroughly mastered, the quality of comprehension can be subject to variation. To see is not always to understand. When the midnight radiance of the indigo light first penetrates your waking consciousness, you may spend a lot of time trying to figure out whether you're Peter Pan, Tinkerbell or just plain moonstruck! Indigo people can be 'away with the pixies' to such an extent that they not only forget to keep their feet on the ground but are likely to forget that they have any feet at all!

In comparison to those who function on the preceding blue level, indigo people are about as different as it is possible to be. Where blue people tend to cling to the past, indigos are always racing off into the future. Most of them are characteristically about half a century ahead of themselves and everybody else.

Because this level is not anchored in the nuts-and-bolts physical reality, the perceptions are abstract and an indigo person will often know things without being able to explain why he knows. This is particularly applicable in the early stages of psychic awakening, when a person will have hunches, premonitions or flashes of awareness but has not yet learned to understand where it all comes from, what it means or how it works.

When a person first begins to experience conscious psychic awareness, the reaction is often one of fear but, once that has been overcome, the awakening psychic is likely to enter a period of euphoria. This can be a dangerous space, particularly if the lower aspects of the personality have not been mastered. There can be an inflation of the ego, a tendency for these people to believe that they know all the answers and that there is nothing anyone else can teach them. This is the mark of an undeveloped psychic who has awareness but no understanding.

A true luminary does not advertise himself from the rooftops as an Enlightened One. He doesn't have to: his enlightenment is self-evident for those who have eyes to see. He leans on nobody for support and feels no need for admiration. Kindred spirits are drawn into his presence on the pure attraction of love, in its highest form.

Indigo people are often spiritual but not religious, Their spirituality comes from direct perception and experience rather than an acceptance of religious formulae. In fact, they can be so impatient with established religious philosophies that they may fail to see the core of truth within the doctrine. Psychic ability does not always equate with spiritual awareness, however, and the fact that a person is psychic must never be taken to mean that he is automatically spiritual. Spiritual awareness, attunement and understanding don't come about by accident but are acquired through a process of effort and application.

Indigo people need to remind themselves that they are here to learn so that they can grow in both wisdom and stature. Psychic perceptions, like our other senses, bring us information about the worlds in which we have our existence. That information needs to be studied, correlated and applied to life *as we are living it.* To accept one form of reality and reject another is no way to gain an understanding of the overall pattern of life. The psychic realms do not represent an escape from the mundane aspects of living and to attempt using them in that way will only result in losing touch with reality.

Concentration on the brow centre and the colour indigo lifts the consciousness out of the physical, removing impediments to the higher awareness such as fears or inhibitions. It expands the mind and purifies the energy streams, thus aiding the higher mental and spiritual processes. It exerts a stabilising influence over the entire system and is even capable of raising the pain threshold.

There are influences abroad today which stimulate the indigo spectrum, with the result that mankind is taking an evolutionary leap into the depths of its own consciousness. This has a number of spectacularly beneficial effects but there is also a reverse side to the coin. Not all of the mind-expansion methods in use today are safe: the drug L.S.D. is a classic example. Some people claim to have found inspiration through its use, but many thousands more have suffered temporary or permanent brain and nervous system damage. Those methods of experimentation simply aren't worth the risk. The only safe way to pass through this portal is through understanding, guidance and purity of motive. Because of the dangers inherent in misguided experimentation, the Enlightened Ones have always warned about the dangers of dabbling with such things. Until the mind's power is properly understood, it is very unwise to play with the instrument panel.

Indigo energy is the gateway to inspiration and represents the intuitive element in man.

The Crown Chakra

The crown chakra is located in the dome of the head, at the anterior fontanelle, which is still open in the skull of a newborn infant and is known as the 'soft spot'. This centre's colour frequency is *violet* (380 nM) and it links us with the *Divine* or *Absolute* plane.

This is the realm of imagination, inspiration and creativeness, the link between the human consciousness and the universal ocean of intelligence known as the cosmic mind. This sphere generates the energies which have inspired our greatest artists, poets, composers and philosophers, the energies which stimulate the faculty of genius. At this level, we move beyond the known universe and begin to experience another realm of awareness; we are in touch with the primordial essence that shapes all forms of life under the influence of the cosmic mind.

As it has often been said, there is a very fine line between genius and insanity. It takes a completely balanced, aware and enlightened personality to cope effectively with the potent energies that exist at this level, where thought is the immediate, living reality. A person capable of working at this level can take the essence of life energy and literally shape it into reality with the power of his mind alone. There is tremendous power here but there is also tremendous responsibility.

There is a pattern to life, in all its forms and at all of its levels. To disrupt that pattern is to generate chaos. A personality that is not sufficiently evolved can become so intoxicated with the sheer potency of this energy that he can be swept away on a power-trip. He will use his power in the form of psychic force, to manipulate and overwhelm others and bend them to his will. This person seeks to establish a kingdom of his own making, rather than to harmonise with the perfection of the system which is already in existence.

A violet person on a power trip is a walking disaster, dangerous and ruthless, a classic megalomaniac. With this type of personality, the violet energy takes on a darker hue to become the deep purple traditionally associated with temporal power.

A violet aura does not necessarily indicate a personality that is more evolved than someone with, say, a yellow aura. People who cannot cope with the realities of life may seek to escape into a world of fantasy images that is totally separated from the established pattern of things. It is vital that we do not lose ourselves in the complexities of our own desires and mental imagery. It is for this reason that the Higher Ones repeatedly urge us to keep checking the reality of our inner images against the pattern of life at every level, so that we can keep in touch with life, growing in balance, fulfilling ourselves and others as we are meant to do.

As David has said, time is a condition of physical existence. There is no past, present or future in the spiritual reality, only one continuous now. Violet exists in this eternal now and, for the violet personality, there is a sense of timelessness that bears no resemblance to the 'live for the moment' motivation of the red level. Red personalities simply disregard the past and future; at the violet level, past present and future are all blended together.

When the personality is balanced and truly enlightened, violet energy manifests as creativity and inspiration, calm but sure and strong. There is a sense of union with All that Is, an elevation of the spirit, the quality of cosmic consciousness. The power to create is used to bring beauty, order and inspiration to others and the influence is selfless and utterly beneficial. Because of its transcendent quality, this personality may seem somewhat detached to the average observer. The truly evolved personality has no need for emotional or sensory gratification, drawing its fulfilment from a higher source. In this respect, detachment does not indicate disinterest or aloofness, it is simply a freedom from lower-self appetites, needs and desires.

The violet level of energy represents the spiritual element in mankind.

CHAPTER EIGHT

Colour and Spiritual Growth

It can be seen from the preceding chapter that our makeup as individuals is inextricably linked, through the chakras and the aura, to a number of distinct energy levels with particular properties and characteristics. There are other levels and other chakras but, at this stage in our development, we are most concerned with the seven primary ones.

It should be borne in mind that we ourselves influence the flow of colour energy through our auras. The colours are determined by such factors as our level of evolvement, education, state of mind and emotions. If we learn to control and manipulate the colours in our auras, the energies thus produced will in turn exert an influence on our capacities and characteristics as individuals. For instance, if you are lacking in physical energy, feeling listless and drained, you can boost your vitality by focussing on the colour red and drawing that energy into your aura. If you are feeling mentally sluggish, concentration on yellow will help to stimulate your intellect.

You can also be affected by the energies that swirl through the atmosphere around you if they are permitted to penetrate your aura. When these effects are positive and uplifting, there is no harm in allowing the energies to be absorbed, in fact they can be beneficial. Basically, however, the idea is to keep your energies maintained in a state of balance from within. All human beings have an energy pattern comprised of frequencies drawn from the seven planes of existence. If just one of those frequencies is blocked or not functioning as it should, there will be an imbalance throughout the whole system and the personality will be incomplete.

If you look through the qualities and characteristics of the energy levels given in the previous chapter, you will be able to see that each level represents a distinct stage in the evolution of the personality. First comes the red-level physical state, related to early childhood, in which the emphasis is on sensory awareness, the body and physical stimuli. Next comes the adolescent stage, in which the focus is on the emotions. In young adulthood, the personality begins to explore the intellect and so it goes on, up the scale, until the personality transcends the physical and enters the worlds of spiritual existence.

It is not difficult to identify the primary stages of growth in terms of physical development, as in the tendency for very young children to explore everything with their senses. Give a young infant a new object to hold and he will invariably put it into his mouth.

Teenagers typically centre their interests around the emotions, fantasising over pop idols, becoming wildly infatuated several times a week, being prone to severe mood swings and so on. At the physical level, however, the stages of development tend to blur as the individual grows older. Every personality contains elements of the energies from each of the seven levels but the proportions of energy in different people are infinitely variable. We can, for instance, see physically mature people behaving like children and youngsters who display levels of wisdom far beyond their tender years.

If we look at the picture from a spiritual viewpoint, the situation begins to be clarified. Firstly, we must take into account that the evolution of a human soul takes place during the course of many physical lifetimes or incarnations, so that physical age can not be taken as an indication of true maturity. In the body of a ninety-three year-old-man there may be an infant soul which is still primarily focussed in the red level. This soul has a number of incarnations to live through before it approaches real maturity. Equally, the body of a tiny infant may be the vehicle for an ancient soul with an infinite degree of spiritual maturity and awareness.

Just for the record, it is the adolescent, orange-level personalities who tend to be attracted towards politics. When we consider that, spiritually speaking, the fate of our world is chiefly in the hands of a group of teenagers, it isn't really difficult to understand why this planet currently has problems!

Progression upwards through the spheres of spiritual growth is a process that will take place naturally over a series of lifetimes, whether the soul is aware of it or not. When you reach a level at which you *become* aware of this process and you begin aspiring to higher levels of awareness and spiritual maturity, you have reached a stage at which you can consciously influence the rate and quality of your growth. The development of psychic abilities is an integral part of your evolution but it should never be allowed to become the primary focus. The key to positive growth is *BALANCE*. The most simple and obvious way to start working to establish that balance is by concentrating on the energies within the aura itself. You can work through the chakras, generating or drawing in energies from each of the levels so that your overall energy pattern contains these qualities in proportion.

There are any number of ways in which this process can be assisted and I could write a hefty book on that subject alone. For our present purposes, however, I will concentrate on a simple meditation exercise. The method given here is necessarily quite lengthy, and I do not suggest that you try to memorise it all. If you are working alone, I suggest that you make use of a tape-recorder. Simply dictate the instructions onto a tape, then sit back, relax, turn on the tape and follow each stage as it is described.

If you are working with a group, you could arrange to take turns, with a different member reading out the instructions in successive meetings. The purpose of this meditation is to stimulate each chakra in turn, suffusing your life energy pattern with the most positive qualities of energy from each of the seven levels. The process should definitely not be rushed. To carry out the exercise properly will probably take as long as ten or fifteen minutes or even longer. We aren't trying to win any races, so take your time and allow these energies to percolate thoroughly through your system.

Although we will be identifying each of the levels by colour, it is by no means necessary for you to *see* each colour inwardly. If you can, that's fine but, if not, don't be too concerned. Remember that we are concentrating on particular *qualities* of energy so the emphasis is more on feeling than seeing. Once again, I will remind you that what you think IS. It is by this power of directed thought that you draw the essential components into your energy system.

The Colour Meditation

Take some time to relax and adjust your breathing to a gentle, comfortable rhythm... now open yourself to the pure white flow of life-giving cosmic Light energy.

Feel the Light flow into your mind, cleansing away all the shadows and producing a sensation of positive upliftment... now, let it flow through your body... experience the feeling of relaxation, purification and well-being... Take a few moments to enjoy and attune yourself to the flow of pure life energy...

Now, allow your attention to centre on the root chakra, at the base of your spine... imagine a point of brilliant White Light in the middle of the chakra, purifying the energy centre so that only the clearest and most positive energies can flow within it...

Feel the point of Light begin to pulse and grow... as it expands, feel it changing to a clear, vibrant red... let the light continue to grow... and feel the pulsations of vitality surging through your body... radiating out from the energy centre like ripples in a pool... feel your blood cells dancing and your body tingling with exuberant life force, giving a boost to your confidence... energy... and initiative.

Take a few moments to enjoy the red energy sensation...

Move the focus of your awareness to the left-hand side of your spine in the small of your back and see a point of brilliant White Light at the centre of your spleen chakra... feel this Light begin to pulse and grow, purifying your Astral energy streams... as the Light expands, feel it changing to a warm, bright orange... with this orange energy rippling outwards through your system, feel its wonderful tonic effect... feel the melting away of any negative thoughts and emotional tensions... they are being washed away in the stream of orange light... feel a clearing of the mind... a sharpening of the faculties... and a positive lift in your emotions... Take a few moments to enjoy the flow of orange energy.

Lift your focus now to the middle of your back, over the kidneys... and tune in to the brilliant point of Light shining at the centre of your solar plexus chakra... as it begins to pulse and grow, feel it changing to a pure, bright yellow... let it spread outward through your system... and feel your mental processes becoming crystal clear... bringing a sharpening of your awareness and a clarity of perception... feel the outflow of a positive force that repels negativity... and attracts the kind of energies that are creative and uplifting... take a few moments to enjoy the flow of warm yellow energy...

Raise your focus of awareness to the level of your heart, between the shoulder-blades... see the point of pure White Light in the centre of your heart chakra... as the purifying light begins to pulse and grow, change the colour to a fresh, bright green... let this refreshing green light pulse out through your system... bringing with it a sensation of renewal... the abundance and fertility of nature... an enrichment within your spirit... inner balance... and an awareness that all is well, the Universe is unfolding as it should.

Feel your heart opening, to pour the goodness of this life-giving energy outwards... letting it bathe the whole of humankind in its richness... give it out as naturally as a flower gives its fragrance... have no fear that your store will be depleted... you are drawing the energy from an infinite source, the well can never run dry and the more you give, the more will be given unto you... take some time to bask in the joy of giving and the renewal and refreshment of the beautiful green world... feel the spirit of Nature itself reaching out to enfold you...

Now, lift your awareness to your throat chakra and focus on the purifying point of White Light at its centre... as the Light begins to well and grow, change the colour to a sparkling electric blue... let it pulsate outwards through your system in an irresistable tide of healing, soothing comfort... feel a quiet strength and stillness within... an awakening of the spirit... and a sense of affinity with the minds of your kindred spirits, who surround you everywhere... let your spirit be nourished in the flow of creative blue energy... and be tranquil, knowing beyond doubt that the course of your destiny is being safely guided by none other than your Creator.

Feel your spirit uplifted... be at peace... know that you are a child of God... at one with your Creator and with the whole of Creation... give the energy outwards... sending comfort, healing and upliftment to the places where it is needed... feel an inner attunement with the souls of your brother and sister spirits everywhere... with all the love you can muster, send them a message with your thoughts and let the message be this: 'Peace be unto you'.

Wait quietly... and feel the flow of love and peace returning to wash over you... and through you... in a quiet but infinitely powerful tide of spiritual fulfilment... rest... and bask in the healing, creative flow of blue light energy.

Now, raise your consciousness to the brow chakra in the centre of your forehead and focus on its centre, in the point of purifying White Light... slowly let the Light expand, gently but thoroughly cleansing your psychic energy streams... now change the colour to indigo... a clear, deep midnight blue... as this colour pulsates through your system, feel the quickening of your intuitive faculties... a purity of thought... and a clarification of your awareness and sensitivity to the higher psychic spheres.

Be assured that you are completely safe... the energy upon which you are drawing is the spiritual Light: clear, strong, pure and protective... in this space you are in touch with only the highest energies in the psychic realms... they come to you in love and will not do you harm... feel the closeness of your spirit guardians... guides... and loved ones, who join you at this level... reach out to them with love and make them welcome... and enjoy the warmth of their loving response... drift for a while in the indigo space.

Now raise your focus of awareness to the top of your

head and tune in to the point of White Light at the centre of your crown chakra... let the Light gently expand and as it spreads outwards, change the colour to violet... as this energy permeates your system, feel yourself uplifted and surrounded by the close, personal presence of your Creator... feel the loving, creative power as it penetrates every level of your being... do not try to direct the flow, just accept it and know that it comes to you from the Highest... to stimulate and nourish the divinity within yourself... as it does its precious work, say to yourself in your mind 'I am a child of God'... and KNOW that it is true... spend a few moments to enjoy the flow of beautiful violet light.

Now pause and focus your attention on the whole of your aura... feel the potency, strength and beauty of the energy pulsing through it as each one of your chakras draws on the infinite energy in its purest and most positive form... let this energy radiate out from you and know that, in its generous flow, you are giving only that which is most beneficial and uplifting... for yourself and for those around you... when you radiate positive energy in this way, negativity cannot reach you because it is overcome and swept away in the tide of goodness... feel the sparkling vibrancy of life energy surging through every fibre of your being... and as the energy radiates outward, feel yourself expanding with it... in a beautiful white-gold stream of perfectly balanced life essence.

Feel a sense of attunement with your Creator... an affinity with All that Is... a pure and unconditional love for life in all its myriad forms... luxuriate in the infinite warmth and love of the Spiritual Light... soak it in... and breathe it out... sharing both the Light and yourself with All that Is... take several minutes to enjoy the feeling of ultimate pleasure and upliftment... and the feeling of absolute Oneness with Life.

When you are ready... slowly prepare yourself for the return to a physical focus... take your time... don't try to rush... as you gradually return your awareness to the here and now, bring the Light with you and keep it radiating, so that it enhances your every thought... feeling... and action within the physical environment... give thanks for the joyful experience you have been given to share and the fresh power and confidence that is yours to apply to your endeavours in life.

Come back gently... take a deep breath... open your eyes... and relax.

* * * * *

When you are dictating this guided meditation, whether it is onto a tape-recording or in a group situation, remember that our normal rate of speech is quite rapid and that the mind must be given time to follow each step in the instructions. You must pay attention to the manner in which you deliver the spoken words. Slow down your rate of speech and pronounce each word clearly. If you rush or mumble, your listeners will be forced to concentrate so intently on keeping up with you and hearing the words that they will be unable to follow the instructions as they should, so the whole exercise will be futile.

In the written text, you will have noticed spaces marked with a row of dots. This has been done to indicate places where it is advisable to pause in the spoken delivery. Wherever you encounter a pause space, stop speaking, count slowly to ten and then continue. This will give the listeners time to absorb the instructions and attune themselves to the progressive flow of energies. At the end of each segment, where the instructions say to spend a few moments soaking in the colour energy, allow an interval of one or two minutes before proceeding to the next level.

In the final stages of the meditation, there is an instruction to 'take several minutes to enjoy the feeling of ultimate pleasure and upliftment... the feeling of absolute Oneness with Life'. After speaking those words, allow at least five minutes before proceeding to the next set of instructions. As you become more familiar with the exercise, you can extend that period of time if you wish. If the instructions given are followed correctly, you may find that some of your listeners are reluctant to come back as instructed and may stay 'out' for some time beyond the point at which they have been told to open their eyes. You will probably also find that, for the participants, the awareness of time is different from the perception of the person who is leading the exercise. For instance, ten minutes by the clock may seem like only two or three minutes to your listeners.

When you have given the 'touch down' instructions, wait a couple of minutes to allow time for the participants to come back gently. Then, if there are some who have not responded, repeat the last set of instructions as follows: 'It is time for you to come back. Take a deep breath, open your eyes and relax.' Wait another few minutes and, if necessary, repeat the instruction again, this time calling the people by name. 'Peter and Alice, we are waiting for you. It is time to come back . . . '

The participants should be aware that they have a responsibility to the rest of the group in this respect. Having taken part in quite a few colour meditations, I am familiar with the pleasure associated with those last few minutes and how tempting it can be to ignore the instructions and continue enjoying a blissful float on my own personal cloud. At the same time, there is a need for self-discipline. Until every member has returned to normal consciousness, the group cannot proceed to the next stage of activities. In addition, if you ignore all instructions to return, there will be a point at which the other members will have to conclude that you have entered a mediumistic trance and they are unlikely to appreciate it if you have simply been indulging yourself.

Having mentioned the possibility of trance, I should now hasten to add some words of assurance for those who may be meditating alone. This meditation, like any other psychic activity, should always be prefaced with the auric cleansing and Invocation for protection and guidance, whether you are working alone or with a group. If you have taken those necessary precautions, you will be in no danger at the psychic level because your guides and guardians will take care of you. If you fall into a trance whilst you are alone, you will gravitate into a natural sleep and wake up normally, quite probably feeling deliciously refreshed and invigorated.

At the psychic level, the guardian spirits will fulfil their responsibilities as requested but, at the physical level, you are responsible for your own welfare. The greatest danger you could encounter would be if some other person were to touch you whilst you are in a trance state, so you should take every precaution to ensure that it does not happen. If you are sharing a house with other people, make sure that you let them know when you are planning to meditate. Be sure they understand that if they find you apparently sleeping, they are not to touch you . . . for any reason. If they need to arouse you, it should be done by calling your name periodically until you respond. If you feel it necessary, lock the door to your room whilst you are meditating.

Spiritual development should be a joyful, uplifting and fulfilling experience but, although it can (and should) be a lot of fun at times, it should never be regarded merely as a game. Psychic energy is both safe and beneficial when channelled responsibly but it is highly volatile in careless hands. Don't fool around with it. Use it wisely and it will serve you well, with positive results in every sense.

It is not necessary to perform the colour meditation every day or even at every meeting of your meditation group. It is simply given as an exercise that has been designed to serve a particular purpose: to help you balance and control the flow of energies within your aura. You can set a routine in which you perform the exercise once a week if you wish, it certainly won't do any harm and, like the exercises given earlier, the more you use it, the more effective it will become. Unlike the previous exercises, however, it is not an essential part of your *protective* routine, simply a tool to be used in the process of your development.

There are any number of effective meditation exercises designed to assist in the growth of your spiritual awareness and I would suggest that you do some reading and research in this respect. If you browse through the contents of your nearest esoteric bookshop, you are certain to find several good books on meditation. Some methods will be suitable for you and some will not but, unless you do some research, your repertoire will be limited and your development program is likely to become boring and repetitious. Don't limit yourself. The more reading and exploring you do, the more you enhance your store of knowledge and thus assist your rate of progress.

For groups, it is always beneficial to have a discussion period following each meditation exercise, giving the members the opportunity to compare experiences and give their opinions of the techniques used. You may find what has been good for some members has achieved little for others. In that case, those who found the exercise helpful could put it on their list for home meditation while the group explores other methods. The idea is to exercise and expand your spiritual faculties so that you become familiar with their functions. In a way, it's like exercising a muscle: the more you practise, the more strong and flexible it becomes.

CHAPTER NINE

Trance Mediumship: Communication with Spirits

'Be comforted. You would not be seeking Me if you had not found me.'

Blaise Pascal

Trance mediumship is arguably one of the most intriguing and mysterious forms of spiritual communication. In some doctrines, particularly within the traditional Spiritualist philosophy, a trance medium is often regarded with something akin to awe, as though to be a medium is to be a part of some spiritually privileged elite. Other schools of thought are more inclined to believe that trance mediumship is unreliable, unnecessary and even dangerous. In practice, as usual, the truth is somewhere in between.

The idea that trance mediumship is the ultimate in human psychic development is a myth. Trance mediums do not possess a level of development far beyond that of their admirers; in fact, there are some who have very little spiritual awareness at all. Without wishing to seem disparaging about the worth of his natural talent, I can cite Roland as an example of the fact that you don't have to know a thing about spiritual reality or psychic phenomena in order to be a good trance medium. Roland himself, were you to speak with him, would not hesitate to reinforce that statement.

When I first met Roland, he was not a believer in psychic phenomena. His attitude towards spirituality in general could best be described as agnostic; he was prepared to acknowledge that there may be some form of existence beyond the physical but he also believed it to be impossible for ordinary human beings to have direct knowledge of it. In his words: 'I'll find out soon enough when I die. Until then, I'm not prepared to ascribe to any theories.'

Within days of our first meeting, Roland had begun to enter trance states. Before a fortnight had passed, I was receiving the first communications from David. Even though I was only a raw beginner at the time, I had enough experience to recognise in David a spiritual teacher of the highest calibre and he has since proven himself many times over. Even though these communications were taking place and he heard tape recordings of my conversations with David, it was a long time before Roland came to accept them for what they are. His disbelief, however, did nothing to reduce the quality of David's communications.

Ten years have now passed since those first communications were received. Even now, Roland will openly state that in addition to regarding himself as anything but an authority on matters of the spirit, he still feels a certain amount of discomfort with regard to his mediumship. His experiences have taught him to accept the truth of a spiritual reality; David's teachings make sense to him and he acknowledges their truth. In that respect he has become a believer but spirituality is not the dominant interest in his life at present. He is happy to give me all the support and assistance that he is capable of providing but he prefers that our trance sittings remain private. He has a profound aversion to what he refers to as 'the goldfish bowl effect' which happens when he knows that people are watching intently in the hope that he will trance for them or studiously *not* watching, which is just as disconcerting. His agreement to work with David and I was made in the knowledge that the work we are doing can be of great benefit to others but it is also conditional on the trance sittings remaining private.

Ask Roland to answer your questions on the subject of spirituality and he will probably follow his normal practice of referring you to me. 'Dawn is the person you should speak to,' he will tell you. 'She's the one who's done all the study: all I do is sit in a chair and go to sleep.'

In all fairness, I have to say that those remarks are more than a little self-effacing on Roland's part. In fact, he has acquired a considerable degree of knowledge in the years that we have been together. However, the point is that his level of conscious knowledge has made *no difference whatsoever* to the quality of his mediumship. For the most part, Roland is a deep trance medium. That is, during trance, he enters a deep sleep in which he is oblivious to the events taking place around him and through him. His body may be quite animated, eyes open, gesturing freely and occasionally even getting up and walking around the room but, when he comes out of the trance, Roland has no conscious recollection of those activities.

There are other levels of trance and other forms of mediumship, some of which Roland has displayed on occasions. For instance, not all deep trance mediums are oblivious to the events that take place during their trances: some mediums have reported viewing the proceedings from a corner of the room, seeing their own bodies functioning independently of themselves. In so-called conscious mediumship, the alteration in consciousness can be so slight that it is almost unnoticeable and seems more like a change of mood. Conscious mediumship is the form that I most commonly experience and I found it disconcerting until I became accustomed to it. I can be halfway through a normal conversation when I become aware that, for the past few minutes, I have been speaking words that seem to be coming from elsewhere. It is my lips that move, my voice that is heard and I am completely aware of what is taking place, yet I am as much a listener as a speaker. The sensation is not an easy one to describe.

Effective conscious mediumship is a little more difficult to master than full trance. Since it is the medium's responsibility to ensure that the spoken words are both true and relevant, he or she must be able to discriminate without censoring. Not an easy balance for anyone to maintain, particularly in the early stages! By contrast, in trance mediumship the responsibility rests on the shoulders of the person who functions as a Control and supervises the proceedings at the physical level.

The first responsibility of a Control is the safety and well-being of the medium: this should come before everything else! He should ensure that everyone present at a trance sitting knows and understands the rules that are to be followed. When a medium enters a trance state, his rate of vibrationary frequency is altered. For instance, our guide David functions at a level much higher than the physical and, in order for an effective link to be made, Roland's frequency needs to be raised. It is necessary for Roland's energy pattern to be synchronised with David's so that the two may be brought together. For the other people in the room, there is no such radical change, although they may feel some alteration, such as a slight raising of the room temperature.

The heightened level of frequency affects every cell in Roland's body as well as the energies within his aura. If anyone were to touch him, even lightly, while he is in this altered state, the results would be both severe and painful, possibly even fatal. The only exception is where David himself deems it necessary for contact to be made, as in a healing session for instance. In that case, David himself will adjust the frequencies so that the contact is harmless for Roland, and David will be the one to say when contact may be made.

If there happen to be other people present when a visit from David is imminent, the first thing I do is warn them to avoid touching Roland, even accidentally. The medium sitting in that chair is my husband and anyone who was careless or thoughtless enough to risk hurting him would find themselves confronted by me... and when it is necessary, I can be implacable!

When you are dealing with the spiritual, psychic and physical welfare of other people, you cannot afford to be careless. It is your duty to ensure that all necessary safety precautions are taken and, should a crisis arise, you should be capable of dealing with it calmly, promptly and efficiently. There is never any excuse for allowing others to be exposed to harm.

A trance medium is a person, not an animated toy. He has fears, needs and feelings and these must always be given every respect and consideration. He does not exist to be used as a glorified switchboard and his talents deserve to be used for a positive purpose, not to be frittered away. The communication transmitted through the medium can be a source of education, enlightenment and upliftment for all concerned. If such a gift is only ever used as a form of entertainment, it is being wasted.

Until a few months after the publication of my first book, Roland and I used to hold open sittings so that people who wished to do so could consult David for advice. Although there were a few who asked serious questions concerning their spiritual evolution, most wanted David to put them in touch with deceased friends or to answer questions about their love life or business interests. After a while, David had a private talk with me and that session was the only time that I have heard pain in his voice.

'I come to offer a treasure,' he told me 'I offer wisdom, teaching and guidance that will help the spirit to grow, to mature and to achieve its full potential but my gift, offered with the greatest love, is rejected. Instead I am asked to perform parlour tricks.'

The grief in David's voice was so tangible that I found myself weeping for him and for the waste of the priceless opportunity he had come to offer which had been discarded as worthless in favour of trivialities. It was from that time forward that we ceased to hold open sittings and conducted our meetings with David in private, much to Roland's relief.

In trance, a medium's body will take on the characteristics and mannerisms of the controlling entity. The process is intriguing to watch because there is usually no outward change in the medium's voice or physical appearance, yet the sensation of observing a totally independent personality is quite distinct, even unmistakable. It is the medium's body which moves and the medium's voice that is heard but it is not the medium who speaks.

At the onset of trance, there may or may not be any external signals. Often the medium will simply appear to have fallen into a natural sleep and will start speaking without any apparent interruption to the normal functions. Sometimes the medium will go through phases of heavy breathing during the onset of trance, almost to the point of hyperventilation. There is usually the appearance of being asleep and there can be characteristic body movements such as a nodding or tilting of the head and/or rhythmic arm movements. Having said that, I shall now utterly confuse the issue by adding that, with any medium, there can be times when the transition is so smooth that you might fail to even notice it, so it is necessary to stay alert!

When a medium first begins to enter trance states, it would be unrealistic to expect fluent verbal communication right from the start. The medium is like a delicate musical instrument which needs to be tuned before it can play. The controlling entity also needs time to become familiar with the mechanics of operating through the medium's body. This was demonstrated to me one night when I had an intriguing visitor: one of David's other 'students', a spirit entity who was learning how to work through a trance medium. My visitor gave me some interesting and amusing insights into the process of working with a trance medium, from the Other Side.

After we had retired for the night, I noticed that Roland had tranced instead of falling asleep. This was not unusual and I relaxed and waited, knowing that if any contribution from me were required, it would be indicated at the appropriate time. For a while nothing happened, apart from Roland pulling a few funny faces, which is also a normal occurrence. Sometimes it is necessary for the controlling entity to loosen the muscles that control the mechanics of speech, which can produce some entertaining facial contortions. This stage of a trance requires no input from me, so all I had to do was watch and wait.

'This isn't as easy as I thought!' The words came in an abrupt burst from Roland's lips and by the startled look promptly enveloping his features, I guessed that the controlling entity was more surprised than I had been.

'I beg your pardon?' I enquired politely.

'Oh, terribly sorry,' replied the entity. 'I didn't expect it to go off like that. You're the guardian, aren't you? Er... I'm supposed to tell you that you know me as David... but that really isn't my name, you understand?'

'I understand,' I nodded, suppressing an urge to giggle. Whoever this entity might be, I had a feeling that I was going to enjoy the encounter.

'These things aren't as easy to operate as they seem, are they?' remarked my companion in a more conversational tone.

'What "things" are you referring to?' I asked.

'*These* things of course... physical bodies. Quite heavy and cumbersome.'

'Oh, I see,' I couldn't help smiling. 'I can't say I've noticed.'

'Well, you wouldn't, would you? You are accustomed to it. Just wait until you have to try it from where I am.'

Roland's eyes abruptly flew wide open, screwed tightly closed, opened again, blinked a few times and focussed on me.

'See that!' exulted the entity, with obvious satisfaction. 'You'd be surprised at how difficult it is to make the eyes work; I've been trying for ages.'

The temptation was impossible to resist, I just *had* to tease a little. 'I don't have any trouble with mine, see?' I batted my eyelashes a few times and gazed at him cherubically. The entity surveyed me with cool speculation for a moment or two, then replied with devastating serenity.

'Yes, but you NEED yours!'

'Touché!' I grinned.

Informal as it was, there was one vital communication given to me by the entity, which told me that the visit had the authorisation of our door-keeper. By saying 'You know me as David,' the entity had effectively told me that it was engaged on a task which carried David's consent and approval. If no such identification had been volunteered, it would have been necessary for me to issue a challenge.

In spiritual terms, a challenge is the equivalent of 'Halt! Who goes there?'. A psychic medium is literally a gateway between different dimensions, and it is vital that such gateways are always carefully guarded. With a deep trance medium, it is the Control's responsibility to function as a guardian at that gateway; therefore anyone who takes on the role of Control should know how to challenge the spirits. The Control should also know how to repel an entity if there is any reason to suspect that it may be of a harmful nature. The basic rule of thumb here is: 'If in doubt, dismiss the entity.' Any spirit from the pathway of Light will know and understand why a challenge is necessary and will always respond promptly and correctly. If such a response is not forthcoming, it is wisest to proceed on the assumption that the entity is not to be trusted.

The form of challenge that I use is my own, not because I invented it (in fact it was taught to me by someone else), but because it suits my purpose. This form of challenge is used by a large number of people and it follows a specific procedure, which begins with the question: 'Do you answer to the name of Christ?'

Unless I get a prompt affirmative answer to that question, my immediate reaction is to summon spiritual assistance. It is always possible that the communicating entity may simply be lost and in need of help, in which case we would carry out a psychic rescue procedure, but it is also likely that it could be a troublemaker. In either case, it is necessary to ensure that events don't get out of control.

The appropriate response to the challenge 'Do you answer to the name of Christ? is an unmistakably affirmative 'Yes' or 'I do'. Even a 'non-Christian' entity will acknowledge the authority of Christ if it is genuinely from the pathway of Light. The question to be asked is not 'Are you a Christian?'. We are dealing with a spiritual energy, not a man-made religion and it is not necessary for a spirit to have belonged to the Christian religion in order to recognise and answer to the Christ spirit. I once challenged a spirit who had last incarnated in ancient Egypt, long before the historical time of Christ and I received this smiling response:

'Yes, I answer to the name of Christ... and Krishna, Ahura Mazda and a number of other names that would be unfamiliar to you. All are manifestations of the one spiritual essence.'

There is one response that *sounds* like an affirmative but it contains a dangerous loophole and I would strongly warn everyone to beware of it. The response is 'I answer to the name of *the* Christ.'

Technically this is correct because the word Christ is not a name but a title which means 'The Anointed One'. Bear in mind, however, that thoughts are more potent than words and that by silently adding the prefix 'anti-' before 'Christ', the whole meaning of the response can be reversed. This is a trick used by Satanic entities and Lord help the unwary Control who allows one of *those* characters to pass through the gateway!

If the answer given to the challenge is not satisfactory, the Control's immediate reaction should be to repel the spirit. This can be done with the command: 'In the name of Christ, *return to your original source!*' The choice of words here is important. Saying 'Go back to where you came from,' is not sufficient. You may be dealing with a low entity that has been causing mischief in our sphere for some time and sending it back to where it came from only means returning it to its most recent location. To send it where it really belongs, you must specifically direct it to its original source.

By issuing this command in the name of Christ, you summon the immediate assistance of your spirit guardians. It is the psychic equivalent of yelling for your big brother when you're being menaced by a bully. Be aware that when you use the name of Christ in this way, you are calling on the highest and most potent level of protective power in our Universe. When you give that command, speak the words with full confidence and authority. Don't be afraid that you may not have enough personal authority to back up your words; if you aren't strong enough to deal with a spiritual aggressor, it is your right to call on more powerful support. I've had to face some awfully mean entities in my time and I have no doubt that quite a few of them could have made mincemeat of me if I had tried to rely on my own resources. The channels of help that are open to me are also open to you and when you need help, all you have to do is call.

If the entity does not instantly obey the command, your spirit guardians will step in and remove it, so be silent and wait. Do not respond to anything the entity might say, simply focus your mind on the presence of your spirit guardians, inwardly repeat the Invocation for protection and guidance, keep your aura filled with White Light and ask for a sign to be given when the danger has been removed. For instance, in such circumstances, David will identify himself to me in a way known only to himself and me, so that I can be sure it's really him and not a clever imposter. He will then tell me 'It is done,' which means that the entity has been removed. Until I get that confirmation, I remain on red alert.

Having dealt at some length with some of the more unpleasant possibilities, I should balance the picture by mentioning that it is quite possible that you may never have to deal directly with a dangerous entity. Just bear in mind that to be forewarned is to be forearmed. You should know what to do in these situations just in case there is ever an occasion when you will need to use that knowledge.

Now, to move into a more pleasant area of thought, let's discuss what to do when you receive a positive response to your original challenge. After all, if you're following the rules, cleansing your energy streams and taking all the correct safety precautions, a positive response is what you should receive. When a spirit has confirmed that it answers to the name of Christ, you should follow with a request for additional information: 'In the name of Christ, state your name and from where you get your authority.'

As an example of a spirit's response to that question, David would say something like 'I am David and I come in the name of Christ.'

Again I will emphasise that the Christ spirit is the authority that I *personally* recognise, so it is the one that I quote. I do not believe, however, that spiritual truth has ever been the exclusive domain of any one man-made religious sect. If you belong to a different philosophy such as Islam or Buddhism, for instance, you will know this spiritual essence by another name. In such a case, you will call on the name that you personally recognise as the Highest. To quote the Theosophists: there is no religion higher than Truth.

Once you have established the bona fides of your spirit visitor, your next step is to ask 'What is your purpose with us at this time?'. Simply to ask 'What is your purpose?' can lead to precise but tantalising answers such as 'I am a teacher. My purpose is to teach'.

You should waste as little time as possible because the spirit can only stay for a limited period at one sitting. By phrasing your question in the suggested way, you will draw a more specific response. For instance, the spirit may say 'I am a teacher. I am here because you wish to learn and you have questions which need to be answered at this time'.

Communicating with a spirit is a bit like talking to a computer. If you do not phrase your questions carefully, you are likely to receive some disconcerting and even misleading answers. The spirit will answer the question as you have asked it, not the question you meant to ask. For instance, if you ask 'Can you tell me if I'm going to lose my job?' the spirit may answer 'Yes' but this should not be taken to mean that you should register for unemployment benefits. The spirit is merely replying 'Yes, I can tell you'. To get the answer you *really* seek, you need to ask 'Am I going to lose my job?'. The spirit will take your words literally.

If the answer given to you by a spirit seems obscure or ambiguous, have another look at the way in which you have phrased your question. You can also ask the spirit to clarify an answer if you do not understand what has been said. When David is teaching me, he periodically pauses to ask me if I have understood what he has been saying. If my answer is 'Yes', he asks me to repeat it back to him in my own words. This tells him whether I really understand or whether I only *think* I do.

If I tell him that I do not understand or if my answers indicate that my understanding is faulty, David will patiently rephrase the information as many times as necessary until I do understand. He never seems to mind how long it takes, which is just as well because there are times when I can be awfully thick! One of the great things about really advanced spirit teachers is that they seem to be blessed with infinite patience and they do not criticise but only advise. They can sometimes be stern but they are never unkind, for their purpose is to raise you up, not to tear you down.

I am well aware of the fact that there are 'spirit guides' who have been known to judge and criticise but there are guides and there are Guides. Some mediums have guides who come from the Astral or Mental planes. This doesn't necessarily imply that there is anything sinister about them, it merely indicates that their knowledge is limited and that they should not be regarded as infallible. They may be links in a chain of communication but if you want to reach the source, you must seek higher.

I have a very devoted and protective spirit companion named David-Michael, with whom I shared a wonderfully happy marriage in Ireland about 500 years ago. He is happy to assist me at any time; however, he is not a guide nor does he claim to be one. He is a loving helper, nonetheless, and the fact that he is not yet a true guide does not diminish his usefulness in the slightest. David is my guide and his level of existence is a long way above our highest frequencies but, even then, he is not the ultimate. As he puts it 'There are those above me whom I call Master.'

On a few rare and special occasions, I have been honoured with visits from some of those spiritual Masters and the experience is absolutely unforgettable. I lack the words to adequately describe the quality of the energies that these beings radiate: the only word I can think of is Sublime.

Through a system of links with successively higher beings, you are effectively in link with the ultimate. This is how the guide system has been designed to function and it works perfectly. For instance, if I am asked a question that I cannot answer, I can refer the question to David. I have not yet come up with a question that David is incapable of answering but, in the unlikely event that I might, he could consult those above him. If I should happen to be menaced by a dark force too powerful for me to overcome, alarm bells are set off all along the line and instantly someone who is capable of dealing with the threat will be at my side to defend me. This system is an example of a 'Big Brother' organisation that really *does* work in our favour!

Highly advanced spirit guides are interested only in helping you to grow and develop spiritually. They are not concerned with things like helping you to sort out your love life or win the lottery. It might be nice if we could coax them into co-operating but that is not their purpose and they are more than adept at fielding our attempts at persuasion when the matter is of no relevance to our spiritual progress.

One of the many wonderful things about the Higher Ones is that the more their wisdom and power increase, the more gentle and serene they become. There is something exquisitely reassuring about knowing that you are in the presence of a being who could annihilate you with a glance, yet knowing beyond a shadow of a doubt that this immense power can embrace you closely without ruffling a hair on your head. Knowing that this power is always carefully watching over you in order to protect you against harm is even more reassuring. I doubt that I could ever adequately describe how it feels to be in the presence of such beings; it is something that has to be experienced to be understood. Try imagining how you would feel if you found yourself holding a conversation with an angel in your living room! Now imagine trying to describe the totality of that experience in words. It's a challenge, isn't it?

The object of spiritual development is to grow in understanding and awareness, balance and control. It would be ludicrous for anyone to expect us to master it all perfectly overnight; that is one of the reasons why the guide system is structured as it is. Your progress is monitored and supervised every step of the way, yet your free will is never overruled and you are not made to feel like a germ under a microscope.

As your rate of vibration is steadily increased, you pass upward through the levels and, at each step, there is a friendly helper to give you safe guidance as you traverse the spheres. The development techniques given in this book are structured on working within this system. Take your time: it is better to learn thoroughly than to push ahead too quickly. Persevere with each step until you are sure that you have mastered it and then move on to the next. You'll get there!

CHAPTER TEN

Countering Psychic Attack

After the publication of *Reaching for the Other Side* I received quite a few letters from people who informed me that I had scared the living daylights out of them with the chapter on psychic attack and psychic rescue. It certainly wasn't my intention to terrify anyone, but it is important for people to know that such things can happen so that they are aware of the necessity to follow the guidelines for safety. I have read far too many books which blithely issue instructions for psychic development without preparing the reader for any possible dangers or giving suggestions on how to deal with such situations, should they occur. There are dark spaces in the lower levels of psychic existence, just as there are areas of darkness in the physical world and, although I have no wish to dwell on an unpleasant subject for any longer than necessary, I would be failing my responsibility if I neglected to explain how to deal with threatening situations.

The possibility that you will find yourself under direct psychic attack by an accomplished black magician is quite remote. You are in much more danger of being hit by a car or mugged by a burglar but, while you are living in this sphere of existence, the possibility does exist and the time to learn how to protect yourself from such an assault is before it happens. If you understand how your assailant works and have a clear knowledge of how to counter any attempt at harming you, there is no need for you to fear.

A number of people have remarked to me that, although they are interested in exploring their psychic potential, they are afraid to do so for fear that they may be exposed to the influence of dark entities. We need to bear in mind that you do not have to open your own psychic channels in order to be exposed to that kind of influence. I have worked on psychic rescues in which the victims have been very young children who wouldn't even know what the word 'psychic' means. In addition, it is worthwhile to remember that not all the dark entities are drifting around in the Astral; quite a few of them are incarnated in physical form, right here on planet Earth.

I have also heard a few people express the opinion that they don't need to go to all the bother of performing White Light meditations and Invocations for protection because it is only possible to be hurt if you *believe* that you can be hurt. That is only partly true. There are people in this world who are skilled in the use of psychic energy, who are motivated by a lust for power and who use their skills as force, to the harm and detriment of others. These are the ones who are known as black magicians and it would be most unwise to underestimate their capabilities.

For those who follow the pathway of Light, the quest is for inner peace, love, truth, wisdom and creativeness. The pathway of Darkness represents the quest for power. That word never stands alone: power is always power *over*. To put it another way, where is the satisfaction in having power if you have nobody over whom you can use it? Power seeks to dominate, to control, to exploit and to consume. If there are no victims for it to feed on, power is useless. In that sense these dark entities, whether incarnated in physical form or not, are parasites... psychic vampires, if you like. Very few of them would openly reveal themselves for what they are but the worth of a tree is judged by its fruits, and the fruits of violence and destruction are violence and destruction. There's a fair bit of that around these days, isn't there?

Open your eyes. Take a good look at the world around you and see what is *really* happening here. The human race has reached a critical point in its cycle of evolution. We stand at the crossroads and we cannot keep wavering in the middle; we must choose one pathway or the other. What we can see happening in this world right now is a polarisation. There are those who are working for the preservation of life and who are opposed to destructive exploitation and there are those who will use any weapon, no matter how terrible, in order to continue looting and destroying and to keep the majority of this planet's inhabitants under their domination. Whether or not they are knowingly using psychic energy in order to achieve their ambitions (and many of them are, though you'd have difficulty making them admit it), they are consciously choosing to carry out acts of darkness.

To a casual observer, it might appear that the destroyers have the upper hand in this world, but appearances can be deceptive. There is ony one weapon that can give a destroyer power over any human being and that weapon is Fear. So long as you can be kept frightened and confused, like a lost sheep in the wilderness, you are easy prey for the wolves. What the Dark Ones fear most is the day when all the little sheep start waking up and remembering who they really are and what a force they can be when they start putting their heads together. Purely from an observer's point of view, it seems to me as though that day is already dawning; the effects are already visible in the world around us if we care to look. Sheep to the right, goats to the left!

Let's get something quite clear from the start: those whom I call the Dark Ones do not need to have a reason for attacking anyone, only an opportunity. They are violent and aggressive by nature and if they don't have anyone else to pick on, they'll fight among themselves. Bear in mind that you don't need to travel into the psychic realms to see these characters at work; the evidence of their activities in this world is all too chillingly clear. Contrary to superficial appearances, however, there are not nearly as many of them as it may seem. Many people who are serving the cause of darkness are doing so in blindness, slaves to their own fear. It should be clear by now that avoiding psychic activity is no way to avoid falling victim to the nasties; in fact, the more ignorant you are about psychic energy, the more easily you can be manipulated.

How we are to overcome fear in the world and put an end to destruction is a matter for deep thought, but it is not the subject with which we are primarily concerned at present. We are concerned with your personal methods of defence against attacks at the psychic level. From the beginning, remember that the only way that darkness can have power over you is if you *give* it power, by fearing it. By the very fact that you fear something, you are indicating that you believe it to be strong enough to overwhelm you and by believing it, you make it so. What you think... IS. In order for that fear to exist, you must believe two basic untruths:

1. That you are powerless
2. That you are alone.

In fact, you are neither powerless nor alone. You have all the hosts of Heaven to call on if you need them and, as far as being powerless is concerned, that is a myth. The most important thing to remember is that you cannot fight force with force. When it comes to the use of force, you are dealing with the enemy's weapons and he is far more experienced and skilled in their use than you would ever want to be. When Christ said 'love your enemies', he was not being idealistic and philosophical; he was pointing out that love in its pure form is the only power than can defeat fear and violence.

The object is to defend yourself against harm, not to go out and slaughter the opposition. All you need to do is deflect any harmful energies that are directed against you: the law of Karma will then return those energies to their source and Karma packs a much more potent wallop than you or I could ever deliver. If you try to *hurt* those who menace you (even though you may be quite justified in thinking that they deserve it), you are sending out a harmful energy and Karma must also return those energies to you. In that case, you would be fighting not one enemy but two: your attacker and yourself. Don't be your own worst enemy; always defend, never attack.

I have always considered it quite ironic to hear the governments of this world referring to their armies as 'defence forces' and speaking of the technology of defence when they are referring to the mechanics of war. In his book *Nineteen Eighty-Four*, George Orwell predicted the use of political doublespeak, where every key word used actually carries the opposite meaning. On a television news broadcast recently, I watched a celebration in Japan which involved a march-past of military troops, heavy artillery, tanks and guided missiles, with fighter planes flying in formation overhead. Under the terms of that country's surrender after World War II, the Japanese are forbidden to have an army, navy or air force. Are they in breach of the terms of this treaty? Our governments inform us that they are not. Officially, you see, Japan's armed forces are not armed forces... they are *defence* forces.

Now, I'd like to ask a couple of questions. Is a bullet from a 'defence' gun any less deadly than a bullet from a 'war' gun? Are 'defence' guided missiles any less lethal? I have a simplistic approach to life and when I see a spade, I don't bother calling it a digging implement. It's a spade. And missiles, cannons and guns are weapons of war!

So to come in full circle, I would like it clearly understood that when I speak of defence, I *mean* defence, not thinly disguised attack. In order to be effective, psychic self-defence has to be totally non-aggressive. Since dark entities have an allergy to the qualities of Love and Light, your regular cleansing and Invocation makes your personal energies quite unpalatable to the parasites, just as garlic is supposed to be unpalatable to vampires. That is your first line of defence.

A direct psychic attack from a dark entity or black magician is an attempt to penetrate your resistance and overcome your free will. If you have reason to believe that you have come under such an attack or that your aura has been penetrated by an alien energy form, the procedure to follow is given below.

First, take a shower or bath and THOROUGHLY CLEANSE your body. After bathing, dry your body with a fresh towel but do not dress. Stand *as you were born* (to use one of David's impeccable phrases!) in front of a mirror. The larger your mirror, the better... but any mirror will suffice.

Look at your reflection and see yourself as a child of the Creator.

For NO LESS than sixty seconds and NO MORE than five minutes, repeat the following Invocation over and over, aloud:

'God above me, God below me;
God before me, God behind me;
God to the right of me, God to the left of me;
God within me.'

This ritual was taught to me by David, who also issued some strict instructions about how it should be applied. The Invocation itself is almost universal and, if you do sufficient research, you will doubtless find it given in other spiritual philosophies. When you use this ritual, you are drawing an extremely high-voltage energy through your body and aura. You may not physically feel this energy as tremendously potent; however, I can assure you that it is. Used in accordance with the instructions, it will burn away any negative energies that have penetrated your aura. If you over-use it, you will start burning out your own transistors. As with many potent natural substances, the correct dose is therapeutic but an overdose can be dangerous.

Do not use this ritual unless you have reason to suspect that a psychic attack or auric invasion is taking place. Do not repeat the procedure more than twice in any one day and discontinue its use when you can feel that the danger has passed. For everyday protection (no, this is not a deodorant commercial!), the normal auric cleansing should be quite sufficient; however, there are some extra precautions you can take if you want to be extra careful.

Sandalwood generates an atmosphere which is reputed to be most effective in psychic protection. It also gives off a pleasant fragrance, so burning a few sticks of sandalwood incense around the house will not only help to repel the psychic creepy-crawlies, it will also make your home smell very nice. You can also dab a few drops of sandalwood oil onto your brow and throat chakras, which will set up a shield in your aura. It should, however, be used in conjunction with your normal cleansing and protective routines, not as a substitute. If you are unsure of where to locate your throat chakra, bend your head forward and run your fingers down the neck, along the spinal column towards the junction with your shoulders. You should be able to feel a bone that is larger than the others, protruding slightly. This is the site for dabbing on the sandalwood oil.

If you think your home has been invaded by something nasty, burn a white candle within a circle of salt until the atmosphere has perceptively cleared. Am I beginning to sound like one of those old village wise-women? If so, don't be too sceptical... many of those old wives knew a lot more than people tend to think! In any case, I am simply passing on some well-tried and proven recipes, given to me by my spirit helpers. The fact that these principles have been used by a diverse assortment of spiritual cultures over the centuries can be taken as a testimony to their effectiveness.

Both salt and fire have been recognised for their cleansing properties since the dawn of time. As with other natural forms of energy, the human race in general seems to be unaware that the effects do not stop at the boundaries of physical existence. We used to understand these things once but we have forgotten and, until recently, all that remained of the old knowledge were the empty husks of superstition. Today we are learning again to understand the meaning behind the words.

Although it is best to be aware that things like auric invasion and psychic attack can happen, there is no reason to become paranoid about the possibility. You could be run over by a car or murdered by a maniac, or The Bomb could be dropped tomorrow but, if you let yourself become obsessed with fear, you're much more likely to drop dead from sheer terror the next time someone slams a door behind you. It doesn't matter where you are or what you are doing, there is always an element of danger. Sensible people take all reasonable precautions to prevent mishaps from occurring and to ensure that they know how to deal with an emergency, should it arise. The same common-sense approach should be taken to the area of psychic activity. If you take all reasonable precautions, it is unlikely that you will suffer any serious misadventures but, should an unexpected threat arise, keep your head.

Don't be afraid that you will be overwhelmed if you happen to encounter something too powerful for you to handle. The guide system is structured in such a way that, if you aren't capable of countering a particular menace, there is always someone close by who can handle it for you. Big Brother is watching over you, remember! At the same time, don't go looking for trouble. If you neglect the safety precautions or decide to pick a fight with the bad guys, you will have to suffer the consequences: that's Karma. Your guides and guardians cannot protect you against the results of your own recklessness, any more than they could protect you from being injured if you jumped into the pathway of a moving bus.

The next obvious question is: how can you tell if a psychic attack or auric invasion is taking place? The symptoms are not always distinct. Tables that do tap-dances around the room, fires that start by themselves and weird bodily contortions can happen, along with a number of other strange and frightening events but, in the majority of cases, the signs are considerably more subtle and not so easily distinguishable. In many cases, the victim is assumed to be suffering from mental illness, emotional disturbances and/or physical complaints of psychosomatic origin. The trouble is that, once a label has been attached to the disorder, people often presume that the problem has been identified when, in fact, the label is only describing a collection of symptoms.

The confusion can be further compounded by the fact that, although the symptoms may be caused by psychic interference, they could just as easily result from a psychological problem or a chemical imbalance within the body. This is where it may be necessary to use a process of elimination to isolate the cause. Psychic interference upsets the balance of energies within the life system and, because these energies are interrelated and interdependent, there can be a whole range of symptoms. There can be a loss of energy, similar to the effects of anaemia. The victim is also likely to become extremely nervous and fearful and may suffer from repeated nightmares. On the other hand, it is equally possible that the victim could become violent and destructively aggressive. There are likely to be severe mood swings, noticeable changes in the personality, disturbed emotions and chaotic mental processes.

Since all of the foregoing symptoms could just as easily be caused by something other than psychic interference, how do you tell the difference? The answer is that, initially, you probably don't. It is usually when other forms of diagnosis and treatment have failed that someone begins to suspect a problem of psychic origin. Let's bear one thing in mind: if the treatment is effective, the problem will disappear. If it persists we must look for other methods of treatment.

I have several naturopath friends who are well qualified to deal with problems arising from chemical or structural imbalances within the body and also very keenly aware of the reality of psychic and spiritual influences. When they find themselves confronted with a patient whose condition does not respond to the standard methods of treatment, their reaction is to look for a psychic cause. In the early stages of our acquaintance, these friends sometimes asked for our help in the diagnosis and correction of a psychic problem such as auric invasion, or possession as it is more commonly called. They also wanted to learn how to deal with such problems themselves, so we were asked to help them develop their own methods of treatment.

Obviously, my friends could not adopt the method used by Roland and me because that procedure requires the assistance of a trance medium and suitable trance mediums are not readily available. We had to work with the basic principles of psychic energy and develop techniques appropriate for the individual practitioners. For someone like a naturopath who is likely to encounter such situations on a reasonably regular basis under conditions which require them to take the active role in correcting the problem, the 'self-help' method given earlier is inappropriate, so we had to develop specialised techniques that were suited to the individual practitioners. Even with the most skilled assistance, however, it is not always possible for a permanent remedy to be effected, for the simple reason that the victim is not always willing to make a personal effort to prevent further infestations from occurring.

To put it quite simply, a person who is competent with the necessary psychic techniques may be able to remove an alien influence from your aura but, unless you are prepared to make an effort to correct the condition that allowed the problem to occur in the first place, there is no way that a re-infestation can be prevented. It is said in the Bible that when an unclean spirit is gone out of a man, it walks through dry places, seeking rest but finding none. Then it says 'I will return to the house from whence I came out' and when it comes, it finds the place empty, swept and garnished. So it goes and takes with itself seven other spirits more wicked than itself and they enter in and dwell there, so the poor victim is in an even worse condition than before. When an invading entity has been removed from a person's aura, it leaves an empty space and one way or another, this space must be filled.

To avoid re-infestation, the individual concerned must ensure that the space is filled with an energy that will keep invaders out. This can be achieved quite simply with the routine cleansing and sealing techniques, which effectively fill the aura with light energy and seal it against further penetration. Unless this is done, re-infestation is a likely possibility.

One of my former students, also a close friend, is a talented clairvoyant who now conducts development classes and works in a counselling capacity to help people with psychic problems. Some time ago she asked for my advice concerning one of her students, who suffered repeatedly from auric invasion. Every time the class got together, my friend found herself obliged to perform yet another psychic rescue. She was seriously concerned, not only for the welfare of the student involved but also for the other students, who were being prevented from learning because so much class time was taken up with psychic rescue.

She had perceived that the student concerned had a couple of physical problems which upset his energy balance and thus rendered him vulnerable to invasion. To correct this situation, she advised the student to consult one of our naturopath friends who also happens to be a skilled psychic. In addition, she explained the need for regular cleansing and sealing of the aura to build up a resistance to further invasion. Despite all of this, the problem persisted and my friend was at a loss, so she contacted me for advice.

'Check with the naturopath,' I suggested. 'I'll wager you will find that your student has not followed your advice and I wouldn't mind betting that he isn't cleansing his aura either. I suspect this person is enjoying all the fuss and attention he's been receiving and has no intention of correcting the problem himself. If this is the case, you will need to be quite firm. Tell him that he is being selfish. Point out that he is not only preventing the other students from learning, he is also exposing them to danger from negative energies and placing a continual drain on your resources. Inform him that if he is not prepared to take the responsibility for his own welfare and show some consideration for others, he cannot expect you to keep shouldering the responsibility for him, nor can the other students be expected to continue tolerating disrupted classes. In short, tell him to shape up or ship out.'

When I heard from my friend again a few months later, she told me that she had followed my advice. The problem student had started visiting the naturopath and cleansing his aura, with the result that the auric invasion had ceased. All students in the class, including the former 'victim' were now making good progress.

Spiritual awareness within the community at large is rapidly increasing, and I can foresee a time when mothers will teach their children the principles of auric cleansing as a natural part of personal hygiene, like washing their hands and cleaning their teeth. When that day comes, the problem of auric infestation will be reduced to a minimum, if not eliminated completely. The problem today is largely the result of ignorance; people simply do not understand how psychic energies operate. They are not aware that their auras need to be cleansed; in fact, most people don't even realise that they *have* an aura.

The development of Kirlian photography and other sophisticated electronic devices has confirmed the existence of an energy field surrounding the human body but, as yet, the amount of knowledge concerning the nature and functions of the aura is stll very limited.

Progress is taking place but there is still quite a long way to go. It has taken hundreds of years for our scientists to reach a level of understanding at which they can begin to comprehend the validity of what the occultists have been teaching ever since the dawn of time. For instance, the comparatively new science of quantum physics has revealed that *consciousness plays an essential role in the nature of physical reality*. This is precisely what the occultists have always taught, except that they express it in more simplistic terms: what you think . . . IS!

Most of the negative aspects of psychic activity in our culture are the results of widespread ignorance. Since ignorance is the cause, it should be readily apparent that the remedy is education. People fear what they do not understand and, because they fear it, they run from it and avoid learning how to deal with it effectively. Auric infestation is a result of fear and ignorance, not only on the part of the victims, but also the earthbound entities themselves. In all the cases of auric infestation that Roland and I have been required to deal with, only about two percent have involved entities that could be described as demonic in the traditional sense. The rest were all poor lost souls who had been wandering around in a state of misery and confusion until they accidentally blundered into some person's aura.

If people learned to understand more about the process of transition known as death and to lose their unreasonable fear of it, there wouldn't be so many lost souls roaming around in the atmosphere. If we all understood how to look after our auras, we wouldn't be so vulnerable to auric invasion anyway. Instead of scaring the wits out of ourselves with a collection of lurid superstitions and horror stories, wouldn't it make a lot more sense to learn about the causes of such problems and take appropriate steps to eliminate them?

Certainly there are demonic entities who will cause damage and destruction if they're given half a chance. There are also dreadful micro-organisms that cause diseases like typhoid and cholera, but running around in a blind panic isn't the way to avoid coming into contact with them. All you would achieve by following such a course would be to restrict your development and cripple yourself spiritually so that you effectively prevent yourself from achieving your potential. In addition, by allowing yourself to become so enslaved by fear that you refuse to come to terms with the reality of psychic existence, you would only make yourself more vulnerable to the very dangers that you most want to avoid.

If you want to make genuine progress you need to use a certain amount of common sense, which means facing up to reality, seeing it for what it is and learning to live with it, without fear. The more you understand about psychic energy and the way it works, the more effectively you will handle it and the less vulnerable you will be to any form of negativity. The knowledge that you need is available but the effort to learn must come from you.

To sum up: in order to cause you harm, an alien energy form must be able to penetrate your aura. Your best defence is to keep your aura clear and sealed at all times and to invoke the continual protection of your guardian spirits. Damage to the aura can be caused by emotional or physical trauma, heavy drugs and alcohol, illness and any influence that lowers your rate of vibrations. If you have been subjected to any of these influences, it is best to suspend psychic activity of an adventurous nature until the damage has been repaired. Concentrate instead on the protective, cleansing and sealing procedures to build up the resistance in your aura. When you have regained your normal state of balance, you can take up the threads again in safety.

If you have reason to suspect auric invasion, perform the Mirror Ritual given earlier in this chapter until the problem is relieved. Incidentally, if it is only some lost and bewildered soul who has stumbled into your aura, the energy generated by this procedure will not cause it harm but will simply remove it from your energy field. The very fact that you are performing this ritual is enough to alert the attention of the Higher Ones and if a lost soul is involved, they will see to it that the soul is taken into protective care and transported to a place of healing.

Your responsibility is to keep your aura clear, sealed, healthy and filled with Light so that the higher spiritual energies that you are seeking to generate will be given a fertile place in which to grow. You have the right to follow your course of destiny and to develop your spiritual awareness and capacities, free from harm, restriction or interference. If another person or entity attempts to take that right away from you, you have only to call on the assistance of the Higher Ones and it will be immediately given. As David has said to me: 'My daughter, it is your right to follow your chosen pathway and if the barrier should be placed across your route, call on us and *it will be removed.*'

Don't be afraid of those who may seek to harm you. Pity them instead because, by trying to injure you, they are hurting themselves most of all. If you are truly following the pathway of Light, you can afford to be compassionate. Be at peace within yourself and be secure in the knowledge that there is never a time when your spirit guardians are not watching over you. Challenges may arise to test you but you are more than equal to them. Each time you overcome another challenge, your growth and spiritual strength is enhanced. The pathway may not be easy at times; nothing worthwhile ever comes easily; but for those who are willing to keep trying, the rewards make it more than worthwhile!

CHAPTER ELEVEN

Spirituality or Religion?

'I don't particularly like the expression "Spiritual Development",' remarked Roland, 'because of the connotations that can be placed upon that term. Spiritual: ergo airy-fairy, or religious... dogmas, doctrines and creeds. I'd prefer something that explained itself to me in terms of the potential that exists within me, the other facets of my being, yet to be explored by me.'

'Connotations give me a pain in the neck!' I grumbled. 'The problem is that it isn't easy for me to define my terms when I know that no matter what terminology I use, someone is going to place connotations on it.'

'That being the case, I'd suggest that you point all this out to your readers,' offered Roland. 'Explain yourself to them so that you are not misunderstood.'

So, dear reader, before we progress any further, let me define my terms. To me, the word Spiritual means 'of the spirit' and as I have mentioned already, Spirit, Mind and Soul are all one. You are not a body who has a spirit, it is the other way around. You... the person who looks out through the eyes of your body... YOU are the spirit. To me, spiritual development means inner growth, expansion and evolution: in short, the development *of* the spirit. Your personal growth, if you like.

What is a Spiritual Essence to me may be Cosmic Energy to someone else. In this respect, one label is as good as another, provided that the meaning behind the words is understood. In this particular field of communication I sometimes believe that we have more problems with labels, semantics and connotations than anything else. If I use the word 'Spiritual', I am likely to raise objections in the minds of people who have had negative experiences with religion. If I say 'Psychic', a good proportion of my listeners will immediately assume that I'm talking about telling fortunes, bending spoons and playing switchboards for the dear departed. If I start talking about the mind and levels of consciousness, someone is bound to demand that I produce my degrees in Psychology to prove that I'm qualified to speak on that subject. Words can sometimes get in the way, which is one of the reasons why the Higher Ones continually remind us that we should *test* everything we are told, no matter who does the telling.

I have said that when you receive a communication purporting to come from a spiritual source, you must always test for truth. You must be sure that the spirit who is speaking to you is a truthteller, not a deceiver. I have told you how to test a spirit communicator; the questions you should ask and the answers that you should receive. Has it occurred to you yet that by writing this book, *I* am being a spirit communicator? Having set the standard of requirements, I should be prepared to abide with those requirements myself or be hoist with my own petard, so to speak. Any spirit, if it is truly of the Light, should be willing and happy to accept that standard. Therefore I think now would be a good time for me to present my own credentials.

If I were to be challenged at the spiritual level, I would answer in this way: 'Yes, I answer to the name of Christ. My name is Dawn and I get my authority from Christ.'

How many of you have just identified me as a Christian? Go back to the chapter on Testing the Spirits and start again. I said 'I answer to the name of Christ'. I did *not* say 'I am a Christian'. There's a difference. You don't have to call yourself a Christian to be a follower of Christ. The word Christ is not a name; it's a title. So we have Jesus *the* Christ, just as we have Elizabeth the Queen or Reagan the President. 'Christ' comes from the Greek 'Christos', meaning The Anointed One. Jesus of Nazareth was *Christed* in the sense that he provided a physical vehicle for the Christ essence, or spirit.

I also believe that there have been other vehicles for the spirit of Christ, apart from Jesus of Nazareth. That same spiritual essence is known in other languages, in other names, but the words we use don't make any difference to the *essence*. At least, they shouldn't!

The spirit that motivated Jesus of Nazareth was also

present in the Buddha and other great spiritual teachers. It's present in all of us, to some extent. To see the Truth, you have to look beyond words. You also have to look beyond religion, philosophy and creed.

The natural laws that were taught by the Nazarene didn't come into existence on the day he was born; those laws have been in existence since before the dawn of Time. That's why he tried so hard to persuade his followers *not* to make a religion out of his teachings but to see them for what they were, simply an expression of natural law. If such natural laws do exist, we would expect to find them operating in the world around us and we would expect to be able to trace their operation throughout our history and they would have been in operation long before the historical time of Christ.

As far back as we can go in recorded history, there have always been spiritual philosophies or religions, all claiming that there is a part of the human being that does not die with the body but enters an afterlife of some description. More recently, the human race has seen the advent of scientists who have endeavoured to persuade us to believe that the whole thing has been a Cosmic Joke, that human life came about by accident and that thought is merely the result of chemical reactions in the brain. Lately however, there has been something in the nature of a quiet revolution; science is beginning to catch up with the old philosophers. As one scientist put it recently, 'We are beginning to realise that scientists and mystics are really looking at the same thing... we just have different names for what we are seeing.'

Something that would have been a 'miracle' to my great-great-grandmother would probably be a fact of life for me today. I can climb into a heavy metal machine big enough to hold about 250 people and, in a matter of hours, I can be on the other side of the world. How miraculous do you think that would seem in a world where the only forms of transport are horses and ships?

David says there really isn't any such thing as a miracle, there is just an understanding of natural law and an ability to work with it. A belief in 'miracles' implies an assumption that immutable cosmic laws can be suspended but that is not the case. To suspend cosmic law, even in the slightest degree, would be chaos, therefore it cannot and does not happen. The greater your understanding of natural law and your ability to work with it, the more 'miracles' you can achieve. With your greater understanding, however, you can perceive that you aren't really working miracles, you are simply applying your understanding of natural law.

Why should we need to make a religion out of it all? We are dealing with *natural* law: it's all around us, within us, in nature... in Life. There's a whole world of experience for us to explore. Seek, as the saying goes, and you will find. We shouldn't need to put restrictions on it.

Not long after my first book reached the market, I was contacted by a lovely Indian gentleman (with the emphasis on *gentle*) who was most eager to talk with me.

'The teachings in your book show a very sophisticated understanding of the Vedantic Scriptures,' he told me. 'It is most unusual for a woman of your background to have such an understanding. How much of the Vedantas have you read?'

When I told him that I had never even glanced at the Vendantas, he was quite astonished. I hastened to remind him that the teachings given in my book were based on the teachings given to me by David. From what I've been told, I understand that David had one or two incarnations in and around India a few thousand years ago, so it's quite possible that he may have studied the Vedantas at some time or another. At the same time, David's teachings are also in harmony with the teachings of Christ and other great spiritual teachers. His understanding of truth appears to be universal.

We sat and talked with Ashok and his wife on a number of enjoyable occasions, deeply engrossed in discussions on spiritual philosophy in absolute accord and harmony, knowing that, although our terminology might be different, we were discussing the same universal truth. I have had similarly enjoyable discussions with a Moslem friend and with a Jew, sometimes even with both of them at once, and still there has been complete harmony and accord. This is because we haven't been interested in squabbling over superficial differences but only in discussing the many things that we have in common.

Labels cause barriers to real understanding. Barriers will only hold you back. Could you define your own personal concept of reality in two or three words? Can you define yourself? If not, how could you possibly hope to define the entire structure of the universe, in this sphere and beyond, all into one small label? Could you even do it in a book?

To have a true understanding of the spiritual reality, which is *your* reality, it is necessary to let go of barriers. Old habits of thinking need to be sorted through and some discarded. The lesson to be learned at this stage of the quest is acceptance. Don't make the mistake of under-estimating this one: it isn't easy. To succeed at this level, you will have to come face to face with all of your worst fears and overcome them. I should add that you will be confronted by your own fears time and time again, whether you are consciously trying to achieve acceptance or not. Life itself will bring those experiences to you; that is its purpose. You have a choice: turn and try to escape from your fears (which is impossible anyway) or face them and make yourself stronger than they are.

When you reach a level of understanding at which you realise that you really have nothing to fear, you will have achieved acceptance.

Bear in mind that being unafraid is not the same as being reckless. It is said that understanding casts out fear and, to me, the reason behind this is simple. When you have understanding and you are at ease with the energies that flow around you, you are in control of your own environment. There is no *reason* for fear.

Not so very long ago, I had a rather lengthy and intense conversation with a couple of Protestant clergymen. Whilst it was never openly mentioned, everybody present at that meeting knew that I was under examination. One of their parishioners had become involved with one of my meditation groups and the clergymen were determined to make quite sure that by doing so, he had not exposed himself to spiritual danger. I might point out that, far from resenting the implied suggestion that I might constitute a spiritual danger, I appreciated the concern of the clergymen for the welfare of one of their flock. If they had merely condemned me without listening to what I have to say or, worse, if they had not cared enough about the parishioner's welfare to check me out, I might have thought them both unwise and irresponsible.

'Where do you believe your authority comes from, to do all the things you have done?' I was asked.

'From Christ,' I replied.

'Are you sure of that?'

'I am positive.'

'Would you call yourself a Christian?'

'Define the meaning of that word and I will tell you whether it applies to me,' I replied. 'But to partially answer your question, I am not a church-going follower of the Christian religion.'

'Perhaps,' smiled one of the clergymen, 'it might be better if you were to define your understanding of the word Christian.'

'Nope. You used the term: *you* define it.'

In the process of defining our terms, we all came to the agreement that we were often using different words to describe the came concept. For instance, one of the clergymen raised an objection to my use of the word 'Psychic'.

'A conventional Christian would reject such a term,' he explained. 'You could stand up in front of my congregation and talk about any of your experiences and, providing that you described those experiences as *spiritual*, they would all listen. Describe the self-same experience but refer to it as *psychic* and three-quarters of the congregation will walk out on you.'

'But the word Psychic means "*of* the spirit"!' I protested.

'You know that and so do I, but the generally accepted term has other connotations . . . '

'Which it will *continue* to have for as long as no-one stands up and corrects the misunderstanding!' I interrupted, somewhat vehemently.

'However, since you prefer it, I will use the word spiritual instead of psychic. Can I ask a favour in return?'

'Please do.'

'Your frequent use of the word "power" makes me

feel uncomfortable,' I remarked. 'In *my* terms of understanding, people who constantly speak in terms of power are not functioning on a very high level. Power is always power *over*... it implies slavery and victimisation, neither of which are qualities appropriate to the Creator.'

'Which term would you suggest we use in its place?' I was asked.

'Energy,' I told them. 'It's all pure energy.'

After a long and very interesting discussion, I was informed that my credentials had been accepted. 'I don't think we're in disagreement on any major issues,' smiled the senior clergyman.

'Don't you? That's good, I'm pleased to hear it,' I smiled in return, with only the slightest hint of impudence. 'Now I've been sitting here answering your questions for about three hours and I think I'm entitled to put forward a few ideas of my own. I'm sorry if this sets the cat amongst the pigeons but I *do* see a major difference between your philosophy and mine, and the issue is of considerable importance to me.'

Whatever the clergyman might have been thinking was carefully screened behind a mask of polite neutrality. 'Go ahead,' was all he said.

'I'll start with a few questions, if you don't mind. Now, you believe that God is Love... right?'

'You know that's true.'

'Just checking. Next question: what is the opposite of Love?'

'Hatred, of course.'

'No it isn't. Hatred is a product of Fear... you hate what you fear, so it's Fear that is really the opposite of Love.'

'What point are you making?'

'Just this: whose work is a minister of religion *really* doing when he climbs up into his pulpit and commands all his parishioners to *fear* God?'

'Ah, but if you look at the Bible definition of the word, you'll see that Fear doesn't have the same meaning...'

'You know that Reverend, and so do I... but do your parishioners? That word... Fear... has certain universal connotations, none of which are pleasant. In any case, the fear is reinforced with threats of hellfire and torment, so I'd say the element of fear is firmly established within the doctrine. The fear may be effective in keeping all those people in line, but it is a philosophy that will breed the most unhealthy of human emotions... we've already agreed that fear leads to hatred, for a start. What have all these things to do with a God of *Love*?

'When you climb into your pulpit, you should raise those people up, not cast them down, Tell them that it isn't a sin to make a mistake or a crime to fall flat on your face, just a crying shame if you refuse to get up and try again. Get them up off their knees, wipe the tears from their eyes and show them that they are loved... that their Creator loves them... warts and all. Help them to *feel* loved... THEN you'll be doing the work of your God of Love, and not before.'

A little breathless and surprised with myself, I sat back and waited for the bombshell to explode. For a few moments, nobody moved. Then the senior clergyman sprang to his feet and reached across the table to shake me by the hand. 'I agree with every word you say,' he beamed.

'You *do*?'

'I will admit that there are still too many hellfire and brimstone preachers around,' he continued. 'But they haven't got the field entirely to themselves. The light of understanding is dawning... even in the Church.'

I caught the hint of a humorous twinkle in his eye and couldn't help responding with a delighted grin. 'Well. Glory be!' I chuckled. 'There's hope for us all yet!'

The matter of religion is an issue of concern to many sensitives. Some are very emphatic in their rejection of religious concepts. Others are deeply religious and sometimes have difficulty balancing the psychic facet of their natures with the spiritual. In either case, there is inner conflict which generates imbalance and distress. So let's look at the subject of religion, as it relates to spirituality.

Late in 1984, Roland and I took part in the making of a television documentary for the Andronicus Foundation. The Foundation's President, Dr. Ian Gordon, is married to a lovely young woman named Sue, a devout Roman Catholic who had begun to experience a conscious psychic awakening only about twelve months earlier. Sue Gordon's story is interesting and is relevant here because it epitomises the intense inner conflict that commonly arises during this stage of awakening. I have a feeling that many of my readers will be able to identify quite readily with Sue.

The very first time I ever laid eyes on Sue, I loved her. We had flown from Queensland to Melbourne in the middle of August, at the tail end of a bitterly cold Victorian winter. At least, it seemed bitterly cold to me having come from the warmth of the north. Friends met us at the airport and drove us to the Gordon's home, where we were to stay. We were looking forward to our meeting with Sue: Ian was an old friend but he and Sue were newly-weds and, although we had occasionally spoken to Sue by telephone, we had never personally met her.

She was standing there to greet me as I stepped out of the car and my first impression was of a pair of massive, fawn-like eyes, brimming with light. Clasping her hands together with only the tiniest hint of nervousness, she spoke softly.

'Welcome,' she said 'To . . . to Here.'

And what a welcome! When Sue opened the door and we stepped inside, I felt myself enveloped in a glorious blanket of warmth. A huge open fire irradiated the living-room and wall-heaters spread the glow to every other room in the house. My face must have reflected my delight, for Sue's face lit up with pleasure.

'I thought you might feel the cold, coming from Queensland. I wanted to make things comfortable for you.'

'Lady,' I grinned. 'You've just made a friend for life!'

Although she was genuinely friendly and solicitous, there was a faint hint of reservation in Sue's manner towards me and, at first, I wondered about it. Later, after she had come to know me better, she explained.

'You have to bear in mind how new I am to all of this,' she told me, referring to the awakening of her psychic faculties. 'For me, it has only been happening for about twelve months and I don't understand it very well yet. When it all started happening, your book was one of the things that helped to save my peace of mind.

'When it first started, I thought I must be going round the bend, so I went to see a psychologist. After she had listened to my story, she asked me whether it had ever occurred to me that I might be psychic. Well of course, it hadn't. I wasn't even really sure what being psychic meant. So, she handed me a copy of your book, told me to go home and read it and come back to her in a week. I can't even begin to describe the way I felt when I read the book... it was as though you reached out and told me it was alright, I wasn't going potty, lots of people have experiences like mine. The *relief*! So you see, to me Dawn Hill was right up there on a pedestal. When I met Ian and he spoke of you as old friends, I felt out of my depth... I was in awe of you, Then when I knew you were coming here, I was torn. Most of me was really looking forward to meeting you and the other part was scared in case you didn't like me. Or worse, if I didn't like you. Can you see?'

I have to admit that the idea of another person being in awe of *me* is one that doesn't sit comfortably with me but, as Sue explained it, I could understand. I've come face to face with some people I admire greatly and found myself lost for words often enough to know how it feels, from the admirer's perspective. I'm just not quite accustomed to being the admiree! Sue's attitude towards me in this respect is quite significant in view of an incident that took place several days after our arrival.

We were filming an 'after dinner discussion' in a rather genteel Melbourne restaurant. Earlier in the evening, Sue had tranced and a message had been delivered on camera by a spirit known to us as Colandrias. This surprised none of us at the time, partly because Sue had been the focus for a number of vivid and dramatic incidents during the filming. Of us all, only Sue was disconcerted by this turn of events. She had expected to play her part on the sidelines and that is where she would have preferred to remain but the Powers That Be decreed otherwise. This had placed a lot of strain on Sue, who was frequently embarrassed to the point of tears by her spontaneous trances on camera. Although she had laughingly accepted her reluctant moments of 'stardom', her unexpectedly prominent role in the proceedings made her uncomfortable.

The crisis came in the form of an innocent question. Our director, standing off-camera, was acting as an interviewer, asking us questions on behalf of the unseen audience.

'Over the past few days working with all of you, it is obvious to me that you all sincerely believe in the truth of what you are saying, yet each one of you also seems to have a strong grounding in orthodox religion. Does this cause any conflict at all?'

I spoke up first. 'I'd like to answer that. I don't see why there should be any conflict. If you examine the principles we put forward and then check the Bible, you'll find the same principles expressed in the teachings of Christ. Our terminology may be a little different but we're talking about the same reality, the same natural laws. There is no reason for conflict.'

'I'd like to answer that question too,' said Sue. 'I'm not as experienced as you, Dawn. I don't see things at the same level and from my point of view there IS conflict. Quite a lot of it. I've never been a fanatic but I've always been deeply religious . . . I even wanted to be a nun when I was little. The things I'm doing now . . . people in my church wouldn't understand. They'd say it's evil. That causes conflict for me.'

'Not all of the people within the church are so biassed, Sue,' I demurred. 'For instance, I have a friend who is a very tuned-in Catholic priest . . . '

With a force that made the cutlery rattle, Sue's clenched fist came down on the table. 'A tuned-in Catholic priest is not PEOPLE, Dawn!' she cried. 'Can't you understand? Don't you know? Can't you understand what it's like NOT TO KNOW?'

Too stunned to speak, I could only watch as Sue turned to face the director, oblivious to the camera that lovingly followed her every move. She had started to cry and her face was twisted with grief as she pleaded to be understood. 'I walk down the street in my home town,' she began, 'and I see people I've known and loved for years. I can see other people with them too, people in spirit who love them very much. You can't see something so beautiful and not *tell* people... can you? So I tell them, thinking it might make them happy and you should see the way they look at me...

'They look at me as though I'm a stranger... an alien,' she struggled to regain control of her voice, openly weeping. 'Can you understand how that feels? To be a stranger in your own world? They treat me as though I'm suffering from some kind of disease. I know that what I'm doing isn't evil but *they* don't. I can see what they're thinking and it HURTS! I'm not the person they know, the person I used to be. They don't know this new person. *I* don't know this new person very well either but I can't go back to being who I used to be. I don't know *who I am* any more... that's why I feel conflict!'

Sue covered her face with her hands. Her shoulders heaved as she struggled for control. Nobody spoke.

As her turbulent emotions subsided, Sue appeared to become aware of the effects of her outburst. Her eyes met mine and she stretched out her hand to me. 'I'm sorry, Dawn,' she whispered. 'I didn't mean to hurt you, it just erupted.'

Bearing in mind that Sue had a tendency to hold me in awe at the time, the fact that her outburst occurred indicates the intensity of her feelings... and her pain.

To a person like Sue, religion is far from being a trivial issue. As she puts it, 'If my Lord wants me to work for Him in this way, I'll do it. I can't say I understand it but I'll do it... as long as I can feel sure that it is what He wants me to do.' Her motivation, her desire to do only what is pleasing to her Lord, is not born out of fear but out of love. Does it really matter what name she calls Him? Would it make any difference if she knew Him as Krishna, or Horus, or Ahura Mazda? In every action she takes and every word she speaks, Sue is the living evidence that her god is a God of Love. Who could possibly call that evil?

My name in Latin is Aurora. In Greek it is something that sounds like 'Adonia'... I think. Therefore if you were to call me Aurora or Adonia, wouldn't you be calling me by name? Words can be wonderful tools for communication, so long as we don't allow them to get in the way. The Mother Goddess, in all her multiplicity of facets, has been given many names: Isis, Astarte, Minerva, Freya and Mary, to name a few. The God of Gods has many names also: Zeus, Ra, Jehovah or Jove, and more. My guide is known to me as David but he has also told me that he is known to others by other names. Why should you and I argue if my name for the Lord of Light is Christ and yours is Mithras? Isn't it more important that we recognise the Light in each other?

Where there is total acceptance, there cannot be barriers. Religious conflict is a barrier to spiritual development . . . just look what it is doing in the world around us, in places like Northern Ireland and the Middle East. If that kind of senseless destruction is the fruit of religious conflict, what does that tell you about the tree from whence it sprang? We don't NEED that kind of insanity: in fact, we cannot afford to perpetuate it.

Now, for all the anti-religious people who are currently sitting back with smiles on their faces, saying 'I told you so', I have news for you too. If you've been rejecting religion completely, you've been making a mistake. It's called throwing the baby out with the bathwater. Try taking a look at the subject from a less emotive viewpoint. What was a religion for the ancient Vikings is mythology to us today. To a Christian, the Hindu pantheon of Gods is mythical and their religious philosophy is based on legend. Ask a Hindu and he will probably tell you that he sees our Bible as being based on legend. It's all a matter of perspective.

Religion represents mankind's attempts to explain the unexplainable. Most religions have their basis in spiritual truth but the truth is often concealed behind thick veils of superstition. It was always the superstitious aspect of religion that turned me off and, for a long time, I wouldn't look at religion at all because I felt deeply disappointed and disillusioned by it. Later, when my own understanding had increased, I started looking at religious writings again and found that I could see the core of truth in them. It really isn't all that difficult to sift the wheat from the chaff and the reward is an added perspective. To reject one aspect of reality is to spoil your chances of learning to understand the entirety. If you are earnestly seeking Truth, you should be able to find it, wherever you look. Some of those old scribes were a lot smarter than we 'modern folk' tend to believe.

Why reject religion out of hand when you could be studying it instead? Don't just study one religion, study them all. Study mythology and legend too. Study philosophy, psychology, quantum physics, study *everything*. Look for a common thread of truth running through them all. That's how you learn, The tapestry of mythology is rich and varied but it is also full of meaning. Every story has a theme and each theme carries a message. It's all there for you, all you need to do is learn to read the messages. Remember: It's not what you see, it's how you see it!

Learn from Life . . . by Living it.

CHAPTER TWELVE

Personal Growth

Spiritual development is essentially personal growth. There is an expansion of consciousness, a heightening of the awareness, particularly on an inner level, through emotions and feelings. Many powerful energies are now coming into operation within the personality and it is only to be expected that their effects will manifest *through* the personality. The process doesn't end there, however; the personality does not stop evolving, there are higher and still higher levels yet to be reached. There should never come a time in your life when you decide that you have finally learned it all and you know everything there is to know... at least, not in this life. The person who thinks he knows it all hasn't even *started* to learn. At this stage in our development, the more we learn, the more we realise how much remains for us to learn.

With the procedures outlined in the earlier chapters, I have given keys that can be used to switch on your centres of spiritual awareness and get them functioning smoothly. The next stage is learning how to focus those energies in ways that produce beneficial results, for you and for those who come into your sphere of influence.

The best way to practise controlling your spiritual energies is to apply them to your life, as you are living it now. The opportunities for practice are as many and as varied as you could ever need. The general rule of thumb is that if any situation in life can cause you to lose control and unleash a bolt of destructive energy, you are not ready to progress to a higher level. Every time you restrain a harmful thought and remind yourself that when you harm another you are harming yourself, you are making progress.

In your periods of meditation, whether alone or with a group, there are exercises that you can use to help you develop the quality of control that you need. An excellent exercise is to focus your mind on something living, such as a houseplant or a domestic animal, and concentrate on surrounding it with all the love and goodness you can muster. Do it daily, over a period of time and observe the results progressively. If you are focussing your energies correctly, the object of your focus should flourish.

Please, *please* do not make the mistake of focussing negative energies onto any living thing. The results are predictable and distressing, especially for the subject of your study. Just imagine how you would feel if someone bigger and stronger decided to experiment on you. If I appear to be laying a heavy emphasis on the qualities of hurtlessness, it is because I see a necessity to do so. You would probably never dream of harming anything if you could possibly help it but there are people who need to be told. At Keene State College, New Hampshire, U.S.A. during the 1960s, experiments were performed by Professor Charles H. Hapgood and some of his students in the projection of energies onto living seedlings. Each student cultivated three trays of plants, giving them identical conditions of soil, water and sunlight. To the plants in one tray, the students projected love and to another, hate. The third tray was ignored to be used as a control. It should not come as a surprise that whilst the plants in the 'love' trays flourished, those in the 'hate' trays failed to thrive.

Then there were the 'scientific' experiments in which a mother rabbit was separated from her newborn litter and electrodes planted deep in her brain so that her reactions could be closely monitored when her babies were being systematically killed, one by one, in a place some miles away. This was done to validate somebody's theories on telepathy. Now in my mind, it is one thing to experiment in a way that will only produce beneficial results but it is something entirely different to inflict pain and distress on another life form, whether or not it is human, There is never any justification for deliberately causing harm. We're supposed to be caring for the helpless, not exploiting them.

In its April 14, 1986 edition, Australia's *People* magazine reported on experiments conducted by an American neuro-surgeon, Dr. Robert White. In 1971, Dr. White decapitated two monkeys and planted the head of one onto the body of the other. During the four days that it managed to survive, the transplanted head showed all the signs of conscious life, eyes following light, eyelids opening and closing, responding to noise and even eating and drinking. The neuro-surgeon considers these results a triumph in the field of surgery and is now looking around for human subjects to practise on, firmly convinced that he has succeeded in discovering a way to maintain the survival of the human spirit (which he believes is contained in the brain cortex!). He believes that by transplanting heads from one body to another, he has achieved what he calls 'the graft of the soul'. I would call it something completely different and my opinion of Dr. White would get me sued if I dared to print it. I will only say that karmic justice might see people such as this reincarnated as laboratory animals!

I cannot help speaking strongly about such things when I can see . . . and feel . . . the suffering that they cause. I can't just see it all happening and not want to have it stopped. I have to admit that when I discussed this matter with David, I found it difficult to be coherent through my tears but the guide had no difficulty in understanding. When I asked him if there were a way in which we could prevent such things from happening, he shook his head sadly. 'For as long as men attempt to place themselves above the Divine, these things will continue to happen,' he told me.

Until the entire human race becomes aware of the sanctity of all life, helpless and innocent creatures will continue to be tormented and a race that condones the perpetration of such crimes against Life must collectively reap the karmic consequences. In order to put a stop to such diabolical practices and to bring some sanity into this world, higher awareness must penetrate the minds of the human race. Alone, maybe I can't accomplish much but I can *talk* to people and I can ask for their help.

Have you ever heard of the Hundredth Monkey principle? It is not, as it may sound, an obscure Eastern myth but a recognised twentieth-century scientific discovery that has been faithfully recorded by Ken Keyes in his anti-nuclear book *The Hundredth Monkey*. During the

1950s, experiments were being performed with colonies of Japanese monkeys, some living on islands off the coast of Japan and some on the mainland. In the course of these experiments, the monkeys were fed sweet potatoes which were dropped onto the dirt. The monkeys enjoyed the sweet potatoes but they weren't too keen on the flavour of dirt; however, because they liked the taste of the potatoes they kept on eating them anyway, dirt and all.

One day, a bright young female named Imo discovered that she could improve the flavour of her potatoes by washing them in water before eating them. She taught this trick to her playmates, who taught it to their parents and, slowly but gradually, the idea spread through the community. Finally, the day came when just one more monkey picked up the idea and that is when the scientists observed something quite remarkable.

No-one knows exactly how many monkeys were involved but, for the sake of simplicity, it is said that when the sun rose that morning, there were ninety-nine monkeys on this particular island who had started washing their potatoes. When the hundredth monkey tuned in, it caused an ideological breakthrough, Not only did all the other monkeys on that island start washing their sweet potatoes, but the colonies of monkeys on the other islands and on the mainland simultaneously started washing their sweet potatoes too! What does that tell you about the nature of consciousness?

When an idea is the 'consciousness property' of a limited number of minds, it exists only as an isolated pocket; however, when more and more minds become involved, we will ultimately reach a point of critical mass where it overflows to permeate the group mind and *everybody* knows it. You can see evidence of this principle in the world of human thinking too. Who had ever thought of using psychic energy to bend spoons and stop clocks until Uri Geller came on the scene? Now children do it just for fun. It is easy for the children: no-one has told them it cannot be done, so they do it.

What do you think would be the combined effect of the necessary number of minds, all united in the projection of positive, healing light energies right through every particle of the Earth's aura? Practise the White Light meditations, feel their effect within your own aura and then imagine that effect magnified thousands of times and beamed out into the atmosphere surrounding this world. It can be done. What's more, for all of our sakes and for the sakes of our children, it *needs* to be done. Think about it.

During the filming of the television documentary I mentioned earlier, I had an experience that I would like to share with you. It was just after sunset and a group of us were meditating on the top of a hill in a location that Ian Gordon's guides had identified as a power centre. We had been told only to go and to meditate and to film whatever might take place during that time. Now, interesting things have been known to happen around me when I sit in meditation groups but I usually see them happening to other people. I have been told that my aura carries an energy that acts as a psychic catalyst and triggers things off in people (as it did when Roland started trancing within days of meeting me). I'm usually not aware of *doing* anything, it all just seems to happen. So I'm more accustomed to watching other people go into trances; it is not something that I would normally expect to do, especially with a television camera staring me right in the face.

We had been sitting for some time in the deepening chill of the Southern evening without anything remarkable happening: this puzzled me greatly because in the eye of my mind I could see scores of golden-white beings of light standing around the perimeter of the clearing in which we sat.

'You asked us to come here... why don't you DO something?' I asked them, with my thoughts. 'Why are you all standing back? We're here with your channel, you can talk to the world through these cameras if you want to... why don't you come forward and speak?'

In answer, I felt myself enveloped in a wave of sadness so intense that I just couldn't hold it all in. There was so much *sorrow*... I could feel myself rocking as though with grief while tears poured down my face unchecked. I could also sense the camera moving into closeup and somewhere inside myself I squealed 'Oh *No*!' but I had already been swept up by the sorrow... and the love.

'Your people do not fully comprehend our purpose,' the words came into my mind and even as I accepted them I heard my own voice speaking. 'People sit in their groups to meditate and they wait for us to come and make things happen. It isn't supposed to be like that. You are the channels, you are the vehicles for the Light and it is through you that the Light must flow. The atmosphere around your world is sick . . . it's polluted . . . and only Light can cleanse it. Open yourself to the Light and let it flow through you, to heal your world. *Do something with it!*'

I have paraphrased the actual words but the message is still clear in my mind and I doubt that I will ever forget the feeling. All those radiant beings really *care*; they want to help and they have so much to give but the true value of the gift is often overlooked. There are a lot of people who think of these spirits as something like glorified genies in little psychic bottles, who exist only to make life a little easier and more entertaining for us. That isn't their purpose at all! They want to help restore balance, beauty and harmony to this world of ours, teach us how to make life better for ourselves and help eradicate the diseases caused by fear. All *we* are asked to do is open ourselves to the Light and let it flow . . . is that so hard?

The meditation group provides an excellent platform for the development of your spiritual gifts, with the opportunity of learning how to attune your minds and pool your energies so that their effect is amplified. You can work with exercises in which energies are projected to each other and discuss your achievements and problems as you go along. When you are looking for suitable exercises, think about the effects that you want to achieve and study the exercises accordingly. Some will help you to reach your goal, others are designed for different purposes.

My name for the following exercise isn't very polite; I call it 'Pig in the Middle' but I won't be offended if you choose to call it something different. In the course of this exercise, each group member will have a turn at being the focus of energies being projected by the other group members. I am assuming that, before the group commences this exercise, every member has carried out the necessary cleansing and precautionary measures to ensure that the energies within the group are as pure as they can be. The method for focussing the energy is as follows:

Pig in the Middle

Each of the focussing members should begin by using their inner awareness to 'imagine' the person in the centre being totally surrounded by White Light, smiling, happy and healthy. Take a few moments to consolidate the flow of White Light energy, from the Creator, through you and out to the person in the middle.

Meanwhile, the person in the middle should be focussing on the flow of Light, inwardly *feeling* the uplifting effect. Remember, if you have difficulty with inner visualisation, don't struggle to see the Light, instead concentrate on feeling the flow. Remember that what you think is: by inwardly placing that Light around the person, you have put it there. Whether you can see it or not makes no difference.

You will next put yourself into a passive frame of mind so as to allow the inward flow of impressions. You are still focussing on the person in the centre but you are opening yourself to receive messages through the atmosphere, with relation to that person. Perhaps you will feel an effect in the region of your emotions, a mood or a feeling. You may receive mental images or find words entering your head. You may sense absolutely nothing at all. Whatever happens, don't try to censor or interpret any of it, just observe and make a mental note of it.

The person in the centre also sits passive, receiving and mentally recording any feelings or impressions. Once again, don't try to interpret anything, just record it in your mind. For this passive, receiving period, allow between three and five minutes. When this time has elapsed, every member should flush their auras through with some White Light and return to normal consciousness. In this part of the exercise, you will obviously need someone to keep an eye on the time and to let the others know when it has elapsed. Usually the person who is being the group leader for that evening is the one who watches the time, with someone else taking over the task when it is the leader's turn in the centre.

Before focussing on the next person, the group should hold a 'debriefing' discussion. Beginning with the person in the middle and proceeding to each member in turn, each person should give a brief account of any impressions received during the exercise. Don't try to make anything significant out of these impressions, simply relate them as they occurred. It is best to avoid placing too much meaning into things at this stage. You will sometimes find several group members sharing an impression with relation to the person in the centre... an excellent chance to play Psychic Snap!

Remember, the exercise isn't finished until everyone has had a turn in the middle. One advantage of having a manageably small group can be seen here, I'm sure. Talk about your impressions, what you learned from performing the exercise. Do a series of experiments with the exercise. For instance, you could go through the exercise once a fortnight or once a month and record everyone's impressions. By comparing the notes from a continuing sequence of the same exercise, you may find that some interesting patterns begin to emerge. It is a pleasant and harmless little exercise but it also happens to contain several basic spiritual principles. By performing the exercise, you make yourself more familiar with those principles, which in turn will help you become more proficient in their use. Don't allow yourself to be deceived by simplicity; the simplest methods are usually the best and most effective.

I'm sure you can see why it is so important that the attitudes and motives of the group members as individuals are of paramount importance. A member who is feeling depressed and frustrated or who is competing for ego-gratification will not be capable of projecting very positive energies; in fact, the energies he *does* project will hold the others back, and might even cause a few headaches and arguments, none of which are conducive to genuine spiritual enlightenment.

Like most spiritual exercises, this one achieves a number of effects. For a start, it generates a lot of positive, life-sustaining energy in the auras of the people involved. It helps to clarify and strengthen your channels of spiritual energy and it helps you to learn how to aim and focus those energies to produce a beneficial effect. In addition, by actively concentrating on a blend of the group's combined energies, you are helping to form the group entity.

The kind of people who seek guidance from me seem to have certain qualities in common. One of those qualities is a desire to use whatever they may have to offer in a way that will bring about the highest good for all concerned. At first, a lot of these folk tell me that they want to be psychic healers. Some of them really aren't born to be healers: their desire to heal is motivated by a wish to serve, to help and to uplift. Sometimes in the process of trying to develop and enhance healing abilities the student will discover that she is a talented teacher or that the creative energies may be channelled in another way, through art perhaps, or music. All you need to do is allow the Light to flow and it will find its own channel within you. I started out wanting to be a healer and ended up being a writer, which is certainly not what I expected back then! I didn't know, in the beginning, that writing could be just as much a channel for spiritual energy as healing or making prophecies. Whatever your own personal talents may be, you can be sure that the Light will find them and enhance them for you. It can get to be a wonderful life.

I can certainly understand the motivation that makes people want to be healers. I went into the nursing profession some years ago because I was tired of just working to earn money. I wanted to do something worthwhile, something that could be of tangible help to others. Nursing was an obvious choice for me to make at the time and I would have been quite content to be a nurse for the rest of my days if Fate had not decreed otherwise. I really loved my patients, even the crabby ones.

The inner feeling that motivated me to become a nurse is the same type of feeling that motivates people who want to be psychic healers. It offers them a way to give the kind of things they want to give: healing, comfort, reassurance and upliftment. Once you broaden your perspective a little, you can see on a broader scale and it becomes evident that life presents you with hundreds of opportunities to put your spiritual energies to work, every day. Because these everyday occurrences are so familiar and commonplace, people don't tend to notice them as readily, yet they are just as important as the bigger and more obvious opportunities.

Let me tell you about a person I used to know. I'll call him Matthew because I know he'd be embarrassed if I used his real name. Matthew worked in a large office complex in the heart of Sydney. On his way to work one morning, Matthew noticed an old drunk staggering belligerently through the crowd, accosting the passers-by with demands for a smoke. Overcome with a feeling it didn't occur to him to question, Matthew walked up to the old derelict.

'Here, Mate,' he said. 'Have a packet. I've only taken one or two out of it.'

The old drunkard accepted the packet in bleary-eyed amazement.

'Have you got matches?' enquired Matthew. The old man nodded.

'Yeah, I've got matches. Er . . . thanks Mate.'

'No worries,' grinned Matthew as he strode off though the crowd.

'I don't know what caused me to do it,' said Matthew, sharing the experience with us later. I'd done it before I really thought about it but I'm glad I did. You wouldn't *believe* the lift it gave to my spirits for the rest of the day.'

'Oh, yes I would,' I demurred. 'It happens to me too, you know.'

It hadn't really cost Matthew anything to give an old man a pack of cigarettes. He could easily afford to buy another pack so he didn't have to sacrifice anything, nor make any tremendous effort. All he did was to allow himself to be moved by the spirit of compassion. The karmic feedback from his action was the immediate lift to his spirits that buoyed him through the rest of his day. That's an example of good Karma in action and it comes from giving *naturally*, just because it feels good and for no other reason.

I don't suggest that we should all start cruising the streets, handing out cigarettes to old winos: the idea is to give what is yours to give, where it is needed, when you see the need. This doesn't mean you have to take a vow of poverty and to deprive yourself of the things you need. It means giving what you can spare, whether it's a kindly word, a shoulder to cry on, a batch of home-cooked scones or any other act of caring. The really important thing is that it should never be given grudgingly. If giving makes you feel unhappy, perhaps it would be better not to give.

Simply by giving out Light, you can give of your best and still have heaps to spare. Think of the wonderful things that could happen in this world if we all saturated the atmosphere with White Light. If you have started feeling the effects of the Light in your own aura and you understand how it works, by dissolving negative energy and transmuting it into something positive, it should not be difficult to imagine the effect this kind of energy could have on the psychic atmosphere around this world.

You have been told that thought is the fabric of reality, that anything created at the level of thought will ultimately be manifest in the physical. You should also, by now, have a basic understanding of the ways in which your thought and emotional energies can affect the other life-forms around you. From the state of our world, it should not be difficult to work out what kind of psychic energies are saturating the atmosphere right now. Unless those negative energies are cleaned away, we will soon reach a point of crisis, beyond which it will no longer be possible for physical life to be sustained on this planet.

There are any number of 'prophets' telling us that we are all about to be engulfed in worldwide cataclysms and that, ultimately, life on this planet will not be able to survive. I realise that is a possibility but it is not the only one. What you think . . . IS. What do you think you are doing when you *believe* in the inevitability of disaster? With your thoughts, you form your own reality; by *believing* in disaster, you will cause it to happen. Surely we are all capable of creating a better reality than that.

Even if you do nothing but beam out White Light energy into the Earth's aura, you will be accomplishing something much more wonderful than you may realise. We don't have to destroy the world when it is possible for us to change it, just by changing the way we think. If you fully understand the White Light techniques we've discussed so far, the method of projection for Planetary Healing is already known to you. All you need to do now is extend your focus.

Planetary Healing is an excellent activity to use at the close of your group meetings or meditation periods. After all, for the past couple of hours you have been concentrating on raising and channelling high levels of energy and you really shouldn't leave all that energy drifting around aimlessly in the atmosphere with no positive direction. That sort of untidiness can lead to messy accidents.

If the single act of giving a pack of cigarettes to an old man in the street can make someone feel high for the rest of the day, imagine what the karmic feedback will be like when you start giving your highest spiritual energies for the healing of the Earth. That, my friends, is called using your energies positively.

Planetary Healing

For a Planetary Healing meditation, begin with the White Light meditation, Invocation and Feeding of the Flame. Let your auras be irradiated and open yourselves to the Light. Feel the Divinity within the Light, as a living presence within and around you. Let this presence lift you up. Let the Light encompass you, then feel it radiating out from you in ever-widening circles, like the ripples in a cosmic pool. Give it all out, as naturally as a flower gives its perfume.

No matter how much energy you give out in this way, you cannot exhaust the supply. In order to flow out from you, the energy must first flow *through* you. By drawing the Light to yourself, you have effectively plugged yourself in to the cosmic battery-charger.

If you like to use visualisation at this point, you can draw whatever mental pictures you like, providing they contain nothing harmful. Some people like to visualise an expanding sphere of White Light spreading out from themselves to encompass their house, their town, then the country, the world and its aura.

My favourite vision is as though I'm hovering at a point out in space and I can see the Earth in the indigo infinity, turning slowly, shrouded in a veil of darkness. At the same time, I can also see row upon row of small white candles, millions of them covering and encircling the planet, all unlighted. Then it happens... one little candle springs alight and, as it does so, it leans across to light the next candle, nearest to itself. The Hundredth Monkey Principle is off and running! From out in space, a mantle of dancing, multi-hued lights spreads outwards over the planet until finally the whole sphere is alive with light and it's like looking at a precious crystal, filled with light. That is what I call *Enlightenment!*

With the use of creative visualisation, you can also imagine the world as we would all like to see it, a garden of beauty, filled with peace and harmony, abundant with life. You can make it a world where fear, cruelty and corruption do not exist and *cannot* exist, where the children of Earth are free to play in the sunshine, tending the earth and being nourished by it in return. Use your imagination to make it as real and as vivid as you possibly can, remembering that you are consciously shaping thought energy, to mould a living reality.

You don't have to take my word for it that all these energies work. I have provided exercises through which you can put these principles into practice and test the results for yourself. *Test* them. When you can feel those energies working within your personal energy field, then you will understand how the effects can be broadened. Words in your head are only words until you put them into practice.

As you can see, this approach to spiritual development is quite different from the old 'seance' idea where everybody sat around waiting for something psychic to happen. You will also find it a great deal safer for the participants.

Don't try to rush your development, particularly at this crucial stage. Patient reinforcement is one of the keys to success. Skimming the surface is a habit that leads to thin ice. Take the time to become thoroughly relaxed and at harmony within yourselves, reinforce the flow of positive life energy over and over until you start flowing naturally with it. Tune in to each other, generate harmony in the atmosphere around you. There are any number of projects here that are capable of keeping you happily occupied for months if you want to get yourself really involved.

By the act of beaming out healing and uplifting energies into the atmosphere, karmic law will bring to you magnified energies of a similar nature. This is how you draw to yourself the spiritual guidance of those who exist on levels much higher than the physical sphere. To put it simply, you will reap what you sow. Heard that anywhere before?

CHAPTER THIRTEEN

Dangerous Pastimes

There seem to be people in this world who believe that, because you know how to make something work, you know everything there is to know about it, which automatically qualifies you to teach other people. If that were true, mankind would never have invented nuclear bombs. I know how to drive a car but if I turn the ignition key and nothing happens, I start looking around for Roland. I don't know a *thing* about all the complicated gadgetry under the hood. I can drive a car but would you expect me to teach you how to be a motor mechanic? I do not claim to know everything there is to know about spiritual energy... if I knew THAT much, I wouldn't be here. At the same time, I have learned enough to be able to see the dangers in certain popular psychic activities and to be concerned enough about those dangers to bring them to the attention of anyone who will listen.

There are a lot of *How to...* books on the esoteric market today: How to travel in the Astral, How to regress yourself and your friends to previous incarnations, How to do Automatic Writing... the list is almost endless. Unfortunately, both for themselves and for their readers, some of those self-styled teachers only know how to drive the car: they don't even see the machinery under the hood. If the advice that they give were not so dangerous, it wouldn't be so bad, but people can get *hurt* by following the instructions given in some of those Do-It-Yourself manuals. That is what causes me so much concern.

Hayley was fifteen when she first wrote to me, not long after the release of *Reaching for the Other Side*. She wrote for advice: the young man who had been her first love had been killed in an accident several months previously and her youth did not save her from the agonies of grief. She grieved intensely and, in an effort to help her, a concerned friend gave her two books about life after death. One was mine, the other was written by a woman who had discovered automatic writing in her attempts to make contact with her deceased husband. She wrote in glowing terms of the comfort and reassurance it gave her to be in regular communication with her husband and she explained in detail how anyone else could learn to do automatic writing. Hayley read that book first.

No prizes for guessing what the distraught teenager did next. She sat down with pencil and paper to try out the method for herself. Hallelujah! The pencil begin to write out messages from an entity who agreed that he was indeed her boyfriend. She poured her heart and soul into these communications but she became confused when the 'lover' lapsed into obscene language and addressed her with contempt. That was out of character with the young man she had known. Then she read my book and became aware of the unpleasant possibility that the entity she had believed to be her boyfriend might, in fact, be an imposter.

Hayley was sensible enough to tell me exactly how she went about obtaining these communications and to send me samples of the scripts. It took less than a few seconds for me to confirm her suspicions. Normally it takes time for me to answer a letter because I have quite a heavy workload but there was an answer on its way to Hayley by return mail. She was in more danger than she knew and there was no time to waste. I told her the truth about the entity that had been deceiving her and explained how, by opening her channels without knowing how to protect them, she had literally invited the creature to take up occupancy in her energy field. I included the necessary instructions for the cleansing and sealing of her aura to evict the unwanted influence and warned her to put down her pen and find something else to do whenever she felt an impulse to try the automatic writing again. I also prayed that she would heed the warning and not allow herself to be ruled by emotions.

A couple of weeks later, Hayley wrote again to tell me that she had followed the instructions and was now ready for more. She wanted to learn and she literally peppered me with questions. I exchanged letters with

Hayley for quite a while and, in that time, she made quantum leaps in terms of spiritual awareness and understanding. I've worked with several young people over the past few years and the speed with which they are capable of learning often astounds me. What would have happened to Hayley, I wonder, if she had not been warned in time?

Hayley told me that the book on automatic writing had made no mention of the possibility that the communicating spirit could be a malicious imposter, nor did it mention the necessity to obtain spiritual protection before attempting any form of contact. It is quite probable that the authoress was not aware that such precautions are necessary. I'm sure her motives for writing the book were pure and that her only intention was to share her newfound joy with others but that doesn't alter the fact that her kind of advice can lead to danger. The harmful misuse of spiritual energy worries me: innocent motives notwithstanding, some things are just plain dangerous and I'd be shirking my responsibility if I didn't say so.

Astral Travel is another subject that fascinates a lot of people and, again, there are any number of books on the market that will tell you how you can start playing this great new game. Many of them will even assure you that it is a perfectly harmless occupation. WRONG!

The term 'Astral Travel' has a specific meaning, which many of the people who use it do not seem to know. If they did, they would not say Astral Travel when they are, in fact, referring to Out of Body Projection. Astral Travel is exactly what its name implies: travel within the *Astral sphere only*. When people speak of travelling into the Astral to reach the highest levels of spiritual existence, they are advertising their own ignorance. The Astral is only one of the spheres beyond the physical and it is not a very advanced one; if you want to reach the levels of pure spirit, you need to aim a lot higher.

I'm not denying that there are places of great spiritual beauty in the Astral sphere: there are, just as there are places of great beauty in this world. The population at the Astral level, however, is merely the out-of-body equivalent of the physical population in this world and there are some characters walking this planet with whom I would certainly not wish to be confronted in a dark corner of the Astral plane. I won't say that you shouldn't travel in the Astral if you want to but it would be wise to be sure that you know what you're doing before you set out.

Are you absolutely certain that, when you release your consciousness into the Astral, you are capable of guaranteeing that you will penetrate the higher levels and not the low ones? Do you feel confident that, if you happened to wander into one of the less salubrious levels, you could handle the situation if you found yourself surrounded by a gang of Astral thugs? Without getting yourself hurt? You will find, if you allow yourself to get caught in such a situation, that your Astral body is capable of feeling pain when assaulted by an Astral energy. I have friends who have come awake in the night to the realisation that they are out of their bodies, in the Astral and surrounded by a pack of mean-looking Astral or Lower Astral characters. It has happened to me on occasions also. It happens to just about everyone... what do you think nightmares are?

I have received many letters asking me to explain an experience in which someone has come awake to a feeling of near-terror and a sensation of a weight sitting on that person's chest. Usually there is physical paralysis associated with the experience so the victim is unable to move or even to cry out. There is also a distinct sensation that whatever is causing the weight to press down upon the sufferer's chest is hostile and capable of causing harm. In extreme cases, such attacks can even involve sexual assault which is physically tangible.

Western mysticism classifies the entities responsible for such attacks as incubi and succubi, incubus being the masculine and succubus the feminine form. I just call them Lower Astral entities. It is obvious to the most casual observer that a non-physical being cannot copulate with a physical body, even when the physical sensations are present, but that does *not* mean that the sensations are imaginary. In fact, the assault is directed upon the etheric body and the aim is to drain off the victim's vital energy.

If you have studied the energy spectrum sufficiently, you will be aware that I am referring here to energies generated at the Physical Etheric or Lower Astral level, in the red range. If your supply of red energy is inadequate, your whole system will be weakened and, if the situation is permitted to continue, it will eventually reach a stage at which your red energy levels are no longer sufficient to maintain the life-force in your physical body. Lower Astral entities feed on that kind of energy and they are all predators. If you can be overcome by fear, your level of vibrations will drop to the Lower Astral level, putting you just where the predators want you. The level of your life-force is directly connected with the gonads and with the sex drive, hence the 'sexual' attacks. In this case, the entity, is tapping into your Root chakra in order to draw off the energy. Charming little characters, aren't they?

At the psychic level, an emotion is a tangible energy. Fear is within the red-orange part of the spectrum and, when you feel fear, you are actually pulsing out energy on that wavelength. Remember that there is no sharp division between the non-physical spheres: like the colours in the rainbow spectrum, they shade into one another. In the red-orange range, you are within reach of entities from the Lower Astral or Physical Etheric and also of entities in the lowest levels of the Astral plane. Not a very pleasant location in which to find yourself. The creatures who congregate at these levels feed on fear and delight in inflicting pain.

If you should ever find yourself in this kind of situation, first start to control the fear. That isn't easy, even when you have a reasonable amount of experience, chiefly because the opponents are quite proficient in the art of causing fear and they are going to do their best to scare you silly. The thing for *you* to remember is that, if they cannot make you feel fear, they can't hurt you. Recognise this and it will help you to control your fear.

If we analyse what happens physiologically when a person feels fear, we are in a better position to exercise control over that fear. Firstly the heart-rate goes up and so does the breathing... the body releases adrenalin for 'fight or flight'. Control the breathing (a conscious decision) and you control the physical panic reaction... you are in control and you are eliminating the fear.

While you are working to get your emotions under control, simultaneously send out a spiritual S.O.S. Focus on your Invocation, repeat the words over and over in your mind and, at the same time, start filling your aura with White Light. You may have to struggle for a few seconds to achieve this but do it... and keep doing it until you are free. You might then 'wake up' abruptly, still breathing rather heavily or your consciousness will simply relocate itself at a higher level and you will drift back into normal sleep quite easily.

If you are a little more experienced, you might simply look at those entities and say 'You can't touch me, you don't even exist in my reality. Shoo!'. Whatever you do, for Heaven's sake don't try playing the knight in shining armour and doing battle with them or you're likely to be creamed. These guys know all about the use of force and they use dirtier tricks than you and I are capable of imagining. The best thing you can possibly do when you find yourself in such company is put yourself somewhere else.

It's all very well to huff and puff and blow yourself into the Astral but have you stopped to consider what you'll do once you get there? Why are you doing it? What do you hope to learn, or to gain? You could visit halls of learning in the Astral spheres... many people do. You might prefer to drift around the physical world, visit all the great cathedrals or even cruise over Mars and explore the canals. Why not Alpha Centauri? You might do anything: the question is, do you have a worthwhile purpose for doing it?

I have read several books on Astral Projection. Most of them provide very practical suggestions as to how you can go about separating the Astral body from the physical while still remaining conscious. Some of them will also offer suggestions as to what you might like to do when you actually get into the Astral. Some will suggest activities like joy-riding... taking over another person's body while that person's consciousness is drifting off somewhere in sleep. I am not joking... I have read such a book myself! It makes you start to wonder where all those nasty little predators I mentioned earlier really come from, doesn't it? Invading another person's body without that person's consent and co-operation is an obscene act of violation: the psychic equivalent of rape.

Another suggestion I have read is that you might like to use an Astral advantage to gain some object that you physically desire, such as a lover. You could visit the object of your affections in the Astral . . . if you're smart, says the book, you might like to use your shape-changing ability to appear before your beloved in a dream as your rival and, in that guise, do a few really rotten things to him. To put the icing on the cake, you can appear in a subsequent dream as his Fairy Godmother. Great fun . . . except for the fact that it is in flagrant violation of Cosmic Law and therefore carries heavy karmic penalties.

What level do you think you would be operating on if you were to carry out those kinds of activities? I'll tell you . . . the red-orange level. At that level, you are prey to the wolf-packs which habitually hunt in that area of the woods and they are bigger, stronger, meaner and more cunning than you. Your spiritual guides can protect you against predators but they cannot and must not protect you from the consequences of your own actions. If you consciously choose to live by the law of the jungle, you throw away your own protection. Get into trouble and you might have to find your way out of it alone. There is a point beyond which the spirits of Light cannot intervene.

Just what kind of Karma do you think you'd be laying up for yourself if you chose to victimise others whilst at an Astral advantage? There are no cosmic policemen who will come along and clap you in chains: there don't have to be. Life itself will deliver justice to you. You reap what you sow. Certain philosophies in Wicca refer to the 'Rule of Three' which states that all of the energies you radiate will be multiplied by three by the time they return to you. Whatever you give to others is going to be at least three times as good (or three times as bad) when it is returned to you. That's worth thinking about.

If you want to and if you feel that your purpose is worthwhile, explore the Astral. Just learn to do it safely, so that you don't get hurt. If you know that a certain course of action is likely to bring you a cosmic kick in the pants, your own instinct for self-preservation will make you avoid it; but how can you avoid something if you don't even know it is there? Make sure you are thoroughly familiar with the Cosmic Bill of Rights before you even think about approaching another being's personal space. Nobody has the right to interfere with Destiny.

That brings me to the subject of Past Life Regression, another increasingly popular New Age activity. Strictly speaking, we could regard Past Life Regression as a kind of spiritual psychoanalysis. The idea is for the conscious mind to visit another time-space in order to review the events of a former life, or lives, so that the primary causes of psychological problems in *this* life can be identified. It is a valid procedure but it also has an element of risk. Unfortunately, some of the practitioners who are taking people into past lives do not appear to be aware of the risks. If they are, they don't mention them in their books or on their T.V. documentaries. To be fair, however, I also know of practitioners who are not only aware but capable of dealing effectively with emergency situations.

It is the hypnotherapist's responsibility to ensure that transitions in consciousness will be made smoothly, without psychic shock or injury. Should the hypnotic subject encounter any situation that causes distress, the therapist should be able to get the person out of that situation immediately. In such a situation, a procedure very similar to the techniques of psychic rescue may need to be employed. Not all therapists are capable of doing that but if you want to visit your past lives in a reasonable amount of safety, I would suggest that you be sure that *your* therapist is qualified.

For anyone who is interested in learning more about past life regression I can highly recommend the books by Dick Sutphen, beginning with *You were Born Again to Be Together, Past Lives, Future Loves* and *Unseen Influences.* Dick Sutphen is a hypnotherapist: he and his wife Trenna also happen to be a highly accomplished pair of spiritual workers. I admire their work and I would love to meet them personally... pity they don't live in Australia!

I have a story of my own which should illustrate the

need for care with such procedures as Astral Travel and Hypnotic Regression. It's quite a long story and some of my readers might even find it a little hard to believe; the response from the critics received by actress Shirley MacLaine when she wrote about her past lives is enough to tell me that. My story also involves a past life, you see. If you prefer to think of it as fantasy, read it as fantasy, I don't mind. Just remember that myths, legends and parables all have their foundations in truth. For me, the story is true. It is *my* life.

This story tells of a chain of events, triggered by a trauma which took place at the end of a former lifetime, events which were carried through into the life I am living now. I'll tell the story piece by piece, as it was revealed to me.

Although I didn't know it at the time, I was given the first thread of the story in a remark made by my favourite 'gypsy lady', Mary Pound, years ago when I was only just beginning to explore my own spirituality. She was clairvoyant, clairaudient, a trance medium and a host of other things apart from being one of my first teachers. She spoke of seeing one of my spirit companions, an Irishman who brandished his shillelagh (an Irish cudgel, to the uninitiated!) and told Mary: 'This lass is my little darlin' and anyone who tries harmin' her will be facin' me first!' At the time, I didn't know enough to ponder the significance of this event. I would probably have been equally pleased to be told that my companion was an old Buddhist monk or a Red Indian. I was simply fascinated with the whole psychic process and wished that I could see as clearly as Mary.

The next thread, apparently unconnected, emerged when I blithely climbed to the top of a stepladder at work one day and found myself paralysed with terror. My head swam, I felt a dizzy, falling sensation and even as I clutched at the ladder, it seemed to sway. I thought I was about to faint and wanted to climb down but I couldn't. I was terrified that if I moved, I would fall.

'It's alright, I've got you. I won't let you fall,' said a voice in my ear. A pair of strong hands grasped me by the arms and, in the care of a big, husky (and rather good-looking) young wardsman, I somehow managed a shaky descent, to be confronted by an exasperated ward sister.

'Nurse, really! If you suffer from vertigo, why on Earth did you volunteer to put those Christmas decorations up?'

I shook my head, partly in denial and partly in an attempt to clear the buzzing in my ears. 'I've never suffered from vertigo.'

'Well, you do now,' she replied in a more sympathetic tone. 'Go take a few deep breaths and get yourself a glass of water. And stay off ladders!'

In childhood I wore jeans and pigtails from the age of about eight because my mother had despaired of ever turning me into a little Dresden lady. I was much more interested in exploring the bush on my own or playing cowboys and indians with my cousins, most of whom were boys. I wasn't a great aim with a slingshot but I could climb fences and trees as nimbly as any boy. I used to scramble up onto the roof of our house when I wanted to be alone with the sky. As a teenager, I tramped over clifftops and waterfalls, so fascinated by the beauty around me that I didn't feel concerned about falling, although I had sense enough to watch where I put my feet. Suddenly, at the age of twenty-nine, I became so terrified of falling that I could not even climb onto a kitchen chair without feeling dizzy. There seemed to be no explanation for it, so I filed it under 'Unsolved Mysteries' and gave up climbing.

Shortly after Roland and I got together, I was visited through trance by the spirit of a persistent Irishman who vowed that I was his long-lost and beloved wife, Eileen. I was disconcerted, alarmed and not impressed! Deciding that my visitor must be a low-level entity trying to cause trouble, I chased him away. When Roland came out of trance and I told him about the incident, he thought it was quite hilarious... much to my disgust.

'I'm sorry, Dawn,' he hiccupped, trying unsuccessfully to conceal his chortles of mirth. 'But the idea of you being pursued by a love-sick spook really appeals to my sense of humour.'

'Yeah? Well, this spook doesn't think he's my lover...

he thinks he's my *husband!* What if he decides to claim his marital rights? Thought about *that?*'

'Kink-*ee*!' crowed Roland. I hit him over the head with my pillow.

'You're impossible!'

A few more years passed and we were working with David and some other spirit beings who were demonstrating the art of spiritual healing. One of these was a character with an Irish accent who identified through the accepted channel by saying 'You know me as David'. After working with him for some time and growing to like him, I asked for his name.

'My name doesn't matter but you can call me Corrigan,' he said. 'As a name, it's as good as another.'

Corrigan rapidly became one of my favourites. He was deft and efficient with his work, yet he always had time for a few friendly scraps of conversation. I always felt a lift during trance sessions when I heard his distinctive greeting. 'Well now, me little darlin', you'll be knowin' me as David but you can call me Corrigan.' (I'll record most of Corrigan's conversations with me in normal speech... I doubt if my writing skills could be equal to the challenge of faithfully reproducing his brogue!)

One night, I was given a very special sitting. It commenced with a visit from David, who told me: 'There is one who wishes to speak with you. I have come to tell you that what is to transpire this night has my blessing.' The latter sentence was a departure from our usual procedure because David had previously only ever remarked that someone wished to speak to me before ushering in the visitor. The fact that he took the extra measure of telling me that my next visitor's purpose had his approval told me that the matter must be of some importance. I was intrigued and had to stifle the stirrings of impatient curiosity as I waited for the exchange of personalities to be completed.

'Well now, my little darlin'.' The beloved voice held a slight texture of hesitance. 'You'll be knowing me as David... '

'*Corrigan!*' I breathed. 'You?'

'Aye darlin', 'tis meself,' he replied gently.

'I don't understand. Why did David need to introduce you as he did?'

'Me darlin', I'm visiting you for a different purpose this time. I've felt a warmth and a friendship coming from you and I wanted to tell you something about myself so that you can know me better and we could grow closer. Would you object?'

'Of *course* not.' I smiled.

'I've a mind to be telling you the story of how I came to be here, working with you.'

'Oh, Corrigan, please do. I *love* stories!'

'Do you now, me darlin'? Well, this is a real life story and it has its tragedy and heartbreak, but it's mostly a story of love.'

Romance! I was hooked. 'Please tell me.'

'It was in Ireland,' he began as I settled back comfortably into my beanbag. 'I had a beautiful wife, me darlin', she was the joy of my heart. I first saw her when she was still only a child, but I knew when I saw her that she was my twinsoul. I watched over her and I waited. When we married, she was fifteen and I was twenty-seven.'

'Wasn't she a bit young to be married?'

'This was five hundred years ago in your time, me darlin'. It was the custom then. We had a glorious life together for fifteen years, then I had to go away and leave her. By the time I returned, she wasn't there.' His voice trailed off.

'What happened to her?' I prompted.

'She thought I wasn't coming back,' he told me sadly. 'She died and I lost her. I've been looking for her ever since.'

'And never found her?'

'There's a problem, me darlin'. You see, she was injured badly and her memory has been affected. She doesn't know who she is and she doesn't remember me.'

I heard the ache of yearning in his voice and my heart was touched. 'Is there any way I could help you, Corrigan?' I asked. He smiled and his eyes were full of love, sadness and an emotion I could not quite identify.

'Believe me, darlin', you help me just by listening,' he said. 'Just by letting me sit with you like this, you are helping me more than you know.'

'There is something I don't understand, Corrigan,' I remarked 'If you were so happy with your wife, why did you walk out on her? Did you have to go to war or something?'

'I'd never have deserted her.'

'But you said that you left her . . . '

'Ah, me darlin', but you don't understand. It was myself who died first.'

I was silent as he continued.

'We lived in a big white house at the top of the cliffs. She came out of the house and found my body. The grief was too much for her and she walked off the cliff.'

'She committed *suicide*?'

'No. She didn't do it intentionally. She didn't even see the cliff; she just kept walking... blind. We were twinsouls. The life in Ireland was to be our last on the cycle of earthly reincarnation. When we left that life, it was intended that we would progress together into the spiritual spheres but, when I went back for her, I was too late. She'd gone. There was only an empty, broken shell at the foot of the cliff.'

'And she is still lost?'

'She was found, but she had suffered serious psychic injuries. Her vibrations were no longer capable of carrying her into the next sphere. She is healing, but she is not yet fully healed.'

'But surely, Corrigan, if you know all this, you must know where she is. Why can't you just go to her and tell her who you are?'

'I have tried. I was too eager and it was too soon. She wasn't ready. I frightened her . . . she didn't recognise me.'

'Can't you try again? Couldn't David help you? Where is she?'

'The Man *is* helping. Because of the damage to her vibrations, it was necessary for her to reincarnate. She is now in your world.'

'Do I know her? Could I help you to reach her?'

'You already have.'

'So I *do* know her. Who is she?'

He studied me thoughtfully for a while. When he spoke in answer, the hesitancy had returned to his voice. 'Her name, when I knew her, was Eileen.'

Eileen! My memory flashed back to the 'lovesick spook' I had chased away years ago. He had told me that I was his long-lost wife and he had called me Eileen. He had also told me his name and it wasn't Corrigan. 'David-Michael O'Shea!' I declared.

He drew a deep breath and nodded. *Bullseye!*

'You are telling me, this time with David's blessing, that *I* am Eileen!'

'Your name is Dawn, me darlin',' he answered me softly. 'But when I knew you as you were in Ireland, your name was Eileen. And you were my wife.'

'When you approached me before, I thought you were a dark entity.'

'You weren't ready, me darlin'. I frightened you. I'd made myself known to you before, but you didn't remember.'

'When did you do that?'

'When I spoke with your friend Mary.'

'That was you?'

'Me darlin',' he smiled. 'Who else would it have been?'

'If I had only understood, I would never have chased you away,' I babbled. 'I can imagine how that would have hurt you. Oh, Corr... David-Michael, I'm sorry. I didn't KNOW!'

'How could you be expected to know? Don't let it bother you, me darlin', you're not chasing me away now.'

'You probably wouldn't go, even if I tried,' I managed a shaky grin.

'Me darlin', I'll not be leaving you again.' His voice was full of bitter-sweet emotion. 'When I left you alone last time, you fell... and you were injured badly. I'll not be letting it happen to you again. I will not intrude on your privacy but I'll be with you all the time. This time when you pass over, I *won't* let you fall.'

Tears sprang to my eyes and I felt myself aching for something just out of my reach... something I had lost and forgotten long ago. Was it my own emotions that I felt, I wondered, or was I feeling for David-Michael? At that point, my transistors started going into overload. 'David-Michael, I'm sure you will understand why I need to think about this and maybe talk with David about it. Not that I disbelieve you, I just need time to get my awareness sorted out.'

'I understand, me darlin'. Take as long as you need. I'll ask only one favour . . . if I may?'

'Name it.'

'May I come and talk with you again, like this?'

'Of *course* . . . me darlin',' I smiled.

Apart from the fact that David had validated David-Michael's story in advance, there was other evidence for such past-life events in my present energy pattern. Eileen had fallen to her death at around age thirty. I had developed a terror of falling at age twenty-nine. The story given to me by David-Michael offered an explanation for the sudden onset and the timing of that phobia.

'Why can't I remember?' I asked David, as soon as I could get him to come and talk with me.

'There is danger for you in the memory,' he replied. 'You have not yet been completely healed and your injuries were much more serious than you know. If you remember and your mind locks into the memory . . . What you think, *is*. It may not be possible for you to be rescued a second time. When there is no longer a danger, you will remember. Until then, your memory has been blocked and precautions have been taken to ensure that you do not spontaneously regress to that life.'

'Precautions? What precautions?'

'I will answer you this way: Several times you have co-operated with competent individuals who have attempted to place you under hypnosis. All such attempts have proven unsuccessful. Do you wonder why?'

'I always assumed that I just don't make a good hypnotic subject.'

'The hypnotic state places you at risk of spontaneous regression, therefore you cannot be hypnotised. That has been set into your energy pattern.'

At first, I found it difficult to understand why such meticulous precautions should be necessary. Apart from the fact that it might hurt momentarily at the physical level, what could be so traumatic about falling off a cliff, especially if you didn't see it coming? There had to be something else, another kind of trauma, something more frightening than mere physical death.

In the process of applying some psychic reasoning, I realised that in the emotional state in which I, as Eileen, had walked off that cliff, I would have left my body at a low frequency of vibration. So *that* was it! I must have become earthbound and suffered some psychic injuries in the process.

Half-curious, half-fearful, I kept pondering the mystery in my mind. Then gradually, as time passed, the memories began. At first I was only aware of fleeting dark images in the depths of my mind, like fragments of a jigsaw puzzle. The first memory was of pain. All-encompassing pain, violation and torment. Shadowy, distorted figures with leering, bestial faces, howling with sadistic glee as they applied more torture. Screaming in my mind: 'Let me die and be out of this!' Then the sickening realisation that I *cannot* die... I have already left my body. Then... nothing. The memory was dim and far away, like an old black and white movie projected onto a distant screen. I knew these things had happened to me but I felt detached from them.

Next, I remembered a recurring nightmare from childhood. Running in panic in the darkness, pursued by a pack of howling, wolf-like creatures. Slipping and falling, trying desperately to reach a house just ahead with lights in the windows through which I could see my family, all unaware of my peril. Trying to call for help but being unable to utter a sound. Then the creatures would catch me and I'd wake screaming, with Mum in her dressing-gown holding me close, assuring me that I was safe and it had all been a bad dream.

I saw, I understood and I stopped probing. It was not the fall from the cliff that had caused the trauma, but the events which followed, when, in a state of distress and confusion, I had stumbled into the clutches of a pack of predators. I understood the reason for the intricate precautions for my protection and David-Michael's fervent determination never to let me wander off alone again.

Knowing what had taken place in my forgotten past explained my fear of falling but did not cure it. Even though I could understand where the fear had originated, I continued to feel dizzy and terrified of heights. In late

1984 when we went to Melbourne to work on the television documentary, I was less than delighted to learn that there was a sequence scheduled for shooting at Hanging Rock where, according to legend, a group of teenage schoolgirls vanished without trace early this century. Ian Gordon and his colleagues had been told by the Higher Ones that the place is a power centre and that we were to go there and meditate, with a camera crew to film anything interesting that might occur.

Hanging Rock is a sizeable geological upthrust in the middle of a surrounding plain; I don't know how high it is but in places there is a sheer drop to the plain below . . . and it's a long way down. I planned to keep my fingers crossed and hope that the guides would help me not to make too great a fool of myself. I was quite relieved to learn that Sue Gordon also shared my fear of heights and we promised to give each other emotional support on the day.

Shooting was set for the Sunday but, on the day before, Ian advised us that the schedule had been changed. Shooting would now be on Tuesday, giving us Sunday free to relax. It was a strange day for me: I felt disturbed, uneasy and restless. Several times during the day I found myself crying for no reason.

'Perhaps you're overtired,' suggested Roland.

'I'm not so sure about that,' countered Ian. 'I don't know why I decided to cancel the shooting for today, except that I felt it would not have been right. Perhaps Dawn's feelings have some connection. Let's try a meditation this evening. Perhaps the guides can tell us something.'

At the commencement of the meditation sitting, it was decided to effect a transfer and a blending of vibrations through the use of psychometry. Sue Gordon handed Roland her engagement ring while I gave her mine. In this way, the blending of energies between both couples was assisted. Both Sue and Roland are trance mediums and they agreed between themselves that Roland should 'tune in' first. He held the ring cupped in one hand as he closed his eyes and waited for impressions.

'I feel as though I'm lifting out of my body,' he told us. 'I seem to be moving with some speed, covering a lot of distance rapidly. Now I'm passing over a city and I think it might be London. At any rate, it's somewhere in England. There are a lot of men with pinstriped suits and rolled umbrellas, it *has* to be England. I'm over water again... now there's more land. You're not going to believe where I am...

'I'm following a pathway up a hill. There are hedges of some kind on each side... it's a sort of roadway. I can see a woman bending down, doing something with the soil... I can't see what she's doing, she has her back to me.'

'Can you get a time period? What sort of clothing is the woman wearing?'

'Nondescript. Something like a scarf or a shawl over her head. Off-white dress, indeterminate style. I'm following the path further. The hedge is opening out and there's a house, quite large, right on the top of the hill. I'm getting closer to it. I'm not far from the sea, I can smell the salt air and feel the sunshine. I feel drawn to go around the side of the house. I can hear voices coming from the back, raised in argument... NO!!'

With a hoarse cry, Roland flung Sue's engagement ring across the room. 'I can't do it!' he was almost sobbing. 'I know where that place is and what I will find. It's too REAL... I can't! I can't go any closer.'

I should have felt concern for him but instead I felt strangely detached. I knew that I could make a reasonably accurate guess as to where he had been, and when, but somehow the knowledge didn't seem to touch me. It was Sue who offered the comforting words. 'Okay Roland, just relax and let it go. I'll see if I can get something more.'

She lowered her head, closed her eyes and concentrated.

'I'm seeing a woman,' she began. 'I don't know who she is, she isn't offering a name but there is a lovely aura around her. She has dark hair, she looks to be perhaps thirty years of age. She's wearing what seems to be a white lace dress and there's something round and white on her head... I can't quite make it out.'

'A pillbox hat?' I suggested.

Sue nodded. 'That's it precisely.' Roland's eyes met mine. Sue had never seen a photograph of Diana,

Roland's deceased first wife, but she was describing her perfectly, dressed as she had been for her wedding.

'Whoever this woman is,' continued Sue, 'She is holding her hands together under one cheek, as though miming sleep. She is saying "This must be put to rest." I don't know what she means... hang on, it's changing. Roland, I'm seeing a house. I think it may be the one you described, the surrounding scenery fits your description. I can hear the voices too but they don't seem to be arguing, it's more like raucous laughter. I'll see if I can get closer.'

'Be careful Sue,' begged Roland.

'It's alright, I'm going around the side. There's a barrier... like a wall of blackness. I can hear the voices coming from behind it but I can't find a way through. Can you all try to help? That's it, there's a tunnel of blue light opening ahead, I'm going through. That wasn't so hard after all... I've reached the corner. A step or two more should tell us... Oh my GOD! Oh no, that can't be happening! They can't... Ian, they can't... you can't DO those kinds of things to people!'

There are no words to describe the sick horror on Sue's face. She was sobbing and obviously terribly distressed, shaking her head from side to side, repeating over and over: 'They can't be *doing* this... it's inhuman. They can't... they can't... '

Alarmed for his wife, Ian intervened. 'What is it, Sue?'

'There are six or seven of the most hideous... THINGS I've ever seen. They've got a woman and... oh Ian, you should see what they're doing to her. You can't DO that to people.'

'What is happening?'

'They've got this woman and... they're doing indescribable things to her... they're trying to turn her into one of them. Oh God, Ian it's already happening... she has the head of a *goat*!'

'Leave it, Sue,' urged Ian. 'Get out.'

'I can't just leave her!' protested Sue. 'If I can get her into my circle of light, she'll be safe. Oh no, it's too late! As soon as the light touches her, she screams... she's writhing with pain!' Sue's extreme distress was palpable and Ian became alarmed.

'Sue, don't risk it. Give a blessing and get out.'

'I can't leave her like that!'

'Sue, get out!' Now it was Roland who spoke.

'I can't stand to leave her in such pain!' cried Sue.

Without quite knowing why, I felt that unless I spoke, Sue would remain focussed into the scene, too overwhelmed with distress to leave the suffering victim behind. 'It's an illusion, Sue, none of it is real. Let it go!' I almost barked. She nodded.

'Alright, but I'll give a blessing first.' She crossed herself, giving a Latin benediction aloud. Then she cried out. 'Ian, they're *burning*! All of them... there's sheets of flame everywhere. Even the woman is being burned. I can't stand the screaming!'

'Get OUT, Sue!' Ian was close to shouting in his concern for his wife.

'Alright,' her voice seemed resigned. 'I can't do any more to help. I'm coming back now.'

'Whew!' remarked Sue after she returned to normal consciousness. 'Does anyone know what to make out of all that?'

'I think so.' I told Sue the story of my life in Ireland, the events related to me by David-Michael, my fragmented recollections and the effects in my present life.

'I'm sure Dawn is right,' added Roland. 'Remember me saying that you wouldn't believe where I was? I meant that for you, Dawn. I had an awareness that I was in Ireland, five hundred years ago. The feeling was so strong that it was as though I was really there and the Roland Hill of today was five hundred years away, in the future. It was so *real*... I could even smell the sea air. I knew that when I got to the back of the house I would see my own body lying on the ground... and I would have to watch Dawn walk off the cliff to her death. It was too real, too immediate. I couldn't face it.'

'Well, I'm grateful to you both for your efforts on my behalf,' I remarked. 'I wish I could say that I feel as though something has changed but I don't. I feel just the same as always and I can't really understand why either of you had to be put through all that.'

'Perhaps it will take time for the effects to become noticeable,' suggested Ian. 'The trauma was very deep-rooted and the changes may be quite subtle. Why not wait and see?'

It was not until several days after we had returned home to Queensland that I was struck by a sudden realisation. On the Tuesday during filming at Hanging Rock, I had scrambled about without once feeling the slightest hint of vertigo, even when I found myself performing a psychic rescue among the pinnacles, only a few metres away from a steep drop. It hadn't even occurred to me to notice the sensation of height. I didn't understand it and I certainly could not have explained it but I was there and it happened.

'Aye darlin', it did my heart good to see you scampering through the rocks with not a sign of fear,' exulted David-Michael on his next visit. 'You're healing fast and it's a joy for me to watch you.'

'Yes, but I don't understand. How was it done? I can understand how the phobia could be healed if *I* had returned . . . to face the situation myself and come to terms with it, but what good does it do if someone else goes back into it? How does that heal me?'

'If you had been the one to return, me darlin', you would not have "come to terms" with it. You would have *identified* with the victim, knowing that it was yourself. Mentally you would have put yourself back into that situation. It isn't easy to explain in terms you can understand but that fragment of your personality had been damaged beyond repair. Understand, me darlin', we're not talking of a woman who lived five hundred years ago: outside of the physical, there is no time. The woman who suffered that torment is not a figure on one of your movie screens, she was a facet of yourself, a fragment . . . a part of you that was still here, inside you. Can you understand?'

'I think so,' I replied, somewhat hesitantly.

'Think of one of the organs inside your body . . . your gallbladder or your appendix. You've had both those organs surgically removed . . . why?'

'They were diseased.'

'Malfunctioning beyond repair, causing pain and endangering other areas of your body. So they were removed by a surgeon. If you had badly injured your leg and developed gangrene, what would the surgeon do?'

'Cut the leg off.'

'Surgical removal. You understand at the physical level, now apply that principle to the burning away of that damaged facet of your personality.'

'Do you mean that Eileen has been burned away, that she no longer exists?' David-Michael shook his head sadly. 'The woman who was seen by your friend, in the clutches of those beasts . . . that was no longer Eileen.'

I cupped my chin in my hands, performing mental gymnastics in an effort to comprehend fully. 'So I've had something like a psychic amputation,' I remarked. 'I can understand it in principle but having a whole chunk of my personality burned away, won't that leave me with the psychic equivalent of a limp? Does this mean I'm now incomplete?'

'Not at all, me darlin',' David-Michael sounded amused. 'Discard your physical limitations. Think of the starfish . . . if it loses one leg, it grows another.'

'I have to grow another personality to fill the space?'

'You've already done it, me darlin'. That is why you needed to enter another physical life.'

Now, dear reader, I won't blame you in the slightest if you find that story a little difficult to digest. You should try coming to terms with it from where I'm sitting! Whether or not you believe it, however, the point is that it is psychically possible. Furthermore, if it is true with relation to me, it is more than likely to be true of some other people as well. I'm not unique. How do you know whether or not you have a similar trauma lurking in your past? Think of the torments suffered just a few hundred years ago by 'witches' under the Inquisition . . . how many souls living in this world today have those memories buried deep in their subconscious minds?

Dick and Trenna Sutphen have encountered situations in which a client becomes deeply distressed and subconsciously blocks the regression process. Less enlightened therapists might immediately start seeking for ways to get the patient around the emotional blockage but the Sutphens have a different method. Trenna is a conscious medium and after forming an energy link with the patient, it is Trenna who travels into that person's past, to identify the situation that is causing the blockage. Once the cause is known, the therapists can devise an effective way of removing the problem. This may have to be dealt with at a psychic level.

This manner of approach has a number of remarkable similarities with the operation jointly performed by Sue Gordon and Roland, not to mention quite a few unseen helpers. I can testify to the effectiveness and the positive benefits of such treatment and I certainly won't advise against past life therapy, PROVIDING that it is performed by people who understand what they are doing at the psychic levels.

What might have happened to me if I had been regressed to that lifetime before the damaged fragment of my personality had been removed? Would a hypnotherapist have been able to bring me out of it, when even my spiritual protectors doubted their chances of achieving it a second time? In returning to that past life of mine, weren't Roland and Sue traversing the Astral plane? If I had stepped out of my body to go wandering without protection and been drawn into that space at the Astral or Etheric level, what would have happened? These are questions you need to think about if you are considering Past Life Regression . . . or even Astral Travel.

To sum up, my advice is that, before you embark on some course of psychic exploration or activity which you have not previously tried, take some time to make yourself familiar with the methods to be used. Weigh those methods against the principles of energy already known to you. Try to analyse the type of energy that would be generated by the procedure. Will it come from the Intuitive level, the Lower Mental or the Etheric? What kind of energies will it attract? Does it lead to an invasion of someone else's personal space or free will? Think carefully.

Occasionally, a friend who is in the process of exploring Out-of-Body projection might say to me 'I'll come and visit you when I get into the Astral.' My reply often comes as a surprise to them.

'You are assuming that you can approach me as freely on the Astral level as you can in the physical,' I inform them. 'If you try it, you are likely to find yourself being confronted by my guardians.'

'But I'm your friend, surely they'd let me pass.'

'Perhaps, if they think your reason is good enough, otherwise you would be turned away.'

'I only want to see if I can actually do it.'

'Sorry. Curiosity isn't a good enough reason.'

To experiment with levels of highly potent energy for the sake of curiosity is not a wise course of action. If you are merely curious, you don't understand what you're dealing with. By all means, have yourself regressed if you think it will help you to improve the quality of your life. Explore the Astral if you think you can learn something worthwhile from the experience, but don't just do it for the sake of idle curiosity. No amount of curiosity could justify the suffering you might have to bear if you make a mistake. It's your life and well-being: don't place it at risk.

CHAPTER FOURTEEN

Creating Your Own Reality, With Your Mind

The spiritual spheres are traversed through the mind. Mental energy is the fabric of life and, with your thoughts, you create your own reality. If those statements are valid, it would be logical for us to expect that we can put them into application to produce physically tangible results. To put it bluntly, we should in theory be capable of changing our own physical reality, that is, the world in which we live.

Did I hear someone say: 'If that is the case, why haven't you altered the world to your own specifications?' A question like that betrays a certain lack of comprehension. There are worlds and there are worlds. For instance, there is your world, there is the world of a starving child in Ethiopia, the world of a murderous urban guerrilla, the world of a prima ballerina and the world of a housewife who happens to write books and talks to spooks as naturally as she talks to physical people. Every living person has an individual view of reality.

Can you possibly imagine what it is actually like to be living in any of those other worlds? Can you understand, in every hate-filled detail, just how it feels to be so full of rage that you just want to destroy and keep on destroying, even if your victims are the innocent and the helpless? Can you get inside the mind of the starving infant or dance in the shoes of the ballerina? Are you capable of imagining any other world but the one you see and feel around yourself? A little perhaps, but only in so far as that other world merges with yours.

If my world is changed, it does not automatically imply that yours will be changed as well. Shall I offer proof? I'd better, or I'm likely to have the sceptics snapping at my heels until I get the next book written. Can I show evidence that my world has been changed through a conscious co-operation with the laws of spiritual energy?

When I wrote *Reaching for the Other Side,* I was a nondescript working-class housewife, living in one of the unfashionable areas of Sydney, with a limited circle of friends. I knew hardly any people who even came close to understanding my outlook on life, and, with those who didn't, I felt ill at ease, threatened and uncomfortable. Roland had a safe job with the Public Service as Audio and Electronics Administrator at the Sydney Opera House on a moderate salary. We had the same problems and worries as any other working-class couple: a mortgage, bills to be paid, never quite enough money and all the other ratrace hassles. Like everyone else, we dreamed of being free of the treadmill and living the kind of lifestyle that we really wanted, instead of the one that circumstances forced us to lead.

Roland had dreamed for years of living in the sunshine and relaxation of Queensland. I didn't really mind where we went, so long as it was out of the big-city smog and hassles. We bought occasional lottery tickets or had a flutter on Lotto and whiled away some pleasant hours discussing what we would do with all the money if we ever won it but, deep down, we knew that we would remain where we were until Roland could retire. I didn't expect things to change very much after the book was published because I knew perfectly well that rich authors are the exception, not the norm.

One evening, we found ourselves entertaining an exotic visitor, a spirit Master from a level equivalent to that of David. To fill in some background details, I had previously been contacted through the mail by a man who told me that he was a trance medium with apparently high-level guides but without a reliable control and unable to question the spirits himself in full trance. He asked, therefore, if I would be kind enough to test the guides for him, so that he would know whether or not to trust them. Something in the vibrations associated with his letter told me that this man, although technically telling the truth, was not quite what he seemed; however, I could detect nothing deceptive or hostile in those vibrations. I agreed to do what he asked.

I won't refer to this person by name because I know he wouldn't like it; instead I'll call him The Wandering Wizard because I know that will amuse him. I will also give the guide a nom-de-plume; we'll call him Rameses. Rameses was charming, polite, informative and witty. In addition, he passed all my tests effortlessly and then told me how I could improve on them, so I liked him. Roland was more than intrigued: it was his first opportunity to observe a trance medium of equal calibre to himself in action. Now he could see the process from a perspective that had not been available to him before. He was fascinated with Rameses and I found it entertaining to sit back and listen to the exchange between them. In his own way, Roland was also testing, asking what to him represented almost unanswerable questions, to see how Rameses would respond.

'Dawn and I have often spoken of leaving Sydney and going to live in Queensland. Both Dawn and I would like to give her spiritual work the time and attention it deserves; that means a 24-hour a day commitment for both of us. Tell me how we could achieve this.'

'Just go,' said Rameses.

'Just like that? With a mortgage that has me in debt up to my eyebrows and a family I love, who need me to provide food and shelter?'

'In this spiritual work of which you speak, who is your employer? What do you call him, Lord God?'

Roland couldn't help smiling. 'I suppose that will do.'

'Very well, so you talk to him. Say "Look here, Lord God, I am one of your employees and I am not happy with my working conditions. Change them for me please and I will be able to offer better work in return." Then it will change.'

'Just like that?'

'If you believe it.'

'Ah, the Catch-22,' smirked Roland. 'I have to believe it will happen in order to make it happen. If I don't believe, it won't work.'

'That is so.'

'This "Lord God" character always seems to have a loophole!'

I smiled to myself. 'Trust Roland!' I thought. 'Always

the sceptic.' Roland hasn't said whether he actually got around to talking with the Boss as Rameses suggested but I know that I did and, just to hedge my bets, I had quite a few talks with David as well.

'Create within your mind an image of that which you desire,' he told me. 'Feed it with your thoughts and with your imagination, bring it alive. Examine every tiny detail to be sure that there is nothing within your image that is of harm, either to yourself or others. Examine it carefully, for the energies you radiate will be returned to you in kind. Choose your image carefully. If you focus on winning the lottery so that you can buy your dream, your energies are in competition with the energies radiated by every other person who is dreaming of a lottery win. If what you want is to be living in Queensland with the time to devote to that which is your purpose, create within your mind that situation. See the countryside around you, feel the air. Put yourself within the vision, inwardly live as though you are already there. This is how you make it real.'

In almost every minute of my waking day, I carried my corner of Queensland within me. When I looked out through the kitchen window, I imagined that I was looking at a sunny landscape, green studded with palm trees and colourful tropical foliage. Roland shared in the dream and did his own inner visualising and Darryl thought we had both gone quite mad when we danced around the living room in each other's arms, singing 'We're going to Queensland.'

To make the dream even more real, we decided to take a holiday in Queensland. Two sunny weeks on the proceeds of my very first royalty cheque. We returned to Sydney with fresh Queensland sunshine flowing in our veins. Over the months that were to follow, the sunshine got bogged down at times but the dream never quite faded.

It is said that the Lord God moves in mysterious ways and I'll vouch for that. Sometimes our greatest blessings are delivered under circumstances that can seem almost catastrophic at face value. When Roland was brought home early one day by a workmate, in a state of near collapse, I certainly wasn't aware that I was watching the unfolding of a blessing.

When Roland was two years of age, he tumbled from a first-floor window to land headfirst on a concrete pathway. At first, he wasn't expected to survive, then it was considered likely that he would never come out of the coma. Later, he was expected to be paralysed for life. At around four and a half years of age, he started learning to walk all over again. At the age of thirteen, he underwent neurosurgery to remove the bone fragments from his brain and place a surgical plate over the hole in his skull. He was given only a fifty percent chance of surviving the operation. When he reached the age of thirty-one, Roland began to suffer epileptic fits. Brain scans were performed but there seemed to be no physical cause for his condition. The specialist assured us that the onset of epilepsy had absolutely no connection with the brain injury. Roland was put on a regime of Dilantin capsules and his condition was controlled for the next six years. Then he started to experience breakthrough seizures and it was after suffering a fit at work that he was brought home by his colleague.

His health seemed to deteriorate quite alarmingly and, before long, he was suffering fits almost daily. In that condition, he was unable to work. He was given sick leave and when that ran out, Sickness Benefits were organised while the medical profession set about isolating the cause of the problem.

Roland was fed a mixture of drugs that had him walking around in limbo, like a zombie, but did nothing to control the frequency of his seizures. C.A.T. scans were performed and the resulting pictures showed a large darkened area at the centre of the brain, roughly equivalent in size to a large golf ball.

'There's your problem,' said the neurologist. 'That dark area is a cyst in the centre of your brain.'

'Can it be removed by neurosurgery?' I asked, clutching Roland's hand tightly. The doctor shook his head.

'This cyst has been caused by scarring and puckering of the brain tissue. One of the ventricles which carry the cerebro-spinal fluid has been pulled out of shape and to compensate, it has filled with fluid. That's why it is known as a compensatory cyst. It could be drained but it would only fill again and the operation would cause further scarring. In any case, it isn't malignant, only troublesome.'

Roland was then subjected to an exhaustive battery of psychological tests known as Psychometrics. The specialist explained that the process was designed to isolate the particular areas of the brain that were most damaged and to determine the extent of the damage. By this time, Roland was having at least one or two fits each day and, apart from performing the most simple functions for himself, was forced to rely on me to lead him around by the hand. Inside, however, his mind was aware and as keen as it had ever been, only his brain was unable to transmit his messages clearly. He felt shamed, humiliated and worse than useless. Until that time, it had always been Roland who had guided and supported me: now the tables had been turned and he was harassed by the fear that the burden would be too much for me.

'What burden?' I crooned as I cuddled him close. 'You ain't heavy, you're my soulmate. Besides, you are giving me a priceless opportunity to repay you for all the care and attention you've lavished on me over the years. We're partners, Pardner. We'll get through this and you will get better.'

'I might *never* get better, Dawn. I might get worse!'

'No, you won't. I won't let it happen.'

'Please don't joke about it.'

'Who's joking? I'm serious. You *will* get better, I know it.'

'How can you possibly know such a thing?'

'I just do.'

The psychometric testing revealed, among other things, that Roland's ability to cope with situations of stress had been steadily decreasing and had now reached a stage where situations of physical, emotional or mental stress could trigger off a fit, or even a whole series of them. He was now having several fits every day and had begun having temporal lobe seizures in conjunction with the epileptic fits. There could be no question of him ever returning to the workforce; he had to apply for an Invalid

Pension. Even though he had not worked for some months, his seizures were worsening and it was clear to me that if he were to have any quality of life, or even survival, he needed to be removed from the stress of big-city living.

'But the mortgage!' he cried. 'We'll be destitute. How will I be able to provide for you and Darryl?'

'It won't be as bad as you think. I've been doing some homework. We can sell the house and even after we pay off the bank loan, we will have a comfortable nest-egg; not a lot but enough to get us established in Queensland. We have to live on the pension wherever we are so it might as well be in the kind of surroundings we both want. Besides, if we get out of Sydney, the cost of living will drop.'

'But it will take months to sell the house. How do we pay our bills in the meantime?'

'I've already contacted the necessary people. All debts will be paid out of sale of the house. They're prepared to wait.'

'I wouldn't know where to start organising it all. I can't even think straight.'

'We can start with a paintbrush. This house could do with some freshening up.'

It took us a couple of months to get the house painted and ready for inspection, then a few weeks more to sell it. Roland had begun to have the breakthrough seizures in late January, 1983. By early in June of the same year, we were living in Queensland. Our funds were sufficient to buy us two hectares in the bush in south-east Queensland and to build a large aluminium shed on it, with a smaller shed nearby to serve as Darryl's 'bedroom'. There was no power, no plumbing and no on-site water. We collected rainwater in an old oil drum and used it for washing. Water for drinking and cooking was carried in twenty-five litre containers from public facilities in the nearest small town and our cooking was done on a second or third-hand wood stove. In the year that we lived there, Roland cleared the ground of stones and dead wood, all by hand. A friend let us have an elderly ride-on lawn-mower on indefinite loan and Roland kept the grass looking like parkland.

At sunrise and at dusk, small shy kangaroos crept from the shelter of the surrounding bush to nibble at the fresh young shoots of grass just a few yards away from our shed window. If we kept still and didn't startle them, we could watch them feeding. Across to the other side of the property was a big old ironbark that I christened my Thinking Tree because I used to sit under it to meditate or to sort out some problem. At around four in the afternoons, the Thinking Tree would come alive with a mass of cheerful pink and grey galahs who fluttered to the ground and waddled around, pecking up the sunflower seeds that I had sprinkled around for them.

There was also a family of magpies, parents and two fledgelings. The parents never quite learned to trust us completely but our handouts of food gained us the friendship of the youngsters. They liked scraps of bread but they were hooked on cheese. They'd walk right into the shed, strut up to the small gas refrigerator and cock their heads to stare at us until we responded by getting some cheese out for them and, after eating that delicacy, they would stroll nonchalantly around our floor, poking inquisitive beaks into dark corners and pecking up crumbs. Roland took several photographs of one of them eating out of my hand. We called them both 'Maggie' because we couldn't tell them apart.

We were disappointed when the fledgelings grew older and the parent birds drove them off to find their own territory but we soon discovered the reason. One morning, there was a flutter of wings and a volley of liquid birdsong. We looked out to see the parent birds standing at a safe distance from our door, with a couple of bemused little fledgelings wondering what all the fuss was about. New babies! And the parent birds had trusted us enough to introduce them to us. We felt honoured... and humbled.

Our pioneer existence lasted for a year, during which time the frequency of Roland's fits decreased and he started to look tanned and wirily fit. At the end of that time, we received a notice from the local council, informing us that we were 'illegally camped' on our land and unless we could build a house within a specified length of time (which we could not afford to do), we would have to leave or be evicted.

At the same time, I was invited to give a public lecture and to attend several private meditation groups in Mackay. 'This will give us a chance to look around,' I told Roland. 'We can drive to Mackay and while we're on the road we can do some exploring, find a place to rent in an area that suits us.'

We didn't have to look far! On our first morning in Mackay, I decided to go for a walk and look around. I had taken no more than a dozen steps when I became aware of a feeling that seemed to come up through the soles of my feet, from the footpath. The feeling enfolded me in a comfortable embrace and gently whispered 'Welcome Home.'

I went back to our lodgings to fetch Roland. 'Come and feel it!' I urged. 'It's incredible.'

For the next few days, we explored Mackay. Everywhere we went, there were friends, people we had met in the groups and at the public lecture, who took us to their hearts and made us feel as though we were with family. When we mentioned that we were considering moving to Mackay, there was a chorus of voices saying 'Please do'.

'Don't worry about accommodation,' said Hazel, one of our new-found friends. 'We have a self-contained flat with two bedrooms, attached to our house. You're welcome to use it free of charge until you find a place of your own.'

So we went back South, loaded up everything we could fit onto our trailer and moved to the North. Our friends found us a pleasant little bungalow to rent at a price within our reach and, before we knew it, we were established in what has to be one of the most beautiful places in the world.

We still have no money to speak of but we are living in the warmth of North Queensland, surrounded with friends who love us dearly. Roland and I are together for twenty-four hours just about every day and the lifestyle is easy. Our little house isn't the most luxurious in the world but after twelve months in the bush, running water, electricity and push-button toilets (not to mention washing machines) are luxuries. We still haven't won any lotteries but we are living exactly the kind of life that we wanted to live, back when it was only a dream in our hearts.

How are we doing so far? Would you say my world has changed? Roland still has seizures but the fits are no longer as protracted or as violent as they were before we left Sydney and he no longer has to take a mixture of drugs. He went through some severe culture shock at first and it took him almost two years to adjust fully to the change in his circumstances. It wasn't easy for him to make the transition from breadwinner to what he has become but he made it, with flying colours.

It may seem that moving to Mackay with a stopover in south-east Queensland is a rather circuitous route, but the year spent on our block of land was far from wasted. If we had come directly to Mackay bringing all our big-city hassles with us, we would probably not have found the environment that now surrounds us. For the first twelve months, we needed the isolation in the bush to clear our systems, bring us back to basics and help us to see our priorities clearly. So, now there is one more two hectare block of land on the market but our sojourn there achieved a valuable purpose for us.

The decision to sell up and move to another state on a limited amount of money and a very small income was a big one, as was the decision to buy the block of land... and then to leave it behind and move to Mackay. Such decisions could justifiably be classified as milestones and they are usually made only after a considerable amount of thought and planning. With Roland so ill and incapable of thinking clearly for more than five minutes at a time, the responsibility of making those choices fell to me. Apart from the fact that my birthsign is Libra, which supposedly renders me constitutionally incapable of making firm decisions, the awareness that a wrong decision could be disastrous for us all was paramount in my thoughts.

Normally, I would have avoided any decision-making on matters of such importance and contented myself with supporting Roland to the utmost in whatever course he chose to follow but Roland was sick and the onus rested with me. If anyone had told me in advance that I would be in such a position, I would probably have suffered agonies of indecision, fearful lest the choice I made should be the wrong one, but, when the situation arose, it was as though the path were being laid out before me in such a way that there really weren't any choices to be made: I just *knew* which course was the right one to follow.

Even before the C.A.T. scans revealed the cyst in Roland's brain, I knew that he would not be returning to the workforce and that we would be moving out of Sydney into a totally different lifestyle. While Roland worried about an impoverished future, I had an inner certainty that even in reduced financial circumstances, we were heading for a life that suited us far better than the existence we had been leading up until then. I'm sure that some of our friends thought I was blinding myself to the truth about Roland's condition, when it was obvious to them that he was deteriorating fast and could not last long if the process continued... and it seemed that nothing on Earth could prevent it from doing so. It was impossible for me to explain to them just how and why I knew that there was no reason for me to worry. Roland himself seemed to believe that I was deluding myself with the optimistic belief that his health would improve, but I knew it would, once we got him out of Sydney and into a suitable environment.

I didn't have a struggle to decide what should be done; the awareness of where we were going and what would happen to Roland's health once we got there was already in my mind. There were really no decisions to be made, only a clear pathway laid out before me. All I did was follow the signposts. I knew that we were taking the right course, just as surely as I knew that Roland's health was going to improve. It was as though someone else had gone ahead to blaze the trail for us, so that all we had to do was follow.

How was it possible for me to be so calm and certain when, under normal circumstances, I should have been reduced to a quivering wreck? I can only explain it by saying that I had learned to trust my own inner guidance.

Whether this guidance came through my own intuition or through some telepathic communication from a spirit guide is immaterial. The fact is that it was there and, by trusting it, I managed to negotiate us all safely through the crisis, with the result that we are now living precisely the kind of life we had wished to lead and Roland's health has improved quite remarkably. There is still no question of him ever being able to return to the kind of life we lived before but he is happy and content in our present life. In addition, Roland is now living in accordance with the wishes he specified to Rameses just a few months before ill-health forced us to dramatically alter our lifestyle.

At first, Roland thought of himself as a useless hulk, thrown out onto the scrapheap, a burden to me and just sitting around waiting to die. For quite some time after we moved to Queensland, he was moody, morose and depressed. All his life, he had been conditioned to believe that in order to earn self-respect a man must work, support his family and achieve financial security. The fact that, in the twenty-four years since leaving school, his life had been a treadmill of going to work, bringing his troubles home from the office, eating, sleeping and worrying had no bearing on the matter as far as he was concerned. It was 'the right thing to do' so he did it without question. Knowing that his inability to work any longer was not his fault didn't bring him any comfort. As far as he was concerned, his life was over and there was nothing for him to do but sit and mope.

I knew that it was natural for him to feel this way but I tried to explain that his previous lifestyle was not the only way to live, nor even necessarily the best way and that the change in his life did not have to mean the end of everything worthwhile. He heard my words but they made little effect on his outlook. For the first six months, I fussed over him, coaxed and flirted with him and generally spoiled him rotten. Then, again acting on intuition, I booted him square in the backside and told him to wake up to himself!

'Just because you can't work the way you used to doesn't mean you can spend the rest of your life sitting on your base and feeling sorry for yourself!' I scolded him. 'You've got an opportunity that thousands of other men would give their eye teeth to have; the chance to explore yourself, discover new ways of living, develop talents you've never had time to exercise before and what are you doing with that opportunity? *Wasting* it, because you'd rather wallow in self-pity!

'Over in the corner you have a very expensive 35-millimetre camera that you bought some time ago because you'd love to be involved in photography. For the past few months, that camera has been gathering dust and all you've got to show for it is a shoebox full of *snapshots!*' That remark hit him right in his delicate masculine ego because he had always been insistent on maintaining that he takes photographs: 'snapshots' were taken by inept amateurs with badly focussed department-store cameras. The best way to goad a Taurean into action is to take a jab at his pride and Roland rose to the bait magnificently!

'Alright!' he bellowed, almost snorting and pawing the earth with healthy Taurean rage. 'Being harsh and unsympathetic is one thing; attacking my Art is quite another. Has it occurred to you in all your brilliant speculations that we happen to be living on a pension and even if I did get out and take the bloody photographs, I couldn't afford to have them developed?'

'Roland, my love, for such an intelligent man, there are times when you can be unbelievably thick!' I replied with a cheerful lack of repentance. 'We have a number of friends who have already said they'd love to have you take photographs for them and I'm sure they'd be happy to pay the cost of processing. You'd get the practice you need and they'd have lovely photographs.'

'Not snapshots?' His voice oozed sarcasm.

'No darling,' I smiled sweetly. 'Not snapshots... photographs.'

'Harumph!' I heard him snorting as he headed for the Thinking Tree. 'Snapshots indeed!'

One of the things I have noticed about life is that when we use what is available to us and do the best we can with what we have, the things we need tend to find their own way to us, apparently by coincidence. Roland's photography is an example. Not only were our friends delighted to have his photographs, but in addition to paying for the processing they usually insisted on giving him a few extra dollars as an appreciation. This enabled him to have his own films developed, without putting a strain on our slender budget.

Roland has never been the kind of person who can be content with mediocrity and just taking photographs was not enough to satisfy him. He wanted to master the art of photography and, to do that, he felt a need to work in black and white because it is a more difficult and challenging medium. He sent a couple of black and white films off for processing but was sorely disappointed with the bland grey results. He was frustrated because he didn't know why he had failed to achieve the result he wanted but didn't know how to overcome the problem.

At around this time, I received a letter from a man named Richard Durham, who told me that he and his wife would soon be visiting Queensland and would appreciate a chance to visit me for an hour or so, to discuss the philosophy of my book, which they had greatly enjoyed. It isn't possible for me to make myself available to everyone who asks for such a visit because my time is limited and my workload heavy but, in Richard's case, I had a strong prompting to agree to his request. Never one to ignore my inner promptings, I wrote to tell Richard that he and his wife would be welcome.

I subsequently discovered that Richard had worked for twenty-five years as a professional photographer with A.B.C. News until ill-health had forced him into an early retirement.

'Be prepared to have your brains thoroughly picked!' I warned him, when he rang to confirm the arrangements for his visit. 'Roland is an enthusiastic learner and there's no way he'll pass up a chance to benefit from your experience.'

'Fair exchange,' chuckled Richard. 'I intend to pick your brains on the subject of spiritual development.'

Roland's black and white photographs elicited a sympathetic grimace from Richard. 'Your problem is in the processing,' he explained. 'Good black and white prints are made in the darkroom and, unless you do your own developing, you can't get satisfactory results. Commercial processors use machines that are pre-set for colour and every film is developed to the same formula. Until you have your own darkroom, I'd suggest that you stick to colour photography.'

Roland accepted his limitations with a philosophical shrug. 'Maybe one day I'll have a darkroom,' he remarked. 'Until then I can work on applying the things I'm learning now.'

Shortly after our arrival in Mackay, we were visited by a young couple named Andrew and Chicky. Andy's brother and his wife, who lived near Brisbane, had been our friends almost since our arrival in Queensland and, knowing that both Andy and Chicky had read and enjoyed my book, they contacted Andy to suggest that he and Chicky get in touch with us. We got along famously from our first meeting and they had not been here long when Chicky happened to mention that, until the birth of their daughter, she had been a professional photographer.

Out came the photographs! Roland and Chicky were soon engrossed in a discourse on f-stops, shutter speeds, depth of field and various other photographic technicalities. Andy and I smiled in mutual understanding and went on discussing spiritual philosophy. Several cups of tea later, Chicky innocently dropped a bombshell.

'Roland, could you find a use for an elderly black and white enlarger?'

Roland's mouth dropped open and he stared at Chicky as though she had just offered him the keys to the national treasury. 'You *bet* I could use it!' he stammered when he finally found his voice. 'But would you really feel comfortable about lending it?'

'Not lend . . . give.' Chicky corrected him. 'I have a new one with a colour head and the old one is just sitting in a box under my bed, waiting for a good home.'

'Oh my!' exclaimed Roland. 'My very own black and white enlarger, for free! I don't believe it!'

'I do,' I commented quietly, mentally blowing kisses to the Man Upstairs.

A week later, we paid a visit to Andy and Chicky. Roland returned with the precious enlarger and a cardboard carton containing several boxes of photographic paper, bottles of chemicals, a thirty metre roll of bulk black and white film and an assortment of other items, out of date but still useful for practice. In short, with a couple of inexpensive exceptions, Roland had been given everything he needed to start off his darkroom. In addition, Chicky gave Roland access to her extensive library of technical photographic publications, which he devoured as fast as he could read. I began to notice new words and phrases appearing in his vocabulary, like 'inverse square laws', 'reciprocity effects', 'densitometry' and other equally impressive tongue-twisters.

Our bathroom now leads a double life, with Roland happily puddling around in his trays of smelly chemicals in quest of the elusive 'black blacks and white whites'. He hopes that one day he might achieve professional status and that the combined income from his photography and my writing might make it possible for us to live without the support of the pension. Even if that doesn't happen, Roland has found something infinitely more precious: himself. There is now a way in which he can bring forth his own inner vision. He is exploring greater depths within himself, creating works of beauty and is no longer the wretched hulk sitting on the scrap-heap, just waiting to die.

There is a passage in the New Testament that can easily be applied here. It comes from the book of Matthew, in which Christ is quoted: 'Do not worry about your living — what you are to eat or drink, or about your body, what you are to wear. Is not the life more important than its nourishment and the body than its clothing? Look at the birds of the air, how they neither sow nor reap nor gather into barns, but your heavenly Father feeds them. Are not you more valuable than they? Furthermore, who of you is able through worrying to add one moment to his life's course? And why worry about clothes? Observe carefully how the field lilies grow. They neither toil nor spin, but I tell you that even Solomon in all his splendour was never dressed like one of these. But if God so clothes the grass of the field that exists today and is thrown into the furnace tomorrow, will He not more surely clothe you of little faith? Do not, then, be anxious, saying "What shall we eat?" or "What shall we drink?" or "What are we to wear?" . . . your heavenly Father knows that you need them all. But you, seek first His Kingdom and His righteousness and all these things will be added to you.'

This passage should not be taken to imply that we can all sit around doing nothing but wait for handouts from Heaven; that isn't the message at all. There is a specific instruction: 'seek first His kingdom and His righteousness.' My dictionary defines righteousness as 'conformity of life or conduct to the requirements of the divine or moral law'. In other words, to be righteous means to live in accordance with the laws of the Creator, which are the laws of Nature. As for seeking the Kingdom of God, where would you look? Again, you can find your answer in the teachings of Christ, in Luke 17:21: 'The kingdom of God is *within you.*' The italics are mine.

David has consistently told me that 'The answers you seek are within you'. For me, all of this ties in neatly with the basic principles of spiritual philosophy and the teaching that, if I attune myself to the Divinity within and live in harmony with natural law, the things I need will flow naturally to me. The events related earlier in this chapter constitute only part of the living proof: I could fill an entire book with such examples from my own life alone, not to mention the other people who have told me of similar happenings in their lives. The events in my own life are the living proof to me of the truth in those teachings.

What applies to me can be applied equally well to anyone else. I have encountered a few people who deny their ability to get the same positive results in their own lives on the basis that they don't have my advantages. 'You're different,' they tell me. 'It's easy for you to be spiritual but you don't understand how difficult it is for ordinary people like me.'

If you will pardon my bluntness, that is codswallop! I'm an ordinary human being like anyone else and it is no easier for me to be spiritual than it is for anyone else. I've had moments when I'd like nothing better than to rip, scream, tear and bust but I've learned, through hard experience, that giving way to impulses of that nature only brings me bad Karma and it makes more sense to stop and think, analyse the situation that confronts me in terms of natural energy and apply the principles I have been taught, in order to find an answer.

Sure, I use my spiritual channels for assistance but so can anyone else if they want to learn how. I don't have any special privileges. What would be the point in me telling you that the application of spiritual principles can help to solve the problems of daily human life if I had never had to cope with anything more serious than a broken fingernail? Because I have faced the same kinds of problems, heartaches and sufferings that afflict any other normal human being, I *know* these principles work.

There may be some people who find it difficult to believe that, merely by focussing on an image within the mind, it is possible to cause the events that brought us to where we are now; but the fact remains that when we were back in Sydney dreaming of Queensland, we could see no way in which it could be possible for us to make the move. When we applied the principles suggested by the guides, a way was made open for us. To me, this is applying spiritual understanding to achieve a physical result. In answer to those who might say that having a cyst in the brain is a heavy price to pay for an agreeable lifestyle, I should point out that our spirit friends didn't *cause* the cyst, Roland did that when he fell from the window.

According to the specialists, the cyst has been there ever since Roland's childhood accident and, whether or not we had been involved with matters of the spirit, it would have started causing trouble as he grew older. The only difference is that having an attunement to the spiritual and an avenue of guidance helped us to negotiate the crisis in such a way that our lives were improved, rather than brought to ruin. Certainly, Roland went through a very difficult time for a while but, again, that would have happened anyway. The point to remember is that, as a result of following that inner guidance, we are now in a situation where Roland is happy and fulfilled, his health has improved to the point where the occasional seizures are little more than a passing nuisance and we are happier than we have ever been before.

As his health and mental ability have improved, Roland has taken more and more responsibility from my shoulders, so that we now have an equal partnership. Prior to the onset of his illness, it was Roland who made all the major decisions and, while he was sick, I made them. Now it's a joint effort, with both of us contributing equally. When Roland told Rameses that he would like to be able to give my spiritual work the 24-hour support it needs, he was talking about a dream. Now it is a reality.

'You are a writer,' Roland tells me. 'Writing is a full-time occupation; so is housework and I don't think it's fair that you should have to cope with two full-time jobs when I don't have to manage even one. If you can take over all the organising and decision-making that you had to do when I was helpless, I can become a good housekeeper. I'm in charge of housework from now on. Go and write.'

Not only is Roland a far better housekeeper than I could ever be, he is my partner and helpmate in other ways as well. He intercepts visitors when I don't want to be disturbed, patiently listens to me reading aloud the pages of script I have produced in my day's work and even edits my manuscripts. He's a wizard at repairing household appliances, knows how to fix things when something goes wrong under the hood of my car and cooks the most mouth-watering spaghetti bolognaise I have ever tasted. He also has the time to pursue his own interests and is making great progress with his photography.

So, from the life of a harassed working-class housewife in a rather dingy suburb of Sydney, I have become a full-time writer living a life of freedom in the glorious tropics with a companion who gives me all the support, encouragement and assistance I could ever need. I am surrounded by friends, most of whom share my spiritual outlook and, for the first time since childhood, I feel as though I am truly at home in this world. So what if we don't have two cents to rub together most of the time? It has often been said that money can't buy happiness and I can assure you that I would not change places with Christina Onassis, for all the money in her bank accounts. I'd say my world has changed, wouldn't you?

Perhaps my lifestyle wouldn't suit you. Every one of us is different and whereas our dream was to live in Queensland and devote the bulk of our time to the spiritual work, your dream is probably for something quite different. Even so, the principles of natural law which brought our dream into reality can do it for you too... all you need to do is apply them, and keep applying them. It *can* work for you.

This doesn't mean that you will never again have any problems to solve: Roland and I have our share of those and both of us understand that it is through facing life's challenges and overcoming them that we learn and grow. We've learned through experience that even the most overwhelming problems can be turned into blessings if we apply the principles we have been taught to use and, when we do this, our challenges don't destroy us. Instead, they help us to gain greater maturity and insight. This kind of spirituality doesn't require us to wait for some misty hereafter before we can start feeling its benefits: we are feeling them right here and now.

CHAPTER FIFTEEN

Suicide, Accidental Death and the 'Lost Soul' Syndrome

Ever since I first became involved with the work of psychic rescue, I have been deeply concerned about the misconceptions that prevail in our society regarding the nature and condition of lost souls. Because these souls *are* lost and wandering around in a state of distress and confusion, they can, unknowingly, cause disturbances for people who are still living in the physical. They can, for instance, become enmeshed within the auras of other people, giving rise to the distressing symptoms associated with possession. Hauntings, either in houses or other physical locations, can also be caused by the presence of an earthbound spirit or even a whole group of them.

The misconception that causes me the greatest concern is the idea, held by many followers of orthodox religion, that all cases of possession or hauntings are invariably caused by malevolent demons. This gives rise to the practice of exorcism rituals, centred around the principle of 'casting out the demons' and binding them forever in the Abyss, a technique which relies heavily on the use of threats, curses and psychic force. It also generates a considerable amount of fear and hysteria in the religious community, which provides a fertile breeding ground for further incidents of possession.

In cases where possession has, indeed, been caused by the activities of a demonic influence, the traditional approach is probably quite effective, at least in the short term. Nevertheless, it also demonstrates a considerable lack of knowledge of the condition of lost souls and, in the long run, that kind of technique and its associated attitudes do more harm than good. A genuinely lost soul, as distinct from a demonic entity, is already in a condition of extreme distress, pain, fear and confusion. The last thing such a soul needs is to be cursed, condemned and forcibly driven into the lower regions of spiritual existence, where it can fall prey to the kind of low-level beings who delight in causing unimaginable torment.

Because of my concern regarding such practices, I went to some length in *Reaching for the Other Side* to explain how an ordinary human soul can become earthbound and the fear and trauma that such a soul can suffer. To illustrate this principle, I used a hypothetical example of a person who had died suddenly in a car accident. I also related the story of one of the rescues performed by Roland and I, which had involved a suicide victim. My intention was simply to explain the folly of judging all earthbound entities as demons and to show how a caring and compassionate approach is infinitely more beneficial for all concerned. In the process, however, I unwittingly generated some fearful misconceptions in the minds of some of my readers, particularly those who had suffered the death of a loved one through an accident or suicide. I have since received a number of letters from people who are most concerned that their loved ones might be earthbound and suffering acute distress, simply because of the manner of their death.

To clear up these misconceptions, we need to refer once again to the principle that our thoughts create our reality. The level of spiritual existence to which a soul will be drawn after death is entirely dependent upon *the state of that soul's mind* at the time of transition. Like attracts like: therefore, the soul will be drawn to a level of existence where the energy frequencies are in harmony with the energy pattern generated by the soul itself.

As an example (and please remember that I am only making up examples to illustrate a point!), let us imagine that we are dealing with a soul who has been terrified of dying and has exerted every atom of willpower in an attempt to stave off the inevitable, clinging to physical life. This soul's own state of mind will keep it firmly anchored to the physical; it may even refuse to recognise the fact that it has 'passed over' and wonder why family, friends and loved ones seem to be totally oblivious to its presence. This state of affairs will continue until the soul recognises and accepts the change in circumstances or is drawn into the proximity of someone who is capable of performing a psychic rescue.

Incidentally, when dealing with a soul in this condition, we usually do not insist that the soul must recognise and accept its physical demise. Instead, we simply say 'You've been very ill and your mind has become confused but you are safe now.' The soul is then taken into the care of a spirit 'rescue team' who take it to a place of healing. The truth of what has really happened is revealed gradually, as and when the soul becomes capable of accepting this information without fear and panic.

Because of the soul's state of mind and the need to create familiar and reassuring surroundings, this place of healing will most likely appear to the soul as a hospital and the spirit helpers as doctors and nurses. As acceptance develops, the illusion falls away and the true situation is revealed. It all happens very gently and the aim at all times is to give reassurance, support and healing to the soul in need.

Fear of dying must be rated as one of the chief causes of the earthbound condition. A person who accepts that death is simply a natural transition from one cycle of existence to another will approach death without fear, understanding that it will simply lead into wider fields of growth and learning. Such a soul is unlikely to become earthbound, regardless of the circumstances under which death occurs. Dying is as natural and inevitable as being born and it is only ignorance of our true nature and purpose that has given rise to all the horror stories about divine condemnation, eternal punishment and all the other ghastly myths that have been foisted on the populace for too long by a succession of religious leaders who ought to have known better, but obviously didn't.

Fear of the unknown has also been exacerbated through the last few centuries of conditioning, in which unspeakable penalties were imposed upon anyone who dared to penetrate the mists of superstition and find out what really lies beyond the veil of death. To carry out such activities, according to the erstwhile 'authorities', is to enter the realm of demons. Small wonder that people have been conditioned to fear death when, to all intents and purposes, it is likely to dump them slap-bang in the middle of all the horrific demons they've been steadfastly hoping to avoid all their lives. It's hardly surprising that so many people cling to physical life for as long as they can possibly do so!

In the natural process of physical death, the spirit's transition is eased through a period of unconsciousness; as one of my spirit helpers puts it: 'You go to sleep in the physical world and wake up at Home.' Sometimes the spirit will awaken in full awareness of what has taken place, in other cases the awareness comes gradually. This is dependent upon the level of understanding and maturity reached by the spirit involved. If it is a young soul who has been largely unaware of the realities of spiritual existence during its earthly incarnation, the transition will be a lot more gradual than for a more mature soul, who has a better idea of what to expect. In every case, the transition process is structured to suit the individual needs and level of comprehension for the spirit who is making the transition.

Even in cases of 'accidental death', this process can still be applied. If you have been involved in an accident, you would not be unduly surprised to find yourself in a hospital so, in the case of an accident victim, he or she will most likely awaken in what appears to be a hospital ward after being 'knocked unconscious' in the accident. As in the case of our hypothetical lost soul, true awareness will gradually arise and the illusion will recede as and when the spirit is ready for it to happen.

Many cases in which a death appears to be the result of an accident are not at all accidental from the spiritual perspective. More often than not, it is the manner and time of departure that was *chosen* before the spirit entered this particular incarnation. Genuine accidents can sometimes happen; as a case in point, we need only refer to the manner of my departure from the life of Eileen O'Shea, in Ireland. The fact that I 'went out' on a low level and subsequently fell victim to an attack by predators is not due to the accident itself, but to the state of mind in which I made the transition. My vibrations were down, causing me to be drawn into the lower levels of psychic existence. At that time, I did not go through the normal phase of unconsciousness; I was simply unaware of what I was doing and I kept on walking, totally oblivious to the fact that my body had gone crashing away beneath me to the foot of the cliff.

In the case of a *programmed* accident, there is usually a period of unconsciousness and, because the event is both planned and expected, there are always spirit helpers on hand to protect and assist. It is an unfortunate fact that some accident victims do become earthbound for a time; however, those cases are far from being the majority and a rescue is always effected at the earliest possible opportunity. It may seem to us as though a considerable period of time has passed between physical death and spiritual rescue but we need to bear in mind that time is a condition of physical existence and, to the spirit concerned, it may seem like only a fraction of a second. As a case in point, I wrote in my last book about a shearer named Jack, who left this life more than twenty years before we performed the rescue procedure that released him from the earth plane. He had no awareness whatsoever of the passage of time. When we asked 'What year is it?', he did some mental calculation based on his most recent physical activities and concluded that it must be 'About 1952...'53?'. When we informed him that in fact it was 1978, his reaction was one of stunned disbelief.

Jack had no recollection either of being ill or of suffering an accident; in fact, he was completely unaware that he had passed over and he had suffered no noticeable distress as a result. The fact that he had unwittingly caused distress to the person in whose energy field he had become entangled did not enter his consciousness, he did not even know that it had happened.

Suicide victims, unfortunately, are more vulnerable to the earthbound condition simply because of the state of mind in which they make their departures from this life. However, it is NOT true that suicide victims are deliberately condemned to the earthbound condition as a punishment for committing a crime against life. I am well aware that, in certain written accounts of communication with spirit entities, the spirits have spoken harshly in judgement of those who take their own lives but, in doing so, those spirits reveal their own lack of true understanding. It is worth remembering that not all spirit communicators are the oracles of wisdom that they represent themselves to be. The fact that an entity may be speaking from the spirit world is not an automatic criterion of spiritual wisdom. Truly advanced spirits do not pass judgement on others, they know better.

Suicide is a tragedy, not a crime. Even to be contemplating an act of suicide is a clear indication that a person is suffering intense distress and hopelessness, to the point of despair. The last thing this person needs is condemnation and punishment!

Pronouncing judgement on others is a human failing, not a spiritual quality. I long for the day when people get down off their self-righteous high horses, stop being so judgemental and start showing some compassion. What we need in this world is more love and understanding, not bigotry, prejudice and 'holier-than-thou' attitudes. The Higher Ones are concerned with order and balance, not punishment; their motivation is love, not pride... and it is pride that makes people think they have achieved such a pinnacle of perfection that they are worthy to pass judgement on others. Let us not forget that not one of us is perfect... yet!

Suicide is an act of despair and, before we start judging any person for committing that final desperate act, it might be better to ask ourselves what made life in this world so terrible for the victim that he or she could no longer bear to remain here? What can we, as a race and as individuals, do to improve the quality of life so that this world is no longer a place of torment for so many people? When we find the answer to that question, suicide will no longer be a problem. Until then, we are *all* responsible and if judgement is due, we must all be judged equally.

I'm not saying it's okay to commit suicide or that it cannot have painful consequences for the victim. The consequences are often painful but they are not imposed as an act of divine judgement: they are a *natural* consequence of the spirit making its transition in a condition of severe mental and emotional imbalance. Those who work in the field of spiritual rescue, whether they work at the physical level or in the spiritual spheres, do not discriminate between a suicide victim and a spirit whose physical death was the result of natural causes. The Higher Ones do give strong warnings against suicide, simply because it renders the victim so vulnerable to entrapment and harm. A victim's guardians cannot act to prevent any such entrapment because it is the result of a free will decision.

By committing suicide, the victim is choosing, albeit unwittingly, to become suspended in the lower levels of spiritual existence, the levels closest to the physical world. Thus the act of suicide solves nothing because the spirit will still have all the emotional problems that existed prior to the act but will be in a position where it is much more difficult to solve them. There is also a strong likelihood that even worse problems will be encountered.

There is a great deal that can be done by loved ones who are still living in the physical world, not only for suicide victims, but for any soul who may be at risk of entrapment. Because we are in the physical sphere, we are close to the levels in which such souls are likely to be wandering. There are also bonds of affinity between the departed soul and its loved ones, which can be used to good effect. Just as we can draw spiritual light into our auras and radiate it out into the atmosphere, we can also focus the light around someone we love. It makes no difference whether that person is living in a physical body or on some other level. Thought is the fabric of reality and the only barriers are those we create within our own minds.

Spiritual healing is precisely what its name implies: healing of the spirit. It works by bringing the sufferer's life energies into a condition of balance. In a physical sense, imbalance within the life energy pattern can cause physical symptoms but the mind and emotions are equally affected. A soul in an earthbound condition is a soul whose energies are out of balance and the projection of healing light can be just as beneficial as if the individual were still functioning through a physical body... perhaps even more so.

By surrounding a departed loved one with Light, we can lend assistance in several ways, to heal, comfort and protect. A spirit who is surrounded with Light has an effective shield against low-level predators. In addition, the presence of Light will help to lift that spirit's vibrations, making it much easier for a rescue to be effected when necessary. The Light acts as a beacon for the spirit rescuers who are always on watch for any soul in need of help.

There is no danger that by sending Light you will override the spirit's free will because the Light doesn't work that way. If any spirit makes a conscious, free will decision to reject the Light and actually enjoys the low-level existence, the Light will simply return to you. There is no power in the Universe that will force a change of heart; however, we are speaking here of souls who are lost, confused and in need of help, not of those who have actively chosen the pathway of darkness.

The method used for the projection of Light is the same as for absent healing, with particular emphasis on self-protection. It is *essential* to commence with a thorough White Light cleansing. Saturate your aura with Light, seal it carefully, make the Invocation for guidance and protection, then tell your spirit helpers *exactly* what you wish to do and ask for their assistance. These precautions are vitally important: we don't want you to risk exposing yourself to any unhealthy low-level influences. Your vibrations must be calm, centred and as peaceful as you can make them. What you feel is what you will project... and attract.

Next, imagine your loved ones as you would like to see them; happy, smiling and surrounded by an aura of the purest and most beautiful White Light that you can possibly imagine. As with absent healing, the Light energy may change colour; if so, don't interfere with it. As you focus, let your love flow. Give out your highest and purest thoughts and emotions, KNOWING that, by doing so you, will actively help that spirit to be healed. Don't forget to flush your aura through with White Light again on completion of the procedure.

The projection of positive healing energies in this way was once widely understood and, no doubt, it is the origin of the practice of saying prayers for the dead, to ease the passage of the soul. Prayer is simply another way of projecting positive thought energy; therefore, it does help to pray for the soul of a departed loved one, more so if you understand how and why it works.

The technique of psychic rescue, performed by trained psychic workers, often involving the use of trance mediums, is usually necessary only when a soul has been earthbound for a lengthy period of time and has begun to cause problems for people still living on the earth plane. This area requires extensive training and discipline, along with the support of a strong and competent team of spirit helpers. It is definitely not an activity that can be recommended for enthusiastic beginners! We can compare it to the rescue of a drowning swimmer, who in his panic will struggle and clutch at the would-be rescuer. Lifesavers are experienced and capable swimmers who are trained to know how to carry out a rescue procedure without being drowned together with the victim.

By the time a lost soul reaches a condition in which this type of rescue procedure is necessary, it can present a very real danger to those who are working to effect the rescue. Additionally, wherever such a soul is encountered, there may also be predatory entities and these will have to be dealt with in a way that prevents them from causing harm. This is an area where no-one can afford to make the slightest mistake and often we do not know whether we will be dealing with a lost soul or a demonic entity until the rescue procedure is under way.

No-one who has any reasonable amount of training and experience with this kind of rescue would choose to go 'ghost-hunting', looking for rescues to perform just for the sake of excitement. Roland and I will perform a rescue only when our guides request us to do so. It really makes me shudder when someone says to me: 'I'd love to see you do a rescue, please let me know when the next one is scheduled so that I can come and watch. It must be so exciting!' There are times when I have to discipline myself not to make some withering remark, such as asking whether the person would like me to arrange for them to watch some open-heart surgery as well, with a rock band thrown in for good entertainment value. We do *not* perform psychic rescues for the purpose of amusement, and sensation-seekers are definitely not welcome!

It isn't at all possible to learn how to perform a psychic rescue procedure by reading instructions in a book; however, there are some basic points which may prove helpful, should you ever find yourself in a situation where a rescue procedure is necessary. Spirit teachers have a wonderful habit of introducing us to new learning experiences by employing what I call the 'deep end' technique, which is like teaching you how to swim by tossing you into the deep end of a swimming pool. It is always possible that your first indication of psychic rescue being a part of your training program will be when you find yourself doing it.

Don't let this idea alarm you too much; your guides will not expose you to such situations if you are not ready or if you are psychologically unsuited to this kind of work. If we all waited until *we* think we're ready to take on something more challenging, I doubt that any of us would make a great deal of progress. By the same token, the guides will not expose us to any situation that is beyond our capabilities. We also have the right to choose whether or not we are prepared to enter a particular field of activity. If you tell your guides in advance that you do not wish to become involved with psychic rescues, you will not be expected to do so.

Your guides will see that you are not exposed to entities too dangerous or powerful for you to handle. The fear that you may find yourself face to face with a demonic entity need not apply because that kind of work is never given to anyone who has not agreed in advance to do it and/or does not have the necessary amount of training and experience. Because this kind of work is so dangerous, it must always be a free will decision on the part of anyone involved and, even then, the guides are obligated to ensure that the appropriate training is given and that the practitioner is competent to handle such work. Needless to say, I am assuming here that you have taken the time to establish an efficient working relationship with a guide who knows how to screen out undesirable influences.

At the risk of overstating the obvious, it should not be difficult to see why all the groundwork explained in the previous chapters is so important. I know of a number of people who are working with 'guides' who are merely human souls awaiting reincarnation. Their level of knowledge and experience is seldom much higher than that of the people with whom they communicate and, from a purely personal point of view, I would be most unwilling to rely on one of those entities to get me out of a dangerous situation.

I can't help feeling concerned when I hear someone say: 'Oh, my guide is Uncle Charlie. He was my favourite uncle and he died about ten years ago.' Uncle Charlie might be a dear old soul and, no doubt, his intentions are good but ten years in the spirit world doesn't make him a guide. Moreover, if he is still hanging around the earth plane it is quite possible that Uncle Charlie himself might be earthbound. There is also the danger that the 'guide' may not be Uncle Charlie at all but a clever low-level impersonator, whose intention is to lead his gullible disciple astray. That risk is always prevalent for anyone who is not careful enough to ensure that he accepts guidance only from the higher levels of spiritual existence.

Before you even begin to think about whether psychic rescue may be your calling, make very sure that you have established your foundations and that you have an efficient working relationship with a reliable and competent guide. Taking risks with your own spiritual welfare is a fool's game.

If you do find yourself in a situation where psychic rescue is necessary, the first and most important thing to remember is: DON'T LOSE YOUR HEAD. Stay calm and don't make any sudden moves or hasty decisions. When it comes to psychic rescue, the role played by the physical participants is secondary to that of the spirit workers, who are in a position to assess the situation with a far greater degree of understanding and accuracy.

In general, it is best not to speak unless the entity speaks to you first. In most of the rescues in which I have been involved, the guides are simply using our energy fields as the channels through which the earthbound entities can be moved from one sphere to another. To speak at the wrong time can interrupt the flow of energy. This may cause the entity either to be cast adrift again or to become stuck within the medium's energy field, a situation for which the medium is most unlikely to thank you. It is quite possible that the entire rescue may be performed without the necessity for you to say or do anything, other than to maintain a flow of positive light energy throughout your aura and generate an atmosphere of calm.

If it is necessary for you to speak, consider your words carefully. It can be a serious mistake to insist that the entity accept the news that: 'You are now dead and it's time for you to move on.' It is equally mistaken to conduct an interrogation to establish the entity's name, rank, serial number, date of birth, last known addresss and what brand of toothpaste it prefers. Such details might be useful for proving the validity of your experiences but that is not the point of the exercise. Strictly speaking, all that information is none of our business and it is quite possible that the entity may not be able to answer the questions anyway. It may be severely traumatised and unable to remember or unable to tell you for some other reason. Remember, we are not dealing here with articulate spirit entities who claim to be guides and who must be carefully questioned in order to establish their credentials. We are dealing with sick and injured spirits who may not even be capable of speaking coherently, much less answering questions.

I am not a deep trance medium and when I am 'channelling' I enter an altered state of consciousness in which I am aware of what is taking place but am slightly removed. It is as though I am watching things happen on a 3-D movie screen inside my head. The experience normally begins with what feels like a simple change of mood and, often, I can be unaware of the true circumstances until I actually start channelling. Usually I find myself relaying information from the Higher Ones: it is rare for me to be used as a channel for earthbound entities. It has happened only twice and on both occasions, the entities were the spirits of young children, little girls.

The first of these rescues took place when Roland was not at home and I was talking with a group of young friends. We gradually became aware of a presence in the house which exuded such a potent aura of fear that we all felt our pulses racing. At first, we thought the house must have been invaded by something unwholesome and we intended to perform a cleansing to drive it away but, as we began our preparations, I felt an unexpected sensation. I could physically feel it, as though a very small body had climbed into my lap to nestle up against my breast. I just had time to say 'I don't think this is a nasty . . .', before I was overwhelmed by a flood of emotion. Before I had time to think about it, I felt tears running down my cheeks while I sobbed like a frightened child. With one part of my mind, I realised that I had somehow taken the lost spirit child into myself. I hoped to Heaven that my companions would be able to handle the situation without frightening the poor little soul even more, for I now realised that the fear we had felt had been a reflection of the child's own feelings. In the other part of my consciousness, I *was* the child, surrounded by darkness, lost and terrifyingly alone.

'Who are you?' the voice spoke suddenly, making me jump slightly. The part of me that was still Dawn recognised it as belonging to Mark, a young man who had himself been used as a channel on several occasions. To the little girl within me, however, it was the voice of a stranger speaking out of the gloom and the only response was another surge of fear. The terrified wailing increased. 'It's alright, I won't hurt you.' Mark's voice was gentler this time. 'I only want to help. Can you tell me your name?'

The child within me struggled to answer and I heard my own voice, breathy and small, sobbing out the words: 'I don't know!'

'Can't you remember?'

'N-no.'

'How did you get here?'

'Don't know.'

'Can you tell me anything that might help? What can you remember?'

Misery overwhelmed the child and great, heaving sighs tore themselves from my body. 'It's dark . . . I'm cold. They won't let me in. I want my Mummy!'

'Oh, it's a child!' exclaimed a soft female voice from amongst the group. 'Poor little thing!'

At the sound of a woman's voice, the child gave forth with a despairing howl. 'I want Mummy! *Mum-mee*!'

'Don't cry, sweetheart. We'll find your Mummy.' It was Mark again and mentally I blessed his good sense. 'Stop crying, look around, Mummy's here, can you see her?'

The child whimpered, then searched. Somewhere on the edge of awareness, I felt rather than saw a pool of soft light surrounding a misty female form. As I perceived it, so did the child. '*Mummy*!' she cried and I felt her struggling to be free. Again I had reason to bless Mark's intuitive awareness.

'Don't struggle, little one, just close your eyes and think you're close to Mummy and you'll be there. Let go and you'll be in the Light... in the name of Christ.'

With those last few words I felt a sudden release and the child was gone. It took several minutes for me to return to normal because the child's piteous distress had touched my emotions deeply. I could sense my companions' eager curiosity but they waited quietly until I was ready to speak. 'It was a little girl,' I told them when I could find my voice. 'Perhaps five or six years old. When you asked for her identity I sensed the name Caroline but I didn't want to speak for fear of breaking the flow.'

'How did she die?' someone asked.

'I don't know. It felt as though there had been violence but it was too indistinct for me to be certain and I'm not sure I *want* to know. Mark, you were beautiful! When you spoke the name of Christ at the end it was like a key that unlocked the door to set her free.'

A puzzled frown creased Mark's brow as he shook his head in denial. 'I didn't speak the name of Christ,' he told me.

'Of course you did. I distinctly heard it; that was what finally released her. You must have done it without thinking.'

'No Dawn, I didn't say it.'

'But I *heard* you!'

'Honestly Dawn, I didn't even mention the name of Christ,' insisted Mark. The other group members chorused their confirmation. 'He didn't say it, Dawn. None of us heard it.'

I had definitely heard the words, yet I had no reason to disbelieve my companions nor had they any reason to deceive me. The only conclusion we could draw was that the words had been spoken but not by anyone physical. It seemed that Mark had also been doing some channelling because he told us that he had surprised himself by some of the words he had spoken. 'I don't know where I got the inspiration to tell the child that her mother was here,' he told us. 'I was saying the words before I had time to think.'

I prefer not to think about what might have happened to that poor, lost, little soul if my friends had attempted to coerce her into answering questions. From my point of view, suspended between the two levels of consciousness, I could see that she knew nothing but darkness and fear. Any attempt to force answers from her might only have driven her away and who knows how much longer it might have been, before she was given release?

Whenever the subject of psychic rescue arises in conversation, I am almost invariably asked 'Doesn't it frighten you?'. I won't pretend that I have nerves of steel but the honest answer is no, it doesn't frighten me. On the few occasions when I have been confronted with a truly malevolent and powerful demonic entity, I cannot say that I would not have felt fearful if I had known in advance what I would be facing. In a case like this, the 'deep end' technique works in my favour. By the time I realise what I'm dealing with, I don't have time to think about being frightened, which is just as well because, in those situations, I can't *afford* to give way to fear.

In a confrontation with a malevolent entity, it is necessary to concentrate so intently that I am unaware of any emotion other than a determination to succeed. Any other possibility is quite simply unthinkable; the trance medium happens to be the man I love and one mistake on my part could be worse than disastrous for him. Once it is over I can afford to let myself go weak at the knees and reach (rather shakily) for a cigarette but, even then,

I prefer not to think too much about what could happen if I made a miscalculation.

Fortunately, that kind of confrontation doesn't happen very often. Usually when I am working on a rescue, the entity is simply a lost soul and even though these entities can, at times, be quite violent and abusive, I find it impossible to feel anything but compassion for them. When we think of the circumstances under which they have been existing, I can't see how any other feeling is possible. Violent or aggressive behaviour in an earth-bound entity is usually motivated by pain and fear. Perhaps my background in the nursing profession gives me some helpful insights in this respect. When people are frightened and in pain, they usually show the worst side of their personalities but, if we look past the superficial unpleasantness and see the cause, how can we feel anything but sympathy?

Earthbound entities are not evil fiends; they are human souls in need of help. Perhaps, somewhere deep in my subconscious, there is a memory of a time when another part of me walked off a cliff and suffered the anguish of a lost and tormented soul. Maybe it is that hidden memory that causes me to rejoice when I am given the privilege of helping to release another. Who knows?

I cannot close this chapter without sharing an experience which must be rated as one of the most unusual rescues I have ever participated in, high in the pinnacles of a place called Hanging Rock. For those who are unfamiliar with the location or who have never seen the movie *Picnic at Hanging Rock*, I shall offer some background information. Hanging Rock is a huge geological upthrust, the size of a very large hill, or a small mountain, depending on how you rate your hills and mountains. I am no judge of heights but the pinnacles tower about a hundred metres above the surrounding plains and, if you are standing at the top, it's an awfully long way down!

I know nothing about the primeval force which thrust those giant pinnacles up out of the earth but the power behind it must have been awesome and spectacular. As the earth fell away from the thrusting teeth of stone, it formed a sloping skirt that now reaches halfway to the top, thickly wooded and quite beautiful. Walking tracks lead up through the trees to an area known as the Platform, which marks the boundary between the wooded slopes and the pinnacles. From here upwards, sightseers must scramble along roughly defined tracks through a collection of great boulders and monoliths, many of which are hollow. In places, as you walk, it is possible to hear a sepulchral echo of your footsteps underneath the stone surface. The place has an atmosphere of brooding mystery and has a fascinating effect on those who try to penetrate its age-old secrets.

The film *Picnic at Hanging Rock* is based on a book which tells of three teenage schoolgirls who disappeared without trace on the Rock, during a school picnic in the early 1900s. There is some doubt about whether the event ever actually occurred; the absence of contemporary newspaper accounts or written records of any kind would seem to indicate that it did not but the story has become a popular legend. I can easily understand how the imagination of a writer could be inspired by a visit to Hanging Rock. There is a compelling atmosphere about the place that can do odd things to the imagination, particularly if you happen to be sensitive to such things.

According to the Park Ranger who spoke with us while we were there, a group of aboriginal people had visited the Rock some weeks earlier and had climbed to the pinnacles, only to come racing down again soon after, terrified and shaking. The leader would say nothing to the Ranger about what they had encountered at the top; he would only vow fervently that none of his tribal people would ever go near the place again. My own opinion, after visiting the Rock, is that the power of its magnetism has the effect of magnifying whatever exists within the mind of the observer and I would not recommend any inexperienced sensitives to go there alone.

We visited the Rock with Ian and Sue Gordon during the filming of the video documentary mentioned earlier. Ian had been told by his spirit friends that the place is a 'power centre' and they wished us to go there with a camera crew and allow the energies around us to direct whatever might happen next. None of us knew exactly what to expect when we got there and we would not have been human if we had not occasionally pondered about the legend. It was obvious that the film crew had been doing quite a bit of pondering! Already perplexed about the odd little things that happened to their camera equipment when we were 'plugged in' to the spiritual energies and about a few other intriguing incidents that had taken place during filming, I'm sure they had moments when they wondered what on Earth was likely to happen next.

'What are you going to do when we get to Hanging Rock?' one of them asked me, only half joking. 'Are you planning to make those three schoolgirls reappear?'

In answer, I raised a teasing eyebrow and gave my version of an inscrutable smile. 'You never know what's likely to happen, my friend,' I purred. 'Anything is possible!'

The film crew chuckled; a little uneasilv, I thought.

It was late winter and, for the entire week of our visit, the skies over Melbourne had been leaden. It had drizzled almost constantly and none of us felt enthusiastic about filming the Hanging Rock sequences in such inhospitable conditions. Earlier in the week, one of the crew had light-heartedly asked me why I didn't wave my magic wand and organise some better weather for the filming.

'Good idea!' I jested in return. 'I'll see what I can do.'

On the morning of filming, the skies were grey and sullen: a continuous light drizzle kept the early morning atmosphere misty, damp and chill. When we arrived at the location, the film crew were waiting for us. They had already filmed some long-distance views of the Rock, to be used during the introductory narration for the sequence. As we stepped from the car, I was greeted with some good-natured teasing.

'What's the matter with that magic wand of yours?' challenged our producer, Ron. 'Batteries go flat?'

'Give it time,' I countered. '*We* haven't started filming yet. Besides, I bet you got some great mood shots of the Rock, with all this mist around.'

'Yeah. Spooky place, this,' he responded in a more sombre tone. I thought I could detect a hint of apprehension in his voice.

Leaving the crew waiting by the road, Roland and

I set out with Ian, Sue and her ten-year-old son, Scotty, to climb to the pinnacles and seek out an area that 'felt right' for filming. We followed the nearest track with Scotty scampering along like a cheerful young puppy, chattering away to Roland, with whom he had formed a close rapport. We climbed steadily for twenty minutes or so, until the trees became sparser and we could almost see the platform ahead. Roland and Scotty spied a smaller track that led off to our left and went charging off to explore it.

'We ought to stay on the main path,' I called after them. The only reply was a cheerful wave from Scotty as he scrambled after Roland, to disappear behind a cluster of large boulders.

'Roland!' I called more urgently. No answer, save for my own voice echoing back from the rocks. Ian and Sue stopped walking, concerned by the sharp edges in my voice. I tried to cover my pangs of unease with a veneer of irritation. 'Roland should have more sense than to go haring off like that... it would be easy for both of them to get lost!'

'They'll be alright, I'm sure.' Ian tried to reassure me. 'Anyway, I think the paths converge up ahead.'

'Even so, it's irresponsible to go off like that!' I grumbled, inwardly surprised at my own agitation. 'We should all stay together.'

Sue laid a reassuring hand on my arm. 'Let's keep going.' she suggested. 'We're sure to meet up with them further along.'

The sloping wooded pathway gave way to rocky tracks that led between huge boulders; we scrambled upwards, periodically pausing to call Roland's name but the calls went unanswered. After a while, Sue began to look a little anxious. Cupping her hands around her mouth, she called Scotty's name and a cheerful reply came back at once. A few moments later, Scotty came scrambling towards us through a fissure in the rocks.

'Where's Roland?' I demanded, now openly anxious. Scotty pointed a nonchalant finger back towards the fissure.

'Through there, on the other track. It's not far,' he told me. My eyes followed the direction in which he pointed and I caught a glimpse of Roland as he passed on the other side, moving like a sleepwalker . . . in trance.

'Oh, my God!' I muttered harshly as I sprang forward.

I am not the most athletic person in the world but I went through that fissure like a mountain-goat, in less than a few seconds. Emerging on the other side, I looked around for Roland. The track opened out onto a large plateau of rock, dotted sparsely with small clusters of boulders and a few stunted shrubs. Nothing else. There was no sign of Roland, yet in the time it took me to reach his path, he would not have had time to traverse the plateau. He had simply . . . disappeared.

I stood statue-still, forcing myself to keep a hold on my reason. The only rock in sight that was big enough to conceal a full-grown man was a single grey sentinel of maybe twelve feet in height, which stood beside me. But I had just come *past* that stone, through the fissure.

'Get a grip on yourself, Dawn,' I scolded myself. 'People don't just vanish into thin air.'

'Oh, no?' argued a nasty little voice in my head. 'This *is* Hanging Rock remember!'

I shook my head, refusing to give the nagging little voice any credence. Then came the sound that turned my spine to jelly . . . Roland's voice, raised in a howl of anguish . . . and the sound came from INSIDE the massive stone sentinel.

'This is it, Dawn,' I said to myself. 'It's finally happened: you have flipped your lid!'

But the mournful cries coming through the rock beside me were all too chillingly real. I stood there paralysed, fighting to stop my legs from buckling under me. 'There has to be a rational explanation for this!' I argued fiercely. 'Rocks don't eat people!'

'Dawn, we've got him,' called Ian from somewhere behind the stone mass. 'Come here, quickly.'

Heart pounding, I stumbled around to the side of the rock that faced away from the fissure. Ian motioned to where Sue and Scotty were standing in front of a large cavity in the stone, within which Roland crouched, deeply in trance, wailing in near desperation. Mentally I sent a 'Priority one . . . Attention!' signal to David and, almost at once, the despairing cries began to subside, first to a miserable whimper and then to quiet sobs. Eventually, Roland heaved a shuddering sigh, opened his eyes and blinked around as though dazed.

'Where did you guys come from?' he stammered. 'What am I doing here?'

'We could ask the same question of you.' I spoke almost harshly, more in relief than exasperation. 'Whatever possessed you, to go running off like that?'

Roland groaned as he stumbled to his feet and looked around, trying to get his bearings.

'I don't know,' he admitted. 'I just had a compulsion...' He broke off and stared almost incredulously at the rock cavity from which he had just emerged.

'This little cave... there's another one like it, back there somewhere,' he declared. 'That's what drew me... there's another clearing and another big monolith, twice the size of this one. It has a cavity too, bigger than this one and higher up. I kept trying to climb into it but it was too high and the rock face is too smooth, no toeholds. I tried for what seemed like ages but I had to give up. I remember feeling an overwhelming sense of despair as I turned to walk away. Then it's all blank... until I woke up here.'

'I think perhaps we've located a likely spot for filming,' announced Ian. 'I'll go fetch the film crew. Sue and Dawn, I think it might be best if you wait here with Roland.' As Ian and Scotty strode off along the pathway, Sue and I looked around for some comfortable rocks to sit on. Roland started pacing restlessly back and forth: I practically ordered him to sit down. 'I don't want you wandering off and disappearing again.' I wagged a cautionary finger in his direction.

'I'll be good, Mum.' He grinned weakly as he arranged his lanky form on a reasonably comfortable-looking rock.

We chatted sporadically as we waited, each one of us mentally trying to calculate how long it would take for Ian and Scotty to return with the film crew. They had been gone for less than ten minutes when we heard a male voice some distance away, calling for Ian.

'That's Ron!' Sue looked puzzled. 'What's going on, I wonder?' She gave an answering call and Ron's voice came back at once.

'Stay where you are. I'm coming.'

A few minutes later with a rush and a flurry, Ron came panting towards us over the rocks. 'Where's Ian?' he demanded.

'He went back to get you and the others, explained Sue. 'Didn't you see him?'

'No, but the other blokes have probably found him by now. What's been going on?'

We explained briefly the sequence of events and Ron pounded a fist into his opposite hand. 'I KNEW it!' he declared. 'When we were waiting back down on the road, I *knew* something had happened.'

'What do you mean?' I asked him. 'How did you know?'

'I dunno, Love. I was standing there, looking up at the rocks and then all of a sudden I just knew that something had happened and you had split up... and I was *right*, wasn't I! I've got the whole bloody crew out looking for you blokes... Jeez, you gave me a fright.'

I was immediately intrigued. 'What made you so scared?' I prompted.

Ron eyed me with feigned patience. 'Let's face it, Love,' he smiled grimly. 'If you all disappeared, you wouldn't be the bloody first, would you?'

'I've arranged to meet the others at the Platform,' he went on. 'They've probably met up with Ian by now. You blokes follow me... and don't any of you go off anywhere else!'

As we trailed obediently in his wake, I couldn't help mentally analysing Ron's state of mind. It was obvious that the man was quite highly psychic and equally obvious that he didn't feel comfortable about it, not right then anyway. We spoke little as we made our way along the rocky path that led back down to the Platform but I resolved to keep an eye on Ron. At Hanging Rock, he was as sensitive to the powerful influences as any of us but he was also untrained, inexperienced and nervous, a volatile combination in such a setting.

The others were waiting for us when we reached the Platform and Ian seemed more than usually animated. We found out why as soon as we came within hearing distance.

'I've found another spot near here,' he called. 'There

seems to be a difference in the energy, I'd like to check it out.' We trooped along behind him as he led us through the rocks to another small clearing, just beyond the platform. 'Here!' he announced excitedly. 'Can you feel it?'

Roland's eyes sent me a question and I replied with a brief shake of the head. Neither of us felt anything particularly significant about the location. Sue however, reacted immediately. 'There's a presence here... it's Kondak!'

Again Roland and I exchanged glances. We had heard of Kondak, who apparently communicates with Sue quite often. He has been described to us as a being from another star system who communicates via telepathy. This explained our lack of sensitivity to the presence. We are certainly not sceptical about U.F.O.s and extraterrestrial beings but we are not particularly attuned to them either and have never communicated directly with them. Sue sat down on a large rock and almost immediately entered a light trance, during which she began to relay a communication.

This sequence required the participation of only one cameraman and sound technician so we decided that Roland and I, along with Ron and the other camera and sound men, would return to the Platform and wait there. As we turned to go, Roland extended a pleading hand towards me. He was shaking, obviously distressed and perilously close to tears.

'I have to go back!' he cried softly. 'Please help me, Dawn. I have to get back to that rock and somehow I've got to get up into that cavity. I have to... I *must*!' he was hovering on the verge of a trance state and I motioned urgently to Ron.

'Something is happening... get your gear and follow us.'

'Right you are; just give us a moment.'

But Roland had already turned and started loping off across the rocks.

'No time!' I called back over my shoulder as I scrambled after him. 'Follow us quickly and *don't lose sight of us*!'

Half running, half sliding, I kept pace with Roland as he shambled along at startling speed. He was now more deeply in trance, only dimly aware of my presence, openly sobbing and muttering to himself. 'I have to find it. I *have* to find it!' It seemed like only a few minutes before we reached the plateau where we had found him before. He stopped and searched around frantically. 'I've lost it!' There was anguish in his cry. I stood back a little, not daring to touch him.

'You haven't lost it,' I panted. 'Use your feelings, let it draw you. Turn around slowly until you feel a pull, then follow the feeling.'

He turned until he was facing back, almost the way we had come but on a slight angle to the right. With a miserable howl, he lurched forward just as the camera and sound men came puffing up to us.

'Back the other way,' I told them hastily as I scooted past.

I searched ahead as I hurried after Roland, seeking for a location that fitted the description he had given to us earlier. We rounded a bend in the pathway and I saw it, the tall standing stone with its cavity near the top. It faced onto a clearing, around which was milling a sizeable group of curious teenagers who seemed to be holding an excited conversation with Ron. Seeing our approach, Ron took in the situation at a glance, clapped his hands together loudly and shouted to the youngsters. 'Out of the way . . . QUICK! Out of sight, and keep quiet.' By the time we reached the monolith, not a single teenager was in sight but muffled giggles from behind the rocks betrayed their presence. 'I said QUIET!!' yelled Ron and the giggles fell silent.

Roland scrabbled at the smooth face of the standing stone, trying to reach the cavity. It was out of his reach, perhaps three metres above the ground on which we stood.

'*Help* me, Dawn! I've got to get in there,' he cried.

'All in the line of duty,' I told myself as I gave him a leg up and then braced myself while he took my shoulder for a foothold to reach the small cave.

I stepped back to watch as Roland crawled into a sitting position within the hollowed-out stone, sobbing and muttering to himself all the while. Then involuntarily, I held my breath. The face that looked out blindly from within the stone was not the face of my husband. As the first tormented howls shattered the frozen silence, I knew what I was hearing. There is no other sound that strikes the vitals with quite the same impact as the dreadful, hopeless howling of a lost soul. I watched the figure of my husband alternately tearing at his hair and beating his fists against the rock; his cries were incoherent but the very sound vibrated with waves of unspeakable torment and hopeless despair. I glanced around quickly to assess the precariousness of Roland's physical position, at least three metres up in the air above a rock surface and another four metres sideways to a sheer drop of about a hundred metres. If the lost soul's frantic struggles should get out of hand, one forward lunge could bring tragedy.

'David, you'd better know what you're doing!' I growled, mentally throwing all of my energies into holding Roland's body safely within the cave. I waited for what seemed like ages but could have been as little as a few minutes, while the figure in the rock above me writhed and struggled, howling in brutal agony. I could not even begin to guess at what inhuman tortures could have caused such terrible desolation. An answering pain began to throb inside me and I felt my throat trying to constrict but I held myself apart from it, still and dispassionate. If I were to allow myself to be overwhelmed by such despair with a sheer drop only a few paces away, I did not care to contemplate the consequences.

Moments stretched into eternity as I waited, scarcely daring to breathe, concentrating my mind on a single command: 'Peace, be still.' Whether the command was meant for me or for the lost soul in the rock I cannot say, but as it filled my mind, peace and comfort filled my heart. Moments later, the anguished cries from above me began to abate. The contorted lines of agony in Roland's face softened, to be replaced with an expression of calm and quiet strength. I saw the characteristic body rhythms that signal the arrival of David and I heaved a great sigh of relief.

'My daughter, I am David,' he greeted me solemnly. 'That one is with me.' I was instantly alert. The statement 'That one is with me' usually means more to come. If a rescue has been completed and all the lost souls gathered up, or if there has only been one in the vicinity, David will say 'It is done', signifying that the atmosphere around us is now clear.

'Are there more?' I asked. He nodded.

'There are *many*.'

I was taken back. What did he mean, there are many? How many . . . and what had brought them here? Almost without realising it, I spoke my thoughts aloud.

'What *is* this place?'

'It is a congregation area,' came the answer from David.

'A congregation area . . . for *lost souls*?'

'That is so.'

'How many could we help?'

'As many as this man could take,' he replied, indicating Roland's body with a brief gesture. I could only answer with a philosophical shrug, 'Okay, you know the limits. Whenever you're ready.'

'Now is not the time, my daughter. This man will sleep.' Roland's head dropped forward onto his chest and I turned to face the wide-eyed film crew.

'What you have just seen is a psychic rescue.' I explained the procedure to them briefly before turning to offer my shoulder to Roland, now awake and indicating that he wished to climb down.

As we settled down, I cast a speculative eye over Ron, who was looking shaken and pallid. He was being uncharacteristically quiet, as though his mind was in a state of numbed amazement.

'Did it shake you up that badly, Ron?' I asked him in concern.

He shook his head and held a hand to his chest. 'Oh, my bloody heart . . . no it wasn't you, Love. It was those bloody schoolgirls . . . didn't you see them?'

'Yes, I saw them but I didn't take much notice at the time.'

Ron stared at me and rocked his head from side to side in apparent disbelief. *'Didn't take much bloody notice!* Jesus woman, what have you got in your veins . . . liquid steel?'

All at once I saw the picture from Ron's perspective and burst into peals of laughter.

'It's not bloody funny!' growled Ron as I subsided into choking giggles.

'Well, is someone going to let us in on the joke?' prodded Roland.

'I can't!' I spluttered. 'Ron will have to tell you!' All eyes immediately turned to Ron, who was looking quite hurt and indignant. 'Look at her laughing... bloke could have had a bloody *heart* attack!'

'What *happened*?' chorused his avid audience, almost dancing with impatience.

'There I am, slipping and sliding all over the track, falling further and further behind because I'm wearing leather-soled shoes and they slip... and *someone* left me to carry this bloody great heavy tripod.' He glared around for emphasis. 'You blokes have all gone galloping off ahead and I'm damn near busting a gut trying to catch up with you after you disappeared out of sight. I came sliding round a corner and there they were!'

'There *who* were?'

'Let me tell them, Ron,' I gurgled, struggling for self-control. 'He came face to face with three teenage school-girls... dressed in nineteenth century costume... straw hats and all.'

'WHAT?' came the disbelieving chorus.

Now thoroughly enjoying himself, Ron resumed his version of the story, 'Three of 'em, just like she says... as real as you, standing there in front of me, at a crossing between two tracks. Just standing there... looking at a bloke as though they think he's crazy... and for a while there, I damn near agreed with 'em.'

'Are you *sure* you saw them?' asked one of the crew.

'Oh, he saw them alright,' I grinned. 'Are they still here, Ron?' I nodded my head meaningfully towards the cluster of rocks from behind which the giggles had issued forth earlier. Ron's eyes sparkled with mischief. 'Alright, you can come out now,' he called and from behind the rocks stepped three giggling teenage schoolgirls, dressed in crisp white ankle-length pinafores and carrying straw hats in their hands. Behind them came several more chortling youngsters, comprising the small party that I had glimpsed climbing towards us as I had gone racing after Roland earlier. I had seen the entire group: Ron had encountered only the three in costume when he came along behind us.

'What did you do when you first saw them?" I chuckled.

'Jeez mate, I nearly died... fair dinkum, I thought I'd had it. I just fell back against this flaming' great rock and yelled "Shit! Where did *you* come from?" and, sweet as pie, they point back down the other track and say "Down there". So I ask them what they're doing here and you wouldn't believe it; they tell me they're on a bloody *school picnic*! Then these other kids come climbing back and I realise they mean a *real* school picnic, not a spook one.' He paused to give me a rather penetrating look. 'I thought you blokes might have set that up as some kind of a joke but I asked the girls what gave them the idea to get dressed up and they reckon they don't know... it was just an idea that came into their heads. Besides, there's no way you'd have known that particular school was planning a picnic here today.'

No, I thought to myself, there's no way I could have known; but I know of someone who could. 'Well?' I asked the question silently and felt my mind filled with the cosmic equivalent of a delighted chuckle. 'We do have our moments of frivolity, my daughter,' came the silent reply.

Later, as we made our way back down the hillside, I tapped Ron's arm. 'By the way, there's something you don't seem to have noticed.' I remarked.

'What's that?'

'Haven't you been looking up at all during the filming? Take a look at the sky.'

Ron stopped dead as comprehension dawned: ever since the commencement of filming, the skies overhead had been clear, blue and sunny as far as the eye could see.

By the time we reached the picnic area below and set up a fire for our barbecue, the sky had clouded over again and a misty rain enshrouded the pinnacles.

'You're slipping,' teased Ron.

'Not at all!' I retorted. 'You only asked for clear skies during *filming*. You didn't say anything about afterwards.'

'There are times when you frighten me, Lady,' he muttered. 'Here, have a cup of coffee.'

CHAPTER SIXTEEN

Witchcraft and Satanism

I have linked witchcraft and Satanism together in this chapter heading, not because I feel that they belong together, but because they are linked in the minds of many other people, even in our relatively enlightened era. In view of the conditioning we are given by society, it is not surprising that so much prejudice still remains. Like most children in a basically Christian society, I was raised on a diet of fairytales which prominently featured the 'Wicked Witch' character. Rarely, if ever, did I find any reference to a *good* witch; they were always evil, ugly old hags who cavorted with demons, cast wicked spells and ate little children for breakfast. Witches, I was taught, are the consorts of Satan and practitioners of the Black Arts. All of this constitutes some heavy mental conditioning!

I didn't consciously set out to discover the truth about witchcraft; life simply brought me into contact with some people whom the average man in the street would classify as witches. I am not speaking here about the colourful, flamboyant characters who love dressing up in Egyptian costume and reading about themselves in popular magazines. I am speaking of the sincere followers of an ancient religion popularly known as Wicca, the Craft of the Wise.

I must emphasise, at the outset, that I am not a follower of the Wiccan faith, nor of any other single form of religion. However, when I see a considerably large number of people being subjected to needless prejudice and hostility, my sense of fair play is aroused. Let's just erase the 'Wicked Witch' fantasy from our minds and start with a clean slate, as it were.

Many modern Wiccans do not like being referred to as witches. As it has been explained to me, the word 'witch' has been applied to these people in the vocabulary of the Christian Church: it has never been their word for themselves. They may feel obliged to tolerate the term but they don't have to like it, even when they understand that no offence is intended. Among my closest friends there are several Wiccans, some who cheerfully refer to themselves as witches and some who can't help flinching slightly whenever the word is used in their presence.

'Wicca is my religion,' one of them explained to me. 'I do not recognise the word "witch".'

Wicca is also known as 'The Old Religion'. It would appear to have been of Celtic origin (although I am inclined to believe that its roots go back even further into our history) and it predates the Christian religion by many centuries. Wiccans can also be described as Pantheists; people who see their God in Nature. My dictionary defines Pantheism as: 'The belief or theory that God and the Universe are identical (implying a denial of the personality and transcendence of God); the doctrine that God is everything and everything is God.'

If you study the philosophies espoused by New Age people, you will find them, for the most part, closely in accordance with that definition. This is not so much a religion as a way of life, although Wicca does include its own form of 'religious' rituals, as does any other spiritual philosophy. It is a philosophy of harmony with nature, attunement with the Cosmos and total respect for the sanctity of all life. Just as it can benefit us to study the philosophies of the 'accepted' world religions, the philosophy of Wicca has a great deal to offer that can enhance the seeker's understanding of life. Despite the fact that its members have frequently been hunted down like animals, subjected to the most inhuman forms of torture and literally tormented to death, the Old Religion has not only survived, it is thriving. To have maintained such a level of vitality and cohesion, it must have something going for it, particularly when you consider the vicious and concerted opposition to which it has been exposed for centuries.

I would not even attempt to explain all the richness and profound simplicity of the Old Religion; I leave that to those who have the wisdom of experience. For those who are interested, however, I can recommend a book entitled *Positive Magic*, written by Marion Weinstein.

I can describe only what I have observed for myself and, from what I have seen, the pure Wiccan faith has nothing whatsoever in common with Satanism. Wicca is a philosophy of harmony and healing; Satanism is the living expression of harm and disruption. Wicca is a love affair with life; Satanism is a denial of life.

Satanists believe that they are a race of super-beings, far superior to the rest of humankind. Some of them have gone so far as to say that all life is unnatural and human life, in particular, is an aberration. Whereas others seek to be at one with all life, Satanists hold themselves apart from it. In a book called *The Occult Experience*, there is a chilling interview between the author, Nevill Drury and the High Priest of San Francisco's Temple of Set, who explains that the ambition of a Satanist is to remain forever earthbound. To melt and be at one with the Creator is for us the ultimate expression of life but, where we see absolute fulfilment, a Satanist sees only annihilation. Therefore, Satanists aim to cheat death by concentrating the total force of their will on remaining firmly rooted to the earth plane.

Whilst I am keenly aware that it would be wrong of me to pass judgement, I have to be honest and admit that the Satanist philosophy is totally at odds with my system of belief. However, we have all been blessed with the divine right of free choice. It is not for me to say how another person should exercise that right, particularly if I expect to be given the right to make my own personal choices in freedom. I have to be scrupulously fair and I have tried my hardest not to let personal prejudice obscure my vision, but I can only describe what I see *as I see it*. To me, it appears that Satanism is a doctrine based on ego, with the acquisition of personal power as its central aim.

As I have said power is an interesting word; it never stands alone. It always has to be power *over*: power to manipulate, to enslave and to exploit. Such a philosophy is in direct opposition to the principles of pure Wicca. Wiccans appreciate the sanctity of all life. This includes the lives of plants, animals, birds and all of the other forms of life (both seen and unseen) which populate this planet and beyond. Followers of the Old Religion are concerned with the care of nature, tending the soil, helping things to grow. They are usually interested in things like natural nutrition, wholistic healing, conservation and peace on Earth. I can't find any reason to argue with ideals such as these. No doubt, there have been quite a few Wiccans who were no better than they ought to be but the same can be said of any cultural group. That is no excuse for conducting a campaign of genocide against the members of the Old Religion or condemning them to persecution by labelling them as servants of Satan. That kind of attitude positively reeks of prejudice!

My Wiccan friends are totally committed to the Light and dedicated to the service of others. They have also been generous enough to share ideas with me and, from them, I have learned much that is of value. I have been taught to judge a tree by its fruits: these people all have a quiet dignity, gentle bearing and a deep personal commitment to the divinity within all Life. They are beautiful, caring people who do not deserve the stigma they are forced to bear. I find it quite astonishing that there are still places where the laws against 'witchcraft' have yet to be repealed.

It is a fairly well-known fact that the philosophy of Nazism is based on the principles of Satanism. Anyone who cares to look for information on this subject will find a number of books available on that connection. Of those I have read, the best is *The Spear of Destiny* by Trevor Ravenscroft. If we take into consideration the fact that Nazism is an expression of Satanism, we must arrive at the inevitable conclusion that, in parts of this country, Satanism is acceptable but Wicca is not. From a purely 'equal rights' point of view, there is something definitely twisted in that kind of thinking.

So-called 'Black Witches', like Satanists, cannot be classified as followers of the true Wiccan philosophy. Black magic is the misuse of life energy for the purpose of gaining power over others. Think very carefully about that definition: not all black magicians are satanists! Strictly speaking, anyone who uses an energy to hurt or destroy for any purpose is carrying out an act of black magic.

I know quite a few people who would be horrified

and deeply offended if I accused them of being servants of Darkness, since they honestly believe they are followers of the Light. It is not the words they speak but their actions and attitudes which clearly betray them. A person may or may not be a witch but this is no indication of that person's motives and intentions. Their souls are revealed by their effect on others. This has no connection with race or creed: there are nice witches and nasty ones, just as there are nice and nasty Christians, Buddhists, Jews, Moslems and Communists.

A commitment to the policy of hurtlessness is the chief distinguishing characteristic of those who follow the pathway of Light, regardless of their religion. Genuine commitment will be clearly evident in the effect people have on those around them. Do they spread love and harmony or do they leave a pathway of heartache and discord everywhere they go? Are they givers or takers? Do they speak well of others or do they enjoy engaging in character assassination? Does their company make you feel uplifted or does it leave you feeling tired and oppressed? Do nice things happen around them or do they attract disaster and misfortune? The answers to such questions will tell you what you need to know about the true motives of the people you are in contact with, just as your own motives can be read in the effects you have on those around you.

If we look only at superficial appearances, we are easily deceived. If we want to avoid people who might be generating harmful influences, we should look at how those people treat others. None of us is perfect and we can all slip now and again but, if there is a continuous pattern of harm and disruption, it would be wise to keep your shields up. By the same token, if a person is generally loving, kind and considerate, what right does anyone have to attack that person's philosophy?

All forms of natural energy are simply that . . . energies. They function in accordance with the known laws of nature and they neither think nor reason: they simply flow as they are channelled. Destructive energy, in its *pure* form, is simply another form of natural energy which has a legitimate function and purpose. It is only when that function is perverted and the energy used in a purpose for which it was not intended that it becomes something evil.

In the natural cycle of life, there is always a destructive phase as well as a creative phase. Life is a continual process of building up and breaking down, recycling and renewal. Just as there have to be creative forces in the generation of life, so there also have to be destructive energies. Look at the world of nature and you can see this principle at work all around you. Your own body survives through a process of metabolism in which there are two distinct phases: anabolism, building up; catabolism, breaking down. Food products are broken down to provide energy for the cells, which in turn age, die and are broken down to be used as components in new cells or to be excreted as body waste. In the natural order of things, this is returned to the soil, thus feeding enrichment back to the earth which, in turn, produces new growth for our sustenance.

The current human lifestyle interrupts the natural process of life on Earth quite considerably and, sooner or later, Nature will have to take some drastic action to restore the balance. From a three-dimensional human point of view, Nature's 'punishment' would be seen as a tragedy of cataclysmic proportions but, from Mother Nature's perspective, it is a simple necessity. Destructive energy in itself is not evil, it is an integral part of the natural cycle of rebirth and renewal.

Within each one of us, there are elements of destructiveness as well as creativity; the choice as to how those energies will be channelled is entirely up to the individual. In human beings, living energy takes on an added quality, the quality of self-determination. Each one of us has the potential to destroy as well as to create. *We* make the choices as to the effects of our thoughts, words and deeds.

The way of Darkness is chosen by those who seek to dominate, to manipulate and to exploit. They seek power over others and, in seeking it, they place themselves into the power of even more unwholesome influences. This is irrespective of the person's outward appearance. They may appear to be robed in sumptuous respectability, pillars of the Establishment. They may even believe that they are what they appear to be, but look to their motives, their habitual companions and their effect on others. Are they occupied by a quest for power? Do they seek to control others? Are they prepared to justify harming some people for the 'betterment' of others? Do they live in a world of disagreement, back-stabbing and fractious infighting? If so, can you honestly believe they are channels for Love, Light and Truth?

The ostracism of Wiccans as 'satanic' is the result of narrow-minded dogmas adopted by proselytising Christians during the Dark Ages; those who perpetrated the witch-hunts, the Inquisition, the Crusades and a number of other bloody purges. The true Wiccans have *never* worshipped Satan: as far as they are concerned, Satan didn't even exist until the Christian religion arrived.

It is not at all difficult for a Wiccan to accept the philosophy of Christ; but the philosophy of many who claim to be Christ's followers astounds them. How, ask the Wiccans, is it possible to follow a doctrine of love, tolerance and harmony and, simultaneously to practise hatred, cruelty and destruction? When the question is asked that way, the answer is fairly obvious, isn't it?

Fortunately there are, today, a growing number of sincere followers of Christ who are working their hearts out to remove the barriers of prejudice and superstition that, in their opinion, have been cluttering up the purity of their Master's teachings for much too long. Some of these people are among my closest friends and you might be surprised to see how well they get on with the Wiccans. A wonderful Roman Catholic priest summed it up beautifully for us all: 'The only difference between your beliefs and mine are the words that we use to express them.' We have all come a long way... but there is still some distance to be traversed.

The Creator gave every one of us the right to make our own choice as to how we express our understanding of spirituality. Are we human beings greater than the Divine, that we have the right to persecute others for their beliefs or to say that they are wrong? Is a red rose any more beautiful than a white one? If we *must* judge others, let us follow the advice of the Nazarene and judge the tree by its fruits, not by the label it wears.

It is not our place to ride forth and do battle with the 'Forces of Evil', which is just as well, because mankind has so far been unable to agree on what is good or evil anyway! Our concern, as individuals, is simply to keep ourselves clear of those whose influence is likely to lead us into harm. If the Light is strong in us, we will be able to recognise the same Light in others, regardless of race or cultural difference. We cannot create a world of peace and fulfilment for ourselves whilst we condemn others to a fate of torment and pain. Karma doesn't work that way. We cannot afford to allow ourselves to be biassed by prejudice.

There is black, there is white and there are countless shades of grey in between. Nobody's perfect and, in condemning the 'evil' in others, we can fail to recognise the Darkness in ourselves. As human spirits, we are evolving but our destiny is not completely predetermined. We can evolve towards Light or Darkness; we choose the direction by the actions and attitudes we display towards others.

CHAPTER SEVENTEEN

New Age Children

I have received numerous letters from bemused and bewildered parents whose children demonstrate a noticeable degree of psychic and spiritual awareness. In most of those letters, I have been beseeched to write some words of wisdom for the guidance of the said parents. Now for a start, I know just enough to be aware that children have a remarkable talent for disproving just about every child guidance theory that has ever been printed. Furthermore, my son Darryl and I are only just arriving at the point where we are beginning to believe that there is hope after adolescence. A child guidance expert I am not and, as a mother, I'd say I rate about average so, once again, I can only write of my own observations. If you find something helpful in those observations, that's wonderful, but please do not regard me as any kind of authority on the subject. I can write only as a mother, and mothers, as we all know, come in all shapes and sizes, with an endless variety of opinions on the topic of childraising.

I gave birth to Darryl at a time in my life when I was struggling very hard to conform with all the requirements expected of responsible young wives of my era. I have to admit that I wasn't succeeding very well but I was trying and, as a result, everything I did with Darryl was done in the conventional way. In accordance with all the 'expert' advice, unless he was hungry or needed his napkin changed I steadfastly resisted the urge to pick him up and cuddle him every time he cried . . . well, most of the time, anyway. Even if I had known about private 'progressive' schools, our income bracket would have excluded that option so Darryl was sent through the government school system.

If he had been a reasonably robust, easygoing sort of a child, he would probably have managed quite well but he was sensitive, selfconscious and a chronic asthmatic. As I watched him struggling to survive the system, I broke my heart for him countless times. Often I had cause to remember the fateful prediction my mother had made when I was still in my teens: 'When you have a child, I hope she grows up to be just like you, so that you can find out exactly how you make me feel.'

At that time, as I recall, I held the opinion that mothers never understand how their children really feel. Now I know that they do... and that is usually the problem! Darryl has always hated being told how much he resembles me and he has been known to expend a great deal of energy trying to prove how different he is: just as I did when people *would* insist on telling me how much I resembled my mother. These days, I take such remarks as a compliment. My Mum not only managed, successfully, to raise four reasonably sane and balanced New Age children, she also did it without going completely round the bend herself. That's a pretty sizeable accomplishment: take a bow, Mum!

I have only one child and I have a healthy respect for any woman who successfully raises several. The investment in terms of energy and commitment is enormous, yet I have friends who thrive on it. One of these friends, Beverly, is currently enjoying the arrival of her second family. From her first marriage, she has two husky sons who have recently entered the workforce. In her second marriage, she has an energetic pre-schooler, a baby just learning to crawl and another infant on the way. Beverly is a tiny, birdlike lady and she is a natural Earth mother. Rarely have I seen her upset over anything; she seems to radiate a gentle aura of peace, love and caring. She practises Yoga, T'ai Chi and meditation and loves getting her hands into the soil, tending the earth and helping things to grow. Motherhood for her is a sacred honour and supreme joy.

Beverly, quite unconsciously, provided me with a living tableau that vividly exemplifies, for me, the image of a New Age mother. When Luke, her pre-schooler was still at the toddling stage, we were visiting the home of a mutual friend. It was a summer afternoon so we sat outside and while we talked, Luke toddled around exploring the garden. He discovered the dog's water dish and squatted down to investigate more closely, paddling his tiny hands in its coolness. Beverly immediately went to his side and I expected to hear the conventional chiding: 'Ugh, dirty... don't touch!'. Instead, she squatted alongside her son and paddled her own fingers in the dish.

'Water!' she said in a tone of delight. 'Wa-ter.' Luke gazed into her eyes for a moment, then gurgled with merriment.

'Wah-ta!' he repeated, grinning hugely as he splashed his hands in the bowl.

Young children are naturally psychic. Some people say this is because children have only recently entered this world and their links with the spiritual spheres are still close. They also have a quality of openmindedness and acceptance that has all but disappeared in many adults. They see the world differently and their life can be endlessly fascinating. I can remember lying for hours on my tummy, absorbed in the search for a four-leafed clover amongst the grass in our lawn. It was one of my favourite occupations and I found quite a few four-leafed clovers, too. I believed implicitly in fairies, elves and pixies and wandered happily through the bushland near our home for hours on end, talking to the tree-people and holding endless mental conversations with the friendly unseen beings who accompanied me everywhere.

Conflict began to arise when I started school and received the devastating news that I had been living in a world of fantasy and 'only babies' believed in pixies and tree-people. Because I did not want to appear foolish, I gave up my belief in such things but it always seemed to me that the world was a sadder place without them.

The system today doesn't appear to have altered much and, if anything, it was even worse for Darryl than it was for me. Rather than aiming to help children discover and develop their natural potential, conventional schooling methods seem designed for the purpose of fitting square pegs into round holes. Those who cannot adapt are rejected as misfits. A large percentage of my readers have made the same observations about the education system and the mothers I have spoken with are seriously concerned about the damage they see being done to their children. It would appear to be a universal problem.

We can't wrap our children in cotton wool and most mothers accept that youngsters have to take a few bumps and bruises along the path to adulthood but most also seem to agree that children are exposed to far too much pressure, too soon. There is also a commonly held opinion that orthodox methods of schooling tend to stifle imagination, creativity and originality. Within that system, there are many naturally gifted teachers who *do* inspire their pupils: I was lucky enough to have several, most of whom happened to be English teachers. My younger brother is another and, even if I do sound like a proud sister, I am going to share a story about him that gives a good illustration of the difference a New Age approach can make.

If ever anyone was born to be a teacher, it is Neville. His godfather, after whom he was named, was also an inspired teacher. I ought to know; he was my teacher for three years in Primary School and I do not recall any of my classmates who didn't adore him and work their hardest in an effort to please him. Within the family we called him Skipper but at school it was always a respectful 'Sir'. Skipper wasn't only a token godfather to Neville: he was my brother's idol, his mentor and his closest friend. All Neville ever wanted was to grow up to be just like Skipper and I'd say he has succeeded.

Sadly, Skipper died before he could see my brother enter Teachers' College but I wouldn't mind betting that, in spirit, he is never far away. There is an attunement between those two souls that physical death could never damage.

Neville chose to be an infant's teacher because, he says, little children are more fun and, besides, the best time to stimulate a love for learning is at the beginning of a child's school life. As part of his training, he was required to do a practical teaching assignment at a government primary school located in a down-at-heel suburb, an area of government housing with high unemployment, divorce and crime rates. The regular teachers at the school sympathised with Neville because the class he had been assigned consisted of a bunch of angry and cynical six-year-olds, already classified as hardened little delinquents. 'They eat prac. teachers for breakfast!' Neville was informed. 'They are virtually unteachable.'

For the first day or two of his assignment, Neville didn't even try to teach the class. He simply sat and talked with them, explaining that, since he would be with them for three months, he would like to get to know them as people. He asked about their interests and favourite occupations and soon discovered that for all of them, the only real interest was in watching television. By unanimous vote, 'Battlestar Galactica' was their favourite series.

'Well,' remarked Neville. 'How would it be if we turned our classroom into the Battlestar? I'll be Captain Adama... who'd like to be Starbuck and Apollo?' He had every one of those 'unteachable' little monsters eating out of his hand before the first week had elapsed! They cheerfully applied themselves to learning their letters and numbers because, as he explained, they needed to know how to operate the Battlestar's computerised controls. All of a sudden, they were the good guys, space age musketeers with 'Captain Adama' as their hero. When Neville's assignment came to an end, the whole class cried as they said goodbye.

'Don't you think he's wonderful?' beamed my mother after proudly relating this story of Neville's achievements.

'He sure is,' I agreed. 'But I would hate to be the poor prac. teacher who had to follow in his shoes.'

The patterns of linear thinking around which traditional systems of education are based simply aren't suitable for New Age children. To be honest, I'm inclined to think they have never been satisfactory for *any* kind of children. New Age thinking isn't based on linear logic; it is lateral, comprehensive and intuitive. Force-fed facts and figures, learning by rote and reciting things parrot-fashion don't relate. Learning needs to be applied to something that has importance in the life of the student.

According to David, if a student cannot learn it is the teacher who is at fault. I have seen practical evidence of this in the life of my own child. According to the state school education system, Darryl was unteachable, unco-operative and unwilling to learn. At the time, he was also on permanent medication, prescribed by his doctors in an attempt to control his crippling asthma. There were four different drugs to be taken three times a day: some were bronchodilators to help his breathing, others were antihistamines, to suppress his allergies. Bronchodilators have a stimulating effect, whilst antihistamines cause drowsiness. From my point of view it was no wonder that Darryl failed to concentrate; half the time, the poor kid didn't even know where he was. In addition, he was in hospital so often that he lost months of school time and fell further and further behind in his lessons. The teachers, struggling to cope with overcrowded classrooms, didn't have time to give him the extra help that he needed. Before he had progressed even halfway through his primary schooling, he was hopelessly behind.

I saw Darryl struggling, agonising over his failures and his 'stupidity' and, finally, accepting the hopelessness of even trying. Time and again I tried to explain him to his teachers, with the result that I was routinely branded as a neurotic mother and Darryl as an overprotected problem child. I discovered natural medicine not long after Darryl entered High School but, although his health began to improve from that time onwards, the damage was done as far as education was concerned. Darryl had been taught to think of himself as a failure and a misfit. When he left school at sixteen, he was barely literate.

Darryl is now almost nineteen and, at the time of writing, he is studying in Sydney, nearing the end of a course in Therapeutic Massage. The course is not an easy one; it involves a lot of theory in which the students must be familiar with the names and functions of the major bones, muscles and nerve centres in the body. He telephoned me a few days ago with his examination results: Theory 82% and Practical 96%. This is from a lad who rarely achieved more than 10% in any examination at school.

Darryl hasn't suddenly become a different person, it is the teaching system that changed. Darryl's teachers are the same wholistic healers who have been our family physicians for a number of years. They told him that he has a natural gift for healing with his hands and inspired him to develop it. The fact that they are also family friends brought him no favouritism in class, in fact, it caused them to be harder on him than on the other students and to expect more of him. These, however, are true New Age teachers, gifted not only with physical skills but with profound spiritual wisdom and insight as well. The proof is in the results my 'unteachable' son has been able to achieve under their tuition.

It is commonly accepted that children are shaped by their environment and that they learn from the example set for them by their elders. For the greater part of their young lives, children evolve in an environment away from the home, over which the parents are allowed virtually no influence at all: school. Psychic children in particular are extremely sensitive and what is commonly classified as the 'normal' rough and tumble of school life can be a life of sheer torment for them. This can give rise to a number of profoundly disturbing psychological effects with which the families have to cope and which can have long-lasting effects on the adult personality, on the way he perceives his world, the way he reacts to it and the way he decides to use his energies. The story I am about to tell is Darryl's but it is not his alone. Although some readers may not wish to believe this, it is a story that could be told by any number of parents with only a few superficial alterations. I know this because of the number of those parents who have told their stories to me.

We moved to Yagoona when Darryl was about eight years old, just completing third class. We had been living there only for a short time when he began arriving home from school looking unusually dirty and dishevelled, often with buttons torn from his shirts. When I queried him about this, he would only hang his head and mutter that he had been in a fight, a confession guaranteed to bring a predictably disapproving response from me:

'How many times must you be told not to get into fights, Darryl?'

No answer from Darryl, just a helpless shrug.

Around this time, we began to be awakened during the nights by the sound of Darryl screaming in his sleep. 'No! Stop it, you're hurting me. Leave me alone, go away! Somebody, HELP!'

I'd go and awaken the child, pallid and sweating from

his nightmare. He could never tell me what he had been dreaming but his ever increasing cries in the night always carried the same theme. It eventually reached the stage where his screams were waking me on an average of every two hours.

He arrived home from school one afternoon nursing a sore hand. When he held it out for inspection, I saw the lead of a pencil embedded in his palm.

'How did this happen?' I asked as I reached for the tweezers to extract the lead.

'Jimmy stabbed me.'

'*What*? Why did he do it... were you fighting again?'

'No, honest Mum. It was in class, this morning.'

'Didn't you tell the teacher?'

'Yes, but he said I was causing trouble and kept me in at recess.'

'Why didn't you show him your hand?'

'I tried to... but he yelled at me.'

I pursed my lips as I dabbed antiseptic onto the wound. 'I think I'd better have a talk with that teacher of yours,' I muttered grimly. Darryl looked horrified.

'No!' he exclaimed in alarm. 'Don't do that, you'll only cause more trouble!'

'Sweetheart, I have to! This time it was your hand but next time it could be your eye. Your teacher needs to know what is really happening when his back is turned. He won't be mad at you.'

'NO!' cried Darryl. 'You don't understand! They'll get me... they'll hurt me worse... '

'*Who*? Darryl, what is going on at that school?'

Now visibly terrified, Darryl burst into tears. 'I can't tell you. If I tell, they'll bash me worse!'

The penny dropped. Schoolyard bullies; I should have known! Having encountered a few of those characters in my time, I began to understand Darryl's predicament. 'You said "they"... how many are in the gang?'

'F-Five.'

'This has been going on for months, hasn't it? Tell me how it started.'

'I wouldn't give them my lunch money.'

'They took your lunch money?'

'If I didn't give it to them, they'd get me after school,' he explained. 'But now they bash me anyway, even after they've got the money.'

I was almost too enraged to speak but I held myself still and spoke as calmly as possible, trying not to upset the child any further. 'Sweetheart, the law says that you have to go to school but this standover racket has to be stopped. If I don't talk to your teacher, this will happen to you every day and those boys will grow up to be criminals. Do you understand? I can't *help* you if I don't talk to the teachers.'

He nodded miserably as he clung, shaking in my arms. The following day, I went to see his headmistress. Although my heart sank when I saw her defensive attitude, I told her the story and asked for her help.

'Please don't let those boys know they've been reported,' I asked. 'I thought perhaps you could ask the staff to keep a discreet watch and catch them in the act.'

'Don't worry, Mrs. Hill,' she told me crisply. 'I know how to handle the situation.'

She telephoned the next day to inform me that the matter had been concluded. 'I'm afraid Darryl has been making up stories,' she announced. 'I have spoken to the boys concerned and they insist that they haven't been bullying Darryl, in fact they are friends. They play together. In any case, I've warned them that if I hear another word about any bullying, they will be dealt with severely.'

'Oh, Darryl!' I whispered as I replaced the receiver. 'What have I done to you?'

That afternoon, two of Darryl's young friends virtually carried him through our front doorway. His shirt was torn, skin grazed, dirty and already bruising. He was unable to stand unsupported, choking for breath and only semi-conscious. I settled him onto the sofa, helped him to use his asthma spray, called the doctor and brought some cool water to bathe his battered skin.

'Okay,' I nodded to his awed companions. 'What's the story... Jimmy and Co. again, is it?'

'They had him down on the ground, Mrs. Hill. They were all kicking him.'

'Didn't anyone try to help him?'

'We did. David got kicked in the head too, but they ran away after that.'

'Where was Darryl kicked... all over?'

'Stomach and chest mostly.'

I wanted to throw up. A kick in the sternum can kill a healthy adult. Heaven only knew what a series of kicks might do to an asthmatic child.

'*I* know how to put a stop to this,' thundered Roland when he came home from work and heard the story. 'I'll wait for those little thugs after school and give them a taste of their own medicine!'

'You can't. You'd be charged with molesting children. The law is on their side. Don't think I haven't considered doing it myself.'

'Well, *something* has to be done before they kill the kid.'

'I know. I've thought about that, too.'

'You're beaten before you start!' he raged. 'The whole bloody system is against you. One person can't fight City Hall, so the school can pretend that none of this is happening and get away with it. It's you against the system and you're only one anonymous little statistic.'

'That's true,' I agreed. 'But *this* little statistic has a voice and there just happens to be a very effective way of dealing with bureaucracies. It's called the Maximum Embarrassment Technique.'

'You're cooking something up, aren't you? What's going on in that head of yours? Tell me.' I told him and the anger in his face dissolved into a broad grin. 'That is so outrageous, it might just work,' he almost chortled. 'Go for it, kid! I think I'm going to enjoy this.'

Next day, I telephoned the headmistress and coolly informed her that my worst expectations had been confirmed and, as a result, Darryl was too sick to attend school. Then I rang the local Child Welfare unit and the Education Department's Public Relations officer. My message to them both was the same:

'I am calling to inform you that I have removed my nine-year-old son from school. I have no intention of sending him back until you can guarantee that his classmates won't beat him to death. Since I'm telling you in advance, you needn't bother to send any of your truant officers to see me... and I'd better let you know that when I finish talking to you, I'm talking to the media.'

And talk I did, to the newspapers, on radio and even on television. Some of the interviewers were sympathetic, others openly wondered whether I might not be over-reacting. In an interview on the Mike Walsh Show the question was asked: 'Are you sure you aren't just being a neurotic mother?'

'How neurotic does a mother need to be?' I shot back. 'I'm not talking about a stand-up, toe to toe fight between two evenly matched opponents; this is five to one.'

'Yes, but children do get into scuffles and they *are* only children; isn't it possible that you are making too much of the situation?'

'They may be "only children" to you,' I argued. 'But from my son's point of view, they are five people who are at least his equal in size. If five blokes *your* size were to beat you up every time you came to work, how long would it be before you reached the stage of not wanting to be here? I don't agree that I'm making too much of it: I wouldn't mind betting that if it is happening to my son, it is happening to other children in schools around the country. I think it's a problem that needs to be aired.'

Mike picked up the challenge. 'Alright,' he said to the cameras. 'Dawn believes there are other children who may be suffering the same problem. If there are parents out there whose children are facing this kind of treatment at school, write to Dawn, care of this channel.'

We kept the Channel Nine mailroom quite busy over the next few weeks with the letters that came from other parents. Some of the horror stories they had to tell brought me to tears.

There was a six-year-old boy who had his front teeth kicked out by a group of brave nine-year-olds who took a dislike to his short haircut. Epileptic children rated high on the school bullies' hit lists; there were numerous stories of continual torment inflicted on them, such as the case of the twelve-year-old boy who was held down while his hair was set on fire. Asthmatics were equally popular targets, a finding which didn't surprise me. As an asthmatic child, I was beaten up a number of times by a particular group of children who enjoyed seeing how I choked for air after a few punches to the solar plexus.

Darryl was given a speedy transfer to another school and it was clearly hoped that I would quieten down once my son's victimisation had stopped. By this time, however, I had the bit between my teeth. Since I had started talking to the media on Darryl's behalf, I saw no reason why I should not continue to talk on behalf of the children whose parents had written to me. The situation soon reached the attention of the Rev. Ted Noffs of Sydney's Wayside Chapel, who is an energetic campaigner for social reform. He felt strongly enough to organise a public meeting and to make sure that it was well attended by the news media representatives.

I don't know whether I was being psychic when I told my audience that if we didn't put a stop to the problem there and then, we would soon see a time when children started killing each other. I only know that my prediction has been proven tragically correct many times since. Children are not only killing other children; it has been reported in newspapers that gangs of marauding youngsters have been known to attack adults and beat them to death, the favoured victims being the old and the helpless. What else can be expected, when we consider the examples being set by the adults in this world?

Children are also killing themselves. I have read with rising concern about the number of youngsters who are choosing to take their own lives rather than continue living in an increasingly brutal world. Some of these suicide victims are as young as twelve or thirteen years of age. Few of them leave notes to explain why they chose to kill themselves: those who have done so write of being unable to face the cruelty and victimisation any longer.

I can bless the powers that be for the fact that Darryl didn't kill himself but there was a time when he came close. His problems were renewed when he started High School. I had tried very hard to convince his teachers that he was not ready for High School when he turned twelve but, once again, the system ruled. In his last few years of primary school after being transferred, he had begun slowly to catch up with his schooling. Had he been given one more year in sixth class, he might have had a chance. As it was, I could see that he was not ready for High School either scholastically or emotionally. I begged his teachers to keep him back for a year but it was not school policy to do so.

Of the two High Schools in our area, Darryl was assigned to the same school to which all of the bullies from his former primary school were assigned. They were *delighted* when they saw him arrive and couldn't wait to begin their campaign of retribution. In addition, Darryl discovered that teachers can also be bullies.

His sports master took exception to the fact that Darryl did not wear a sports uniform on the allotted day and, as punishment, Darryl was made to run eight laps around the sports oval. This cost him a few more days off school because the over-exertion brought on another asthma attack. It was also illegal for students in public schools to be ostracised or pressured in any way for not wearing school uniforms.

The following week, I sent a note to the teacher, informing him that Darryl's lack of a sports uniform was due to the fact that I could not afford to buy one at that time. I also wrote that, as he was a chronic asthmatic, I would appreciate it if Darryl were not subjected to punishment, particularly of a physical nature, for a situation in which he was not at fault. After reading the note, the teacher informed Darryl that regardless of what I had to say, HE was the boss at school and Darryl would run the eight laps as before.

This time, Darryl had a companion, the son of one of our neighbours, also lacking a sports uniform. His reason was that he had only just returned to school after having a surgical operation to remove a bowel obstruction. His doctor had ordered no physical exertion and, therefore, his mother hadn't thought he would *need* his sports uniform, particularly when he was able to show the teacher a doctor's certificate.

Darryl's mathematics teacher took a very dim view of his inability to cope with his work and regularly held him up for ridicule by the whole class, on account of his 'stupidity'. Once again, we started waking in the night to the sound of Darryl's screaming nightmares or the sound of violent retching, coming from the bathroom. The situation worsened rapidly and it came to a head one day, when Darryl scored ony 4% in his mathematics test. His teacher went to great lengths to berate him scornfully in front of the class.

'Go home and tell your parents what a miserable failure you are,' he sneered. 'I can just imagine how proud of you they'll be.'

Obediently and with immense trepidation, Darryl delivered the awful news to me.

'Don't be too upset about it,' I soothed. 'I didn't get very good marks for maths when I was at school either. I got 5% once.'

It was then that Darryl told me what his teacher had said. As he spoke, his chest began to heave and huge tears welled up in his syes. His face crumpled, then he broke. The howling of a tormented soul is gut-wrenching enough at any time but there are no words to describe the way I felt when I heard those agonized howls coming from my twelve-year-old son. All I could do was cry with him as I held him close to me, cursing myself in my helplessness to ease his pain.

It was probably a mother's instinct that woke me that night to hear muffled, surreptitious noises coming from the kitchen. I went to investigate and found Darryl at the sink with my sharp kitchen knife in his hand, trying to muster up the courage to slit his own wrists.

'Darryl, NO!' I cried, aghast. 'You *mustn't*... that isn't the answer.'

The knife fell from his nerveless fingers and he flung himself against me, sobbing. 'I can't face it any more, Mum. I can't go back there!'

A few weeks later, Darryl was admitted to Rivendell, a Health Department treatment centre for 'depressed adolescents'; youngsters who cannot cope with the stress of their environment. He was assessed initially by a team of child psychiatrists and psychologists and, as part of the program, parents were also required to visit the counsellors for regular discussions. By this time, I had decided that somehow I must have failed Darryl badly and I asked the counsellor where I was going wrong.

'You aren't,' I was told. 'If Darryl's home life is contributing at all to his problem, it is only because it is *too* good.'

'How can it be too good?'

'The contrast between his home life and what he has to face at school is quite dramatic. He's a sensitive child who simply cannot cope with the rough environment outside his home.'

'But what can we do about it? Surely we don't have to start treating him badly at home just to even the balance!'

'Not at all,' smiled the counsellor. 'We need to help Darryl learn enough confidence to cope with the environment.'

Darryl spent six months at Rivendell and I have nothing but the highest praise for that institution and for its staff. They made Darryl feel that he was worthy to be loved, that people cared about him and that life could be enjoyable in spite of its hardships. When he was discharged, the social worker arranged for him to be transferred to the other High School in our area. Although he never managed to achieve any remarkably improved scholastic results, he managed to muddle through without any more trauma. Now that he no longer has to contend with the school environment, he is beginning to improve his chances in life. Although, in view of his past history, it may seem incongruous, I believe Darryl is one of the lucky ones. So far, he has survived; there are many youngsters who do not.

Recently, I conducted several seminars, during which I had the opportunity to meet a number of my readers in person. During intervals in the course of the lectures, I spoke with a number of people individually. One of these was a lady named June, who was still grieving for her teenage son, who had committed suicide two years earlier.

'I still can't understand why he did it,' she told me. 'We're a close and loving family and he didn't seem to have any problems with us. He had a few hassles with life in general but we thought he'd grow out of it. I keep wondering what we missed. Where did we go wrong?'

'Probably nowhere,' I replied softly. 'I've been asked the same question by other parents who have suffered this tragedy. It's natural to feel that way but I don't think families are to blame: it's the world *outside* the home that does the damage.'

When the seminars were over, I received a beautiful letter from June, a part of which I will quote here:

> On Monday I opened a children's Art Show . . . the whole school had painted and drawn pictures of the world and animals that they loved. When you told the story of the Hundredth Monkey on Sunday, I thought 'Of course! That's what I'll tell the children when I open the exhibition.'
>
> Children's art always shows a happy world, children playing, sun shining, flowers large and colourful, trees always there and, after the story, Dawn, I was able to tell these *four hundred* children to carry out their own experiment to visualise the happy world they wanted in their minds just before they went to sleep. Wasn't that wonderful!!!
>
> The teacher friend who had asked me to open the show said she was going to carry that through with her class. Yesterday, my friend brought me letters from everyone in her class telling me how much they had loved the story and giving me their love.

Before I went south to conduct those seminars, David told me that, if every person I reach with my message could in turn reach only two more people who could pass on the message to two more, the possibilities are endless. This one woman *alone* has reached four hundred open-minded and enthusiastic children with the message about Planetary Healing.

In the teachings of the Nazarene it is said that, in order to enter the kingdom of Heaven, we must become 'as little children' and yet our system seems designed to stifle all the best natural qualities of childhood, turning bright, inquisitive youngsters into little more than robots, programmed with anger. We can't change the system overnight but our children could help. It is for us to teach them that they have the power to do so and to help them understand how to use it wisely, for the highest good of all.

What this world really needs is a mother! It has long been said that the hand that rocks the cradle rules the world and I think it's about time that we women let our voices be heard, not in strident militancy but in all the finest qualities of mother-love. We can teach our children that they don't have to be helpless pawns in a man-made system: they have the ability to *change* things, just by thinking about it. Just imagine the transformation that could be wrought by a single generation of children, all focussing their purest and most exuberant energies into the creation of a paradise on Earth!

I am not suggesting that we teach our children to play with psychic energy. On the contrary, I firmly believe that it would be not only unhealthy but dangerous to emphasise the merely psychic aspect. I have come into contact with several youngsters who have been treated as though they are specially gifted simply because they happen to be psychic. I have seen, among them, far too many cases of over-inflated egos, which all too often leads to power-tripping.

Bearing in mind that sensitive children can suffer harassment, causing great pain, frustration and unresolved anger, it would be more than dangerous to acquaint them with the idea that psychic ability could give them power over their tormentors. Spiritually, we may be dealing with some very old souls but, as physical children, those souls must develop both intellectually and emotionally before they are capable of handling the concept of unlimited power. Power without responsibility is a dangerous weapon in anyone's hands and children should not be encouraged to play with dangerous weapons. We do not want to produce a generation of power-happy young tyrants. If we truly want to serve the needs of our children, we need to consider more than helping them to learn how to use their spiritual abilities wisely. We also need to work at creating the kind of environment they need, to help them grow up healthy in mind and body, secure in their surroundings and at harmony with all life.

There is an excellent book for children of all ages, entitled *Manual on Using the Light* written by John-Roger. In simple, childlike fashion, it sets out the qualities and uses of the Light, which the writer equates with the Holy Spirit. It is an inspiring book for both children and parents, with the added advantage that it is not expensive to purchase. It explains how people can work with the Light to bring healing to those who are sick, to resolve disputes, lift ourselves out of depressions and generally improve the quality of life for ourselves and those around us. There is nothing in the book that could stimulate negative activity and I firmly believe that its influence on anyone who reads it can only be for good.

At the time of writing, *Manual on Using the Light* can be obtained in Australia from: Baraka Educational Foundation Inc., P.O. Box 123, Currumbin, Queensland 4223.

Overseas readers will need to contact the publishers: Baraka Books, Ltd., 453 Greenwich St, New York, New York U.S.A. 10013.

Because of their sensitivities and the pressures to which they are exposed, psychically sensitive children tend to be highly strung. If there is no release for the internal tensions, pressure will build and serious problems develop. Teach them how to relax, both physically and mentally. The relaxation exercise and 'Magic Hands' meditation given earlier are as suitable for children as for adults. The period while they are settling down to sleep is a good time for parents to sit with young children and guide them through these exercises. This helps the child to find a safety valve for the release of tension and also promotes more restful sleep.

Rather than teaching children to play psychics, it would be far better to help them learn how to hold a balance between their spiritual sensitivity and the requirements of this physical existence. It would also be better not to heap praise on them for being psychic or to give them the idea that it makes them special in any way. Instead, we need to emphasise the naturalness of psychic energy and point out that, even though many other people do not understand or even recognise these abilities within themselves, everybody has them.

Teach them about the cosmic laws: the reality of thought energy, the law of attraction and, of course, the law of Karma. A child who understands that like attracts like and that all of our thoughts, words and deeds must come back to us can understand why we need to control our baser impulses and concentrate on the highest good. If a child understands the Why, he shouldn't need an endless list of Do's and Don'ts. Of course, you can guarantee that any normal child will test everything to the limit and do a great deal of learning from hard experience but at least, if he knows how the cosmic laws operate, he will be better equipped to understand the lessons that life brings to him.

As parents, we cannot dictate to our children or turn them into something they do not want to be. We can try... but the results are likely to be disappointing and frustrating for all concerned. Our function is to do our best to help them understand and come to terms with their environment, to teach them the skills of survival and to help them to discover and develop their highest potential. We can also learn from them. The most successful mothers I know don't talk *at* their children but *with* them; this involves listening as well. Discovering the world afresh through the eyes of a child can be a most enjoyable and enlightening experience and it helps to keep us all young at heart.

Because sensitive children are so prone to external influences, they need to know how to cleanse and seal their auras. I can foresee a time when all young children will learn this basic and very essential technique as naturally as they now learn to clean their teeth and wash their hands. With any of the meditation techniques suggested in this chapter, parents can strengthen the bonding between themselves and their children by doing the exercises with them regularly each day, sharing together in the flow of the highest and purest loving energies possible.

Most importantly, we must take a good hard look at the world we are bequeathing to our children. If the children are to grow up as happy and fulfilled as we want them to be, many things about that world need to be altered. A world that is such a living hell that a child would rather die than continue living here is badly in need of change. Just as children have the power to alter things, so do we: I can think of no better reason for doing so than the happiness and welfare of our own children. It's time we stopped thinking of ourselves as anonymous statistics and started to realise that mothers not only *matter*, they have a great deal of power to influence this world for the better. We don't *have* to sit back helplessly while our children are munched up by The Machine; we have the ability to change things and to teach our children to do the same. Remember the Hundredth Monkey principle: it might be your child who becomes the Hundredth Monkey. Who knows? It might even be you!

Prayers of the right kind can provide an excellent means of focussing thought energy. Prayer is a way of talking to the God Within and it is good to encourage it in children. If you are seeking a 'special' prayer to teach them, it would be difficult to find a more beautiful and inspiring example than the Prayer of St. Francis of Assisi:

> 'God make me an Instrument of Your peace;
> where there is hatred, let me sow love;
> where there is injury, pardon;
> where there is doubt, faith;
> where there is despair, hope;
> where there is darkness, light;
> and where there is sadness, joy:
> That I may seek to console rather than to be consoled, to understand rather than to be understood, to love rather than to be loved.
> For it is in giving that we receive; in self-forgetfulness that we find our true selves,
> in forgiving that we are forgiven,
> in dying that we are raised up to life everlasting.
> God, make me an instrument of your peace.

And when all else fails, remember the Mother's Motto:

'LOVE IS THE ANSWER: WHAT WAS THE QUESTION?'

CHAPTER EIGHTEEN

A Message

I have sometimes been accused of emphasising my own ordinariness to the point where it begins to sound like false modesty, yet there are still quite a number of people who insist on expecting me to behave like Wonder Woman. When I have proved that I am every bit as human and fallible as anyone else, those people cannot forgive me and I am accused, at the very least, of being a fake. This is in spite of the fact that I am constantly asking to be accepted as a *normal human being*.

A few years ago, when the Upstairs Management first informed me that I was to write books that would help other people to discover and develop their spiritual qualities, I spent a lot of time checking to make sure that the Cosmic Computer hadn't confused me with somebody else. In this great big world, I'm sure there are many people who are much more saintly and wise than me and I was afraid that, as a fragile human, I'd do something stupid and mess up the whole project. David assured me that there had been no mistake and that my very human-ness is an essential part of the message, so I took his word for it and wrote the first book.

It is very important to me that people know me as I am and not in some false image. At the same time, I am well aware that, in my particular field of communication, it is easy to be branded as a 'guru'. Some people enjoy wearing guru badges but I do not. I am not and have never been a guru, nor have I any intention of becoming one in the future. Ego trips and personality cults not only leave me cold; I consider them to be spiritually unhealthy. My time in this world is not unlimited and there are things I want to achieve. I do not have time to waste on silly games.

Saints and gurus always seem to be regarded as something more than human: as semi-divine and far beyond the sphere of mere mortals. They are supposed to have special gifts or qualities that ordinary human beings do not possess. If we follow this line of reasoning, we have to arrive at the conclusion that what works (or *seems* to work) for the guru need not necessarily work for the ordinary human being and that therefore, we need a guru to intercede for us in some way. That may put money into the guru's bank account and Rolls-Royces in his garage but it doesn't do a great deal for the promotion of true spirituality.

The whole point is that you don't *need* a guru. There isn't a person anywhere in the world who has any powers or abilities that you don't have. In that respect, we have all been created equal. It doesn't matter whether you are an Indian swami, a University professor, a truck driver or an everyday housewife; you have the same channels of communication with your inner source, the God (and the Goddess!) within you. If those channels don't seem to be working for you, it's probably because, somewhere in your mind, you are saying 'I can't'. Well , you *can*! Any one of us can develop those channels and use them beneficially if we put our minds to it.

If I were some kind of angelic being, the whole point of my message would be lost. It's easy for angels to be spiritual, but what do they know of the trials and tribulations associated with being human? I'm not claiming to be an angel. I'm not even a saint. I am a *human being* and I intend to go right on being cheerfully, deliberately and defiantly human. If I swear occasionally or tell an earthy joke and other people can't handle it, they are the ones with the problem. Anyway, I usually relax to that extent only when I'm with my friends who don't mind because they're all human too. I am not in this world to conform with someone else's false image of what they think I should be. I am quite happy to be myself and I have every right to do so.

I am not a supporter of spiritual anarchy but I think the 'pardon me for being human' attitude has worn a bit thin for all of us. Being human is an essential part of our spirituality, it isn't something we should all deny or which should make us feel ashamed. If the Creator had wanted us to be anything other than human, we wouldn't *be* human.

I spent the first thirty years of my life struggling to be what other people thought I should be and all I succeeded in doing was to become hopelessly confused. For a start, what is approvable and desirable for one group of people can be totally unacceptable to another. Whatever we do, there will usually be people who do not understand. To give an example: anyone who spends a reasonable amount of time in company with Roland and I will know that we are very 'cuddly' people. We express our love for each other and for those who come close to our hearts by hugging and cuddling. With very close friends we even kiss and most people accept this as being quite normal. Others do not and I can never quite make up my mind whether to be offended or amused when they react as though we attend sex orgies every time there's a full moon.

To a certain extent, I can understand the confusion some people feel when they become acquainted with me at a personal level. If there is any such thing as the conventional image of a psychic, it is an image that I do not fit. I don't tell fortunes, bend spoons or relay messages from the dear departed and I have a healthy aversion to the performance of psychic parlour tricks. I don't condemn people who do such things; in fact, I imagine that they fulfil a valid purpose by proving that such things are possible but their purpose is not mine. The only thing that worries me about such performances is that they usually contain a strong element of showmanship, which causes a lot of people to regard the supernatural as little more than an offbeat form of entertainment.

People have many preconceived notions about 'psychics', which is one of the reasons why I do not like being labelled with that tag. I would prefer to be known simply as a writer who happens to make a study of psychic and spiritual awareness. At the same time, I cannot criticise people for holding the same preconceived notions that I used to hold before the Man Upstairs decided to correct my thinking. Even when *Reaching for the Other*

Side was first published I thought it was David's intention to make himself available to those who wished to seek help with spiritual healing, psychic rescue or simply advice. I had the idea that we would continue to hold trance sittings in the pattern of the circles conducted by people such as Hannen Swaffer, at whose meetings the famed guide 'Silver Birch' delivered his teachings.

I was therefore more than a little taken aback when our trance sessions with David came almost to a standstill once the book had been published, especially when I was being inundated with requests for healing and/or consultations with David. I didn't understand David's motives at all and, to be quite honest, there were times when I felt hideously embarrassed, as though I had promised something I couldn't deliver. Even though I had specifically pointed out in the book that healing is not our primary purpose, I couldn't blame people for seeking our help when all other available forms of treatment had failed. At the same time, I could not agree to hold sittings for people when the guides had made it clear that they would not co-operate.

I even argued with David about this on more than a few occasions, trying to make him understand how much these people needed his help. In answer, he explained that he did understand but to answer every individual request for healing was not the way to give the help that is really needed, for the maximum number of people.

'My daughter, what is the saying which begins "Give a hungry man a fish . . .?" ' he prompted.

' "Give a hungry man a fish today and he will be hungry again tomorrow but teach him how to catch his own fish and he need never be hungry again," ' I replied obediently.

'Do you not understand the principle?'

'I understand, but how do I explain it to these other people?'

'My daughter, you are the writer. Need you ask me how to write?'

David's message is that his purpose is not to encourage people to depend on him but to help them find the magic within themselves. He has pointed out that, even if we spent the rest of our lives healing people, we would leave this world no better than we found it when the time comes for us to return Home. By contrast, if we can help people learn how to heal themselves and to correct the imbalances of life in our world, we will have given a legacy that will go on helping long after we have ceased to exist here even as a memory. That is David's purpose and it must be mine also.

When it comes to addressing the problems of human life, there are two different lines of approach. We can keep trying to stick Band-Aids over the symptoms or we can look for the causes and find ways of resolving them. The second approach makes the most sense to me. If my kitchen sink keeps overflowing, I am not going to concentrate all of my energies onto mopping up the floor. It makes more sense to clear the blockage in the drain so that the sink won't keep overflowing. That way, I only have to mop up the spillage once.

If it is apparent that the major cause of problems in this world is ignorance of natural laws, it would seem to me that the answer lies in learning to understand and work in harmony with those laws. We can't force other people to learn if they don't want to; all we can do is make the knowledge available and try to teach by setting a good example. We are not responsible for the free will choices of other people, only for our own.

It has always seemed to me that there are far too many people in this world telling everyone else how they ought to be living. The principle seems to be 'If everyone would be reasonable and do things my way, we wouldn't have any problems'. That would not be a balance, it would be a dictatorship. It's like saying that all roses have to be pink.

Everybody knows this world of ours is in big trouble and everyone would like to be able to help make it better. The trouble is, we have all been indoctrinated with a single self-defeating thought: 'I'm only one helpless little person, what can I do?'. Well, all we little people can do quite a lot once we get rid of the idea that we are helpless and isolated. If you have understood the principles that have been explained in this book, you will know that, when you work in harmony with the laws of nature, you are anything but helpless and certainly never alone. It is only when we try to bend those laws in the interests of self-gain that we start getting into trouble.

It is within our capability to create a world that is free of fear and suffering and we don't have to wait until everyone else comes round to our way of thinking before getting started. We don't have to demonstrate in the streets or ram our personal philosophy down anyone else's throats; all we have to do is work with the natural laws. Those laws are neither numerous nor difficult to understand, basically all we need to remember are three principles:

- Thought is reality.
- Like attracts like.
- Energy moves in a cycle that inevitably returns it to its point of origin.

I have learned to understand that the Spiritual Light is a living essence with the power to cleanse, heal, nourish and uplift. I have been taught further that, when I give myself as a channel for the Light and allow it to radiate through me and into the world around me, all my needs are answered and my world becomes brighter, happier and more beautiful. For me, those lessons aren't just words in a book: I *know* they are true. I know the Light is real because I am *living* in it.

I can't give the Light to anyone else; it isn't mine to give and, in any case, it is already in you. It is there in abundance, all you need to do is open yourself to it and let it flow. You don't even have to tell it what you need because it already knows. You cannot cultivate the Light by holding it in, only by giving it out. Your thoughts create your reality and like attracts like. Try offering yourself as a channel for the Light, asking no more than that it be free to flow wherever it is most needed, for the highest good of all. That way, the Light will automatically work for *your* highest good. It may not always bring you the things you want to have but it will bring what is best for you. It will work *with* you, but not *for* you.

If you want to live in a world that is free of fear and

oppression, picture a world in which every living creature has the same freedom. You cannot create one world for yourself and a different world for others: nothing worthwhile can ever be gained by making others lose.

The price of freedom is freedom and the price of love is love. In Cosmic Law, your payment is made in advance so, if peace and love are what you want, peace and love are what you should be giving.

I have heard it said that fighting for peace is like copulating for virginity. I have to admit that, when I heard this saying, it was expressed in earthier terms but I think the essential message is quite clear and to the point. I have also heard it said that we can't rid ourselves of wars by hating war, only by loving peace.

I would not by any means classify myself as a radical feminist but I think that women have advantages when it comes to working for the creation of a world of peace and plenty. A woman's purpose is to give life and to nurture it, not to destroy; therefore, the qualities of giving and nurturing life are inherent in us. I personally find the idea of breeding children for use as cannon fodder abhorrent and I doubt that there is a normal, loving mother in this world who would disagree with me. The problem is that we've all been conditioned to believe that we can't do anything to change the system and, as long as we believe that, we won't even try. That isn't only a problem, it's a tragedy for the whole of humankind.

I have said before that this world needs a mother's influence and I'll keep on saying it. Motherhood knows no racial, social or religious barriers; it is concerned only with the welfare of our children. Mothers all over the world have a great deal in common and if we were to combine our energies, we would be a force to be reckoned with!

When I look at the people who currently hold the reins of government in this world, I see, for the most part, a collection of greedy, quarrelsome spiritual juveniles playing very dangerous power games with our lives, the lives of our children and the life of this very planet. To add insult to injury, these little boys in big men's breeches would have us all believe that we have no say in the matter. They will tell us how and where to live and even decide when we should cease to live, if they so choose. If we complain too loudly, they bring in the heavies to put us out of action... and they would like us to believe that they are acting for the highest good of all. We all know that isn't the truth but we have been taught to believe that there is nothing we can do to alter the situation. It is 'God's will'. It may be the will of the gods of greed and corruption but it certainly isn't the will of a God of Love!

If we were to saturate our atmosphere with spiritual Light, the influences around those who govern our nations would be more pure and genuinely motivated by the highest good. When the influences that cause people to hate and destroy are no longer present in our atmosphere, they will not be present in our world. If we teach these principles to our children and practise them ourselves, we can do more good in the space of one generation than the whole succession of man-made governments throughout the history of mankind.

I am speaking especially to mothers because we have the opportunity to teach these things to our children, who are the next generation. In taking a female approach, I am not excluding the hosts of menfolk who would happily support our mutual cause; I am simply pointing out that, as mothers, we can shape the thinking of generations to come. As it is said in the theme from *Time*, if we want to change our world, we must change the way we think. If we teach the coming generations to live by the principles of balance, harmony and natural law, this world has a future and so do its children. Remember the cycle of reincarnation: there is every chance that you will be one of those future children. What sort of a world do *you* want to inherit?

If it seems to you that I am talking politics instead of spirituality, you haven't understood what I've been saying in the preceding chapters. Spirituality is not attained by ignoring the physical but by manifesting the spirit *within* the physical. We cannot say that events in this world aren't important because 'this world is not spiritual': that simply isn't true. This world is a *part* of the spiritual universe and, at present, it's a very sick part! If we don't use our energies wisely and start setting it to rights, how can we expect to qualify for entry into higher spheres?

We have the power to shape this world with our thought energies and, until we can demonstrate that we are capable of using that power responsibly, we cannot progress upwards. If we cannot live in harmony within this limited sphere, what kind of unholy chaos could we create with the infinitely more potent energies that exist on higher planes? We need to learn how to manifest our highest and most beneficial spiritual energies right here in the physical and we need to learn fast because, the way things are going, we don't have a great deal of time.

In this world right now there is a polarisation of energies between the destructive and the creative, the takers and the givers, the lovers of life and those who would destroy it all. It is time to choose sides! It's time to heal the damage, put an end to the exploitation and start giving something back to Life. All we need to do in order to achieve this is to *change the way we think.*

When we think of all the wonders that we could be performing together, the idea of bending spoons or telling fortunes begins to look rather trivial, doesn't it? This is why I am not particularly interested in playing psychics in the conventional way or in teaching others how to do it. There is so much more that we could be achieving if we work together as one, for the highest good of all. I'm not talking pious platitudes or Utopian fantasies. I am speaking about a living reality, our reality. We don't have to cringe back in fear while our planet is poisoned, our wildlife wiped out and our children sacrificed to the gods of greed and brutality. We have the power to stop those things from happening and there is no force on Earth that can stop us from using that power, because it is all in our own minds and in the life around us.

I'm not asking anyone to make great sacrifices for the good of humankind. Remember the law of Karma: the energies you give out will be multiplied and returned to you, so if you give for the highest good, the return will be for your highest good. That can hardly be classified as self-sacrifice, particularly when your gift to Life can be something as simple and effortless as spending a few minutes each day in a meditation for planetary healing. What can you lose?

When I wrote *Reaching for the Other Side* I asked my readers to write to me, to share their thoughts and experiences, to tell me about the things they need to know and the answers they seek. Thousands of readers responded and, largely from reading their letters, I have been able to assess the needs that I have set out to answer in this book. I have been delighted and encouraged by the response and my only regret is that I do not have the time to answer every letter. Nevertheless, I am very interested in reading what you have to say. More than this, I *need* to hear from you because I cannot do my work in isolation. My books are written for you and, unless you tell me what you want to know, how can I be sure that I am giving what you need?

If you enclose return postage, I will do my best to answer your letter but I cannot make any promises on that score. I am already receiving more letters than I can answer and, at present, my level of income does not allow me to hire a secretary. I personally read every letter I receive and I answer as many as I can but my workload is heavy and there are only twenty-four hours in a day, so please forgive me if you don't receive a letter in reply.

Please do not write to me in care of my publishers. They are lovely people but they have their own work to do and it isn't fair to expect them to function as a mail forwarding agency as well. If you feel inclined to write, my postal address is:

P.O. Box 151,
Mount Pleasant,
North Queensland, 4740
AUSTRALIA

A word of caution: be careful with the Postcode number, there is more than one place named Mount Pleasant in Queensland! I hope you have enjoyed this book and that it has provided at least some of the answers to your questions. I also wish you happiness and fulfilment on your chosen pathway.

MAY THE LIGHT BE WITH YOU!